Organizing Men and Power

Rand Mᶜ Nally Series in the Organization Sciences

Organizing Men and Power:
Patterns of Behavior and Line-Staff Models

Robert T. Golembiewski

University of Georgia

Rand Mᶜ Nally & Company   Chicago

Rand McNally Series in the Organization Sciences
Robert T. Golembiewski, Editor

Abrahamson, *The Professional in the Organization*
Cornog, ed., *EDP Technology for State and
Local Government*
Golembiewski, *Organizing Men and Power*
Golembiewski and Gibson, eds., *Managerial Behavior
and Organization Demands*
Press and Arian, eds., *Empathy and Ideology*

To Peg

*for her work toward that which might be between us and
    between others
for her acceptance of that which had to be
for her courage and dignity when we had vainly hoped for
    better from the world
in short, for Peg herself.*

Contents

Introduction

This book challenges a long-current myth in organization design, the persistent notion that "staff" in cooperative enterprises should be outside the chain of command, that it should and does provide service rather than exert control, and so on. This "old" theory is challenged here.

Why study the staff concept? And how shall it be done? On the broadest level, this study is motivated by experience with various structural forms in organizing work, many of which seem to be part of the "new" theory of organization necessary to meet the evolving challenges to cooperative effort that have outmoded the old theory. This general motivation supports an analysis having multiple components that build toward structural redesign. They may be outlined as follows: to build from these structural innovations, some having longish histories; to extend these innovations into a coherent model, as far as that is possible; to marshal the existing research that establishes the superiority of the new model for organizing effort; and to analyze in detail the probable behavioral consequences of the new model in areas where more research is necessary.

In sum, this study integrates a broad range of materials from the frontiers of management thought about organizing. The novelty of the new model lies basically in bringing together an array of relevant experience and in explaining why many structural innovations "have worked." That is to say, the discovery of new and undreamed of structural worlds is not the major preoccupation of this book. The integration of available experience with diverse structural forms and the explanation of that experience—these matters do dominate the book.

If it has definite limitations, this effort need not be denigrated. The "traditional theory of organization" to many approximates a dogma, unflinchingly and often unreflectively held. Integrating useful structural innovations is thus more than a necessary job. In significant senses, it is *the* crucial task. That is, the heart of dogma is rejection of the inconsistent. Consequently, progress in structural design depends upon a demonstration of the limits of the dogma, as well as upon the demonstration of the efficacy of specific structural arrangements inconsistent with the dogma. For if the dogma survives, any successful innovative arrangements will be regarded as but exceptions to good practice. This does not take one very far. The main stress here, oppositely, is that many structural innovations need not be measured against the traditional standards. In fact, these innovations themselves set different standards for good practice.

The preceding paragraph implies the delicate balance which this argument attempts to respect. The innovative model developed in succeeding paragraphs is offered as a prescriptive guide for management based on what we presently know. At the same time, the model is an analytical target designed to challenge research. The danger is not so much that the model plunges far beyond the track laid by available research. Rather the real danger is that the prescriptive usefulness of the model under diverse conditions will not be tested by empirical research. Some probable boundary conditions of the new model seem clear enough, research presently underway may isolate new boundary conditions, and research should permit greater specificity than was possible here. But the existing and in-process research are but small samples of what is required.

The basic motives of this volume are dual, then: to develop a model of line-staff relations that will permit more effective managerial action given what we now know, and to provoke empirical rejection or refinement of that model.

Six subsidiary reasons further motivate this analysis. First, I argue that working myths ought to be scrutinized every once in a while, and all the significant myths should receive an especially thorough going over, is only to verify what everyone believes to be correct. Man's history encourages this effort; it is studded with some extraordinary aberrations that received faithful support because no one thought to challenge their reasonableness. On this score, there is ample reason to subject the staff concept to scrutiny. For the traditional notions of staff rest on very fragile supports indeed. Moreover, the confusion in the literature concerning interpretations of the traditional staff concept provides motivation aplenty for a root-and-branch analysis.[1]

---

[1]Theo Haimann, *Professional Management: Theory and Practice* (Boston: Houghton Mifflin, 1962), p. 190.

Second, compelling evidence suggests that line-staff relations worsen as staff activities become more important to organization success.[2] The combination cannot be accepted with equanimity, suggesting as it does that the prevailing concept stops considerably short of an effective structuring of line-staff relations.

Third, the staff concept requires a kind of analysis that has not been fashionable of late. That is, the flush of discovery of "informal organization" has tended to obscure the significant role played by the formal structure in influencing behavior. Or, alternately, that discovery cast the formal structure as a villain in inducing aberrant behavior or in limiting the development of mature individuals. Indeed, a commentator with Simon's stature felt constrained to explain (somewhat belligerently) his stress upon the formal structure, since it was so out of tune with current emphases.[3] However, enough is now known to permit these categoric propositions. The formal structure often significantly influences what the informal organization will be, whether it will coincide substantially with the formal structure or whether it will depart from it radically; and the proper formal structure may facilitate healthy adaptive behavior of individuals in organizations.

Fourth, the design of the staff concept tends to be accepted as a given, if a given to complain about. For example, numerous observers note the stresses induced by staff activities, if all do not go to the length of a semiserious Parkinson. Brech puts the matter more forthrightly than most: "The more one endeavors to scrutinize the 'line and staff' concept analytically the more one comes to the conclusion that . . . it is an arbitrary and artificial notion whose implications have never been thought through." But even Brech is solidly in the ranks on the question of redesign: "The conclusion has, reluctantly, to be drawn that the puzzle must remain unresolved, unless the view be accepted that the label serves no useful purpose and is therefore banished from the management vocabulary."[4]

Why redesign languishes in neglect must remain problematical. A substantial literature critical of the traditional staff model exists, however, and it must be extended to redesign a structure. Otherwise, over the long run, the critical literature merely carps. The present effort attempts to do more than carp.

[2]Robert C. Sampson, *The Staff Role in Management: Its Creative Uses* (New York: Harper, 1955), esp. pp. 1-10.
[3]Herbert A. Simon, "Comments on the Theory of Organizations," *American Political Science Review*, XLVI (December, 1952), 1133n.
[4]E. F. L. Brech, *Organization: The Framework of Management* (London: Longmans, Green, 1957), p. 52.

Fifth, administrative times have changed radically since the days of the early development of the staff concept which reach back at least to the mid-1700's. To paint with an extremely broad brush, we are entering the epoch of the "educated society." Organizations cannot stand apart from this rush of history. Indeed, the needs of our great bureaucracies have helped propel us into this epoch. Thus if it takes more training to be an engineer today than it did in the past, much the same is true of a wide panoply of lower-level operations in organizations. In sharp contrast, the traditional guides for organizing work have a developmental history with roots deep in what can be called "uneducated society." The organization structure and managerial techniques appropriate there are hardly suitable for what Drucker sees "as the central social problem of twentieth century America": the "integration of the professional into the business organization."[5]

Sixth, our fund of knowledge concerning behavior has increased beyond all but the wildest expectations of early students of organization. This knowledge literally begs to be put to service in analyzing the traditional staff concept and in designing a more adequate one. However, the scope of the task will leave us satisfied with relatively small incremental advances toward an increasingly sophisticated concept of staff and a supporting theory of organization.

---

[5]Quoted in Louis B. Barnes, *Organizational Systems and Engineering Groups* (Boston: Division of Research, Graduate School of Business Administration, Harvard Univ., 1960), pp. 12-13.

Chapter 1
Conceptualizing Line-Staff Relations: Ideal Models and the Neglect of Power

There has been a recent outpouring of works about organization. "Readings in," "theories of," and "notes on" are common leads to voguish titles. Some studies move toward an integration of what is known about the personality, or about groups, as such knowledge modifies or rejects notions about organization which have been veritable dogma. Spurred by recent advances in mathematics and computational techniques, still others exploit interests in simulation, system-building, and other newly opened research territories.

This outburst of research and theorizing defies simple cataloging, but particular significance must be accorded the attention given to line-staff relations in the contemporary reevaluation of structure and techniques in management. The increased size of administrative units and heightened complexity of management have upgraded the importance of staff services, and pleas for the solution of the "staff problem" have become increasingly insistent. For example, one student noted:

> Staff experts must now re-equip themselves. They have a new and larger contribution to make in modern management—a creative staff role. This new kind of staff leadership asks that staff people be the vanguard of modern management. This new role calls, too, for a radical change on the part of line administrators in their use of staff specialists.[1]

Sampson sees no real alternative to significant changes in line-staff relations. "Staff specialists can hide their heads in the sand temporarily," he grants grudgingly, but only if they ignore this datum:

---

[1]Robert C. Sampson, *The Staff Role in Management: Its Creative Uses* (New York: Harper, 1955), p. 3.

"...some companies are already falling apart at the seams because of conflict between line and staff."[2] Sampson's judgment seems acute.[3]

This attention to staff has been largely abortive. The typical remedy for reducing line-staff conflict, for example, is more of what seems to cause it: more of the prescription that staff is and should be advisory. McGregor has made the point delicately in his discussion of the "subtle and complex process" of providing professional help. His primary emphasis is that "help is always defined by the recipient." McGregor holds that an action taken by the staff for the "good of the organization" is the root of many line-staff problems. He explains that many headquarters staff units offer or impose their services in a paternalistic manner and rely on inappropriate methods of control. When such offers or impositions are rejected, McGregor notes, the "recipients of the 'help' ar seen as resistant, stupid, indifferent to organizational needs, etc."[4]

The explanation implies the lameness of the advice. Line-staff problems certainly would be reduced if staff always allowed the recipient to define help. But why contrary staff behavior does occur and must occur are interesting questions. This analysis seeks to answer these questions in terms of structural arrangements and managerial techniques having two consequences: They create problems between line and staff that need not exist, and they also compound other problems that may be expected in any organization. Consequently, calling for changes in staff behavior is no substitute for appropriate changes in structure and techniques.

Like the golfer watching the line of a putt similar to his, one can "go to school" on the experience of contemporary attention to staff. Basically, the common criticisms of staff have been both too hopeful and too narrowly conceived. Of course there would be no line-staff problem if staff acted as most observers prescribe. This is hardly helpful, however. The practical questions are not so iffy: (1) Should and can staff reasonably be expected to behave as the traditional model prescribes? and (2) If not, what changes are necessary in line-staff relations to permit a reasonable chance of their successful activation in operating situations? Appropriate answers also may be adumbrated here. These two answers, in fact, constitute a thumb-

[2]*Ibid.*, p. 176.
[3]Edmund P. Learned, David N. Ulrich, and Donald R. Booz, *Executive Action* (Boston: Division of Research, Graduate School of Business Administration, Harvard Univ., 1951), p. 155.
[4]Douglas McGregor, *The Human Side of Enterprise* (New York: McGraw-Hill, 1960), pp. 163-64.

nail summary of the results of this study: (1) No; and (2) Fundamental changes in the traditional concept are required: The traditional concept is not likely to be approximated in practice, and, if it is, the organization is not likely to be better off for it.

Orthodox Staff: *The* Model of Three Models

This summary is more easily phrased than it is supported. To get on with providing support, then, the focus will be upon three ideal models of line-staff relations. They illustrate the full range of models that could guide the development of structural relations, and the three include that one model which has in fact guided most efforts at organizing.

Emphasis upon "models" breaks with tradition. For it was not fashionable for those in the hard-headed business of organizing for action to acknowledge that they were theoreticians, or model-builders. Fashion, however, does not change matters. Any prescription for action implies a theory — or a model — of how one's purposes are to be fulfilled. Like the literary lightweight who learned that he spoke prose, in short, one can be surprised that organizing implies a theory or a model. Like our literary character, however, the organizer only has the choice of becoming better or worse at what it is that he does and must do. Lately fashions have changed. Thus McGregor bluntly notes: "Every managerial act rests on . . . theory."[5] And few voices are raised in opposition.

This treatment strives to be fashionable and accurate. Hence its interest in three models of staff-line relations that have influenced thought and action about organizing. Their shorthand designations suggest the major characteristics of these models: the Colleague concept, the Alter Ego concept, and the Neutral and Inferior Instrument concept. The three models support the demands of accuracy in several senses. Thus all three models have received at least a modicum of support and thus require treatment.

Moreover, outlining the several ideal styles should prove satisfying to the observer of organizations, for reality often demands greater complexity than that encompassed by any single model. Thus the emphasis upon three staff models helps avoid the impression that a strawman has been set up which subsequent analysis can demolish easily. That is, two theses underlie this chapter: (1) that the literature about staff is not monolithic, and practice is even

---

[5]*Ibid.*, p. 6.

more variegated, but (2) that, nevertheless, in terms of central tendencies, one concept of staff-line relations has been emphasized sufficiently to permit reference to it as *the* model.

Finally, the contrast between the models will serve the purposes of this analysis in attempting to be constructive as well as fashionable and accurate. In a crucial sense, the description and analysis of the three ideal models is the benchmark for structural redesign. The Neutral and Inferior Instrument model supports the critical emphasis of this treatment, and the Colleague and Alter Ego models will serve more constructive ambitions toward the design of an alternative model of structural relations.

One further note seems appropriate by way of introduction. This chapter will not differentiate staff in terms of the designations commonly assigned to agencies ("general staff," for example) or to individuals ("chief of staff" or "assistant-to," for example).[6] Normally, these designations aim at solving problems of line-staff relations by baptism. Calling Mr. X an "assistant-to" rather than a staff man does not solve the problems of authority and communications that Mr. X's position induces, whatever it is called.

Solution-by-baptism will be foresworn here, the emphasis being upon the three possible models covering the full range of the relations of any two individuals or units providing different contributions to cooperative effort. This approach will permit meeting the problems of line-staff relations head-on, rather than obfuscating them with verbalisms. Whether the staff units are considered to be "auxiliary staff," "personal staff," "general staff," "control staff," or what have you, the three ideal models cover the full range of their relations with line units.

Staff: The Colleague Model

The Colleague model of staff, first, implies formal authority independent of, and sometimes superior to, the line. Consider the German practice of sending direct representatives of headquarters into critical battle areas, not as line commanders but as chiefs of staff. These chiefs of staff participated in, and sometimes assumed, command. Their relations with line commanders were fluid. As one commentator describes them:

---

[6]These designations, for example, are employed in Ernest Dale and Lyndall F. Urwick, *Staff in Organization* (New York: McGraw-Hill, 1960), pp. 89-109.

> Always the commander commands through the chief and
> the chief's orders even older subordinate commanders
> have to follow without murmur. . . . How far the chief
> can go in issuing orders without the knowledge of his
> commander is a question that can be decided only be-
> tween the two and cannot be judged by any outsider.[7]

The concluding sentence is crucial. The relations of the staff man
and the field commander cannot be described simply. They will be
determined "only between the two." Moreover, the Colleague
concept of staff does not hide the relationship of a superior staff
official who is a direct representative of headquarters with a subordinate line official in the field. Indeed, the traditional notions of
line do not apply. For the Colleague model implies a bargaining
situation, and the traditional line-staff distinction permits no such
indeterminacy.

The Colleague model of line-staff relations, then, does not prescribe *a* particular pattern of behavior. Indeed, three patterns of
behavior (if we neglect differences of degree) could develop under
the Colleague model. They are shown in Outline 1.

	Characteristic Role		
	I	II	III
Staff Units or Individuals	Subservience	Dominance	Consensus About Alternation of Roles
Line Units or Individuals	Dominance	Subservience	

Outline 1

Role III seems the one most suitable for the Colleague concept of
staff. However, Role III also offers significant opportunities in line
and staff activities to develop any other pattern of relations which is
at once their own, is congenial to them, and is sanctioned by the
formal structure. The German experience cited, for example, implied Role II. In any case, the bases of alternation would be such
features as: experience of the participants; their interests, training,
and skills as they apply differentially to different problems; or
personality characteristics that might make a particular task attractive or repugnant to one or another of a set of line-staff officials.

The fluidity of the Colleague concept has a useful set of intended
consequences. Consider only this intended consequence of the

---

[7]Hans von Seeckt, *Gedanken eines Soldaten* (Berlin: Verlag für Kulturpolitik, 1929),
p. 163.

model: to encourage the active participation in command decisions of individuals whose formal positions encourage orientations to problem situations that differ in terms of jurisdiction and pressure of time. In terms of jurisdiction, the field commander would tend to emphasize conditions dominant in his problem area, the staff man to incline more toward overall policy and strategy. Temporally, the here-and-now would tend to be of most concern to the field commander. A longer-run view would tend to influence the staff colleague.

This first concept, then, attempts to provide for the integration of the "part" and the "whole," which is one of the base problems of administration. In the case of a personnel staff service or similar organization-wide activity, for example, the whole would be the functional area, the part the personnel matters of any administrative unit. But this first concept of staff does not attempt to handcuff organizationally either the commander or the Colleague staff man. For, by implication, to do so risks the inadequate expression of either particularistic or overall considerations. And both must be expressed adequately for effective functioning.

Staff: The Alter Ego Model

A second concept of staff implies less indeterminacy. It may be called the Alter Ego model. To illustrate, the United States Army's *Staff Officers' Field Manual* notes that the "staff of a unit consists of the officers *who assist the commander in his exercise of command.*" Such assistance is of an intimate nature. For the staff officer is enjoined to "live inside the mind of the commanding general, and know what his policies are, even though they have not been announced."[8] This "living inside of" may be reflected, for example, in orders signed by the staff officer "in the name of the commander." Field Marshal Montgomery's *Memoirs* give a precise picture of the relations involved. De Guingand, his Chief of Staff, would have a clear role: "every order by him," Montgomery explains, "would be regarded as coming from me and would be obeyed

[8]War Department, *Staff Officers' Field Manual: The Staff and Combat Orders* (Washington, D. C.: Government Printing Office, 1940), p. 1, is the source of the description. This author's emphases. The nature of the assistance is described by Richard M. Leighton, *History of Control Division, ASF: 1942-45* (Washington, D. C.: Historical Section Control Division, Army Service Forces, April, 1946, mimeographed), p. 205.

instantly." These are no mere words. During the major battle of the African campaign, for example, Montgomery retired early. Unanticipated difficulties soon developed, and De Guingand acted. As Montgomery explains: "de Guingand rightly issued orders for a conference at my Tactical HQ...and then woke me and told me what he had done. I agreed."[9]

The Alter Ego model, then, restricts behavior far more than the Colleague concept. The alter ego's orders are to be obeyed, but these orders merely articulate for the commander. There is no provision for the bargaining implied in the Colleague concept. The staff man, rather than asserting his own personality, ideally assumes that of the commander.

Staff: The Neutral and Inferior Instrument Model

Despite the reputation of these two staff concepts for getting results,[10] American students of organization—of both the government and business varieties—generally have chosen a third concept. It can be characterized as the Neutral and Inferior Instrument concept (NII) and is very familiar. White notes in his influential text that "line authorities . . . are the central elements of any administrative system. . . ." Staff comes off more poorly. White also notes that "staff and auxiliary agencies are necessary in a large and complex organization, *but they are secondary.* They serve the line; the line serves the people."[11] Thus staff in this concept is: "outside the lines of command"; "deliberate organization for thought rather than execution"; and "purely advisory."

The NII model sharply delimits behavior. Illustratively, no orders may be issued by the staff official who respects the Neutral and Inferior Instrument concept. Nor need such orders be obeyed, *in theory,* even if issued. In contrast, the two previous concepts (and especially the Colleague concept) include ample room for staff work inside the lines of command, for execution as well as thought, and for action as well as advice.

The NII model is by far most commonly prescribed, and this despite wide awareness of its significant practical limitations.

---

[9]Bernard Law Montgomery, *The Memoirs of . . . the Viscount Montgomery of Alamein* (Cleveland: World, 1958), pp. 93-94, 118.
[10]Alvin Brown, *The Armor of Organization* (New York: Hibbert, 1953), pp. 92-97.
[11]Leonard D. White, *An Introduction to the Study of Public Administration* (New York: Macmillan, 1955), p. 195.

Dale's comprehensive study found that advice and service were the legitimate "staff activities found in the majority of companies surveyed." Direct command over line units, Dale reports, is formally given to staff units or officers only in "certain exceptional cases."[12] That this formal obeisance to the NII concept exists along with (as Dale observes) full realization that *in fact* staff units can control or influence events is a combination that invites attention. For it suggests that the NII model has both very strong *and* very curious support. The curious sources of support will be discussed in subsequent chapters. The immediate purpose is to analyze three general types of support of the NII model.

Support by Verbal Manipulation. The NII model is not some mere abstract concept. Obeisance to it can be illustrated by any number of examples drawn from industry and government or from the worlds of practice and study. This does not mean that practice and study are dull monoliths. Incredible industry has been devoted to developing variations of the NII model, oppositely, and these are often spectacular to behold. The verbal gymnastics required usually are complex, sometimes gracefully so, sometimes in ungainly ways. But—as with the aerialist performing over a net—the spectator is assured that things will turn out well. Variations of the Neutral and Inferior Instrument model, that is, feed on that model and nourish it. That is all.

For example, many students have attempted to reconcile verbally the patent fact that staff often does have the power to influence (if not decide) with the NII model's intent that staff should not have this power. A common gambit assigns the "authority of command" to the line and the "authority of ideas" to the staff. Although it is not immediately clear why the basis of influence (command *vs.* ideas) should differentiate units of an organization, Ordway Tead supports the position with a flair. He notes that line officials issue orders consistent with their own operating responsibilities. Staff officials stand apart: They (Tead explains) "justify themselves as they are able to influence fellow executives at all levels by virtue of their factual or technical mastery." Although the point apparently does not apply to the line, Tead puts matters in a fatherly way: "It has been wisely said that 'a demand for an exercise of authority is a confession of weakness.'" Tead cannot sustain the argument, however, emotional appeal and all. He leaves the conceptual barn door wide open when he notes that, "the relation of the top personnel officers to the president of the company may on occasion

---

[12]Ernest Dale, *Planning and Developing the Company Organization Structure* (New York: American Management Association, 1952), p. 100.

be one of delegated powers which he exercises for the president not by advice giving but by direct dealing with line officials."[13]

Much the same point applies to Humble Oil Company's variation on the NII model which instructs that "The Staff Man Doesn't Turn In Half-Baked Ideas."[14] This emphasis upon "completed staff work" does not violate the traditional concept, on the face of it. But it does imply some serious potential limitations on line supremacy while it illustrates the verbal magic often used to disguise line-staff contradictions. Thus if staff work is "completed" in the sense that a single proposal, worked out in detail, is offered to a line executive for his approval or rejection, staff leverage could be enormous in influencing policy. Determining which decisions will not be made, in short, is at least as important as approving or disapproving a proposal that has been fully worked out.

Support by Neglect: Three Key Questions. The fragility of much of the support-by-variation of the traditional staff model accurately reflects the fact that discussions often are couched in terms which subtly or grossly foreclose analysis. For example, Mooney and Reiley explain that "The staff is purely an advisory service. . . . This difference from line command is implicit in the very meaning of the word staff, which is something to support or lean upon, but which of itself has no authority to decide or initiate."[15] That is, the analytical jig is up before the analysis begins. The power of words is considerable, and staff is a word not congenial to probing analysis even at the most trivial level.

While it may be uplifting to argue that men should not be what they are, the costs are great. Thus the verbal manipulations supporting the NII model neglect three important questions: (1) What are the pressures which force staff personnel to depart from the traditional model? (2) Can these pressures to depart from the traditional model be overcome in most cases? and (3) When these pressures to depart from the traditional model are neglected or overcome, is increased efficiency the probable outcome? There is no need to feign inconclusiveness or fabricate suspense. Subsequent analysis supports a negative answer to questions (2) and (3) based upon a detailed analysis of question (1). The vehicle will be a comparative evaluation of the NII and Colleague models of structural relations.

This is a sweeping conclusion but hedging is not necessary. Even

---

[13]Ordway Tead, *The Art of Administration* (New York: McGraw-Hill, 1951), p. 104.
[14]National Industrial Conference Board, Inc., *Improving Line and Staff Relationships* (New York: National Industrial Conference Board, Inc., Studies in Personnel Policy, No. 153), p. 73.
[15]James D. Mooney and Alan C. Reiley, *Onward Industry: The Principles of Organization and Their Significance to Modern Industry* (New York: Harper, 1931), p. 62.

defenders of the traditional staff concept despair of "yes" answers to questions (2) and (3). Sampson, for example, argues essentially that the traditional staff concept be preserved. Thus he notes that there "are no staff controls *as such*," but on the same page Sampson stresses the need to violate the NII model. Consider his section subtitled "Clubs to Control the Line." Sampson observes that when staff technicians fit men to systems, they in effect reduce the control of line supervisors over activities in their organization units. "Line" is still "responsible," however. "Staff standards and controls result in authority for staff people," Sampson concludes, "and consequent decreases in authority, discretion, initiative, and opportunity to think creatively on the part of line people."[16]

Whatever the verbal trappings, in short, the traditional distinction remains inviolate in the usual treatment of staff. The critic can be pardoned for concluding that he has heard all this before, then, whatever the elegance with which the various arguments are developed. And he can usually find that observation and prescription are worlds apart, as in Sampson.

Support by Default. Critics of the traditional model also often take the easy path. They contribute support by default, or by condescending tolerance. Thus one commentator noted that it is incredible to expect staff men to behave consistently as the talented eunuchs for which the NII model calls. At least their identifications with their programs will encourage more backbone.[17] However, only infrequent attempts have sprung from such observations toward the design of an alternative staff model.[18]

Default or tolerance can no longer be suffered or, to mean the same thing, need not be suffered. The NII model, straightforwardly, dares an effort at redesign and is ripe for it.

Three Staff Models: An Overview

Analytical patience counsels consolidating the modest gain of having distinguished the three staff models. The immediate contribution to this end involves stress on the uses of the models. The specific demonstration will be dual. That is, the usefulness of the three models in describing the complexity of staff structural ar-

---

[16]Sampson, *op. cit.*, p. 198.
[17]Willard Hogan, "A Dangerous Tendency in Government," *Public Administration Review*, VI (Summer, 1946), 235-39.
[18]Gerald C. Fisch, "Line-Staff Is Obsolete," *Harvard Business Review*, XXXIX (September-October, 1961), 67-79; Edward C. Schleh, *The Results Approach to Organization* (New York: Society for the Advancement of Management, 1959).

rangements in organizations will be sketched. Moreover, the usefulness of the three models in interpreting the evolution of the German General Staff will be outlined.

Using the Three Models: Describing Actual Staff Units

The three ideal models of structural relations at once serve to simplify this study while they permit a substantial complexity. Consider that staff in operating situations need not be pure types. For example, the Industrial Engineering Department at Mergenthaler Linotype is organized so that it reflects the NII concept in some of its staff operations, while it seems to approach the Colleague model in others. Three basic distinctions between organization units, then, are recognized: "line," "staff," and what is called "line-staff" at Mergenthaler. The staff group at Mergenthaler in the Industrial Engineering Department works on future planning and the development of new techniques. The staff-line group plays a more active role. It installs new systems, sets up new systems or techniques, and maintains contact with operating problems. The line group includes all activities that are centrally concerned with production but which are not directly engaged in production.[19]

The usefulness of the present approach via three models is briefly this. It provides a reasonable and simple framework for analysis, while it admits the more mixed conditions that often prevail in operating situations. The three models will not describe every existing staff unit, to be sure, but they will describe many such units in great detail. This limits the following analysis. For example, Chapters III and IV contribute an unflattering evaluation of the degree to which the NII model helps ameliorate certain common tensions between line and staff. To the degree that some actual staff unit departs from the NII model, the less strictly the analysis applies to them.

Using the Three Models:
Describing the Evolution of the German General Staff

The three ideal models also imply a continuum of types of line-staff structural relations. Not surprisingly, then, some organizations have experienced the full range of the three models of relations.

---

[19]Normand Provost, "Industrial Engineering at Mergenthaler Linotype," in *Line-Staff Relations in Production* (New York: American Management Association, 1957), pp. 130-31.

This seems to be the case with the German General Staff, for example, as the history of that administrative unit is reported by students such as Ralph N. Traxler.[20] A thumbnail history conveniently documents this point, while it also reinforces the distinctions between the three ideal staff models and demonstrates that not even the originators of the staff model could make do with the NII model. Traxler's account will be relied upon heavily, particularly since it is supported by other investigations.[21]

The forerunner of the German General Staff, the Prussian General Staff, knew its lean days. Two factors particularly limited the early administrative potency of the Prussian General Staff. The "general staff" concept aroused the suspicion of line officials who then as now feared that the staff would infringe upon their prerogatives. Moreover, the development of the General Staff implied entrance requirements built upon technical competence rather than noble birth. This not-at-all-veiled threat to the established Prussian military tradition was not taken lightly.[22]

Given this unfavorable environment, the model of staff adopted for the Prussian General Staff was not really in doubt. The Neutral and Inferior Instrument concept came to characterize the General Staff's relations with other army units. Hence the insistence by early heads of the General Staff—Wilhelm von Gneisenau, for example—that the prerogatives of the field officials of the line be scrupulously respected. The General Staff was restricted to planning and even so gave wide latitude to field officers. This respect for decision-making by the line was a major factor which in the long run led to a degree of acceptance of the General Staff.

Of course, the picture is not one of blacks and whites. Thus even in the early days of the General Staff, field commanders who supplied technical information as their major responsibility actively supported the General Staff.[23] By and large, however, the General Staff had to scratch vigorously for its support. One technique suggests the nature of these long-range attempts to build support: the rotation of line officers through the General Staff. The technique also suggests the difficulties facing the General Staff. Rotation through the General Staff was not always enthusiastically

[20]Ralph N. Traxler, Jr., "A Model of Modern Administrative Organization: The German General Staff," *Journal of the Academy of Management*, IV (August, 1961), 108-14.
[21]Bronsart von Schellendorf, *The Duties of the General Staff* (London: Kegan Paul, 1877), esp. pp. 1-3.
[22]Walter Goerlitz, *History of the German General Staff, 1657-1945* (New York: Praeger, 1953), p. 35.
[23]*Ibid.*, p. 39.

Conceptualizing Line-Staff Relations:

accepted. The villain seems to have been the very staff model respected in early General Staff operations, the NII concept. Thus Traxler observes that the system of rotation was long in coming and for an apparently good reason. It was "only natural," he notes, that few would seek out staff as a place to serve. "Line operative officials often felt 'demoted' when they were promoted to a staff job," Traxler concludes. "Their main complaint even today is that the staff job is dull and not accepted by line operatives."[24]

Events after the first two decades permitted the General Staff to develop beyond the limits of the NII concept. Fantastic increases in the complexity of the technology of war provided perhaps the major encouragement. Thus the General Staff increasingly was pressed into training. Moreover, consistent with Clausewitz' thesis that war was too important and complex to leave to the military as traditionally conceived, the General Staff became an increasingly important advisor on the tailoring of military plans to general governmental policy. For example, the King underscored this developing role of the General Staff in the 1820's when he requested that the War Minister consult the General Staff before deciding upon a policy issue.[25]

This second phase of the development of the German General Staff demonstrates that the Alter Ego model began to characterize line-staff relations. The role of the General Staff had expanded significantly. The expansion, however, was conceived as a means of extending the personality of the line, as a magnification of the faculties of the line through specialized services such as training, advice, and planning. That is, matters had not developed so far by the 1820's that the General Staff was considered to exercise line authority. Illustratively, although the War Minister was requested to consult with the General Staff before making a decision, nothing more than an advisory relation was involved. Authority to decide was still with the line official. Similarly, the General Staff had little leverage for influencing local field commanders in matters of organization and procedure. Although field commanders might accept advice from the General Staff, for example, there was no formal provision for feedback via reports of action by line units.[26] Consequently, the General Staff as Alter Ego trained, advised, and planned. But line supremacy was patent.

Matters changed quickly. By the mid-1860's, the Alter Ego model seems to have been abandoned essentially. Indeed, a royal order of

[24]Traxler, op. cit., p. 110.
[25]Goerlitz, op. cit., p. 57.
[26]Traxler, op. cit., p. 112.

1866 went so far as to empower the Chief of the General Staff to issue operational orders to carry out war plans.[27] The not altogether happy experience with the Danish campaign of 1864 seems to have encouraged the royal order. Whatever the cause, however, the consequences were clear. The Colleague concept characterized line-staff relations. Recall the description given earlier of line-staff relations in the German army which is consistent with this conclusion: "How far the chief [of staff] can go in issuing orders without the knowledge of his [line] commander is a question that can be decided only between the two and cannot be judged by any outsider." The judgment of Traxler is, if anything, even more pointed in supporting the characterization of the third phase of General Staff development in terms of the Colleague model:

> For the first time all the organic functions of administration were under one administrative policy making unit. This meant that the functions of planning, organizing and controlling were now the prerogative of the technically trained policy making group. Operative managers were freed from making decisions in a vacuum that locally might be wise but could upset an over-all scheme. The Staff now had evolved into much more than an advisory group. It had become the chief administrative officer because it had final authority over the organization and control functions.[28]

This minihistory does more than demonstrate the usefulness of the three ideal models in describing the evolution of a staff unit. The evolution also suggests the kinds of forces that commonly encourage staff to behave in a wider field than the NII model permits: the desires of top management for greater control, the commitment of staff to a program whose cultivation requires power, and staff leverage that derives from its special skills and its orientation toward the long-run and the universal, as opposed to the line's bias toward the short-run and the particularistic. Administrative times have not changed, as will become abundantly clear.

Staff$_1$, Staff$_2$ . . . Staff$_n$: A Concession to Complexity

To this point, this analysis deliberately has avoided discussing kinds of staff units. The reasons were not frivolous, but the time has come to present a representative typology of such units. This

---

[27]Goerlitz, *op. cit.*, p. 86.
[28]Traxler, *op. cit.*, p. 113.

concession to complexity will be made with as little fuss as possible. The presentation will be in outline form, reflecting the comprehensive treatment of Davis. Davis defines "staff" broadly "as those activities which are supplementary to the primary functions of an organization," and isolates these varieties of staff:[29]

I. General Staff

Davis explains that the general staff is an extension of the manager's capabilities, and therefore must operate within an area as broad as that of the manager himself. The assistant to a manager illustrates a general staff man, aiding the chief and serving as his agent. Davis concludes: "His function carries no authority over others. Since he cannot delegate to others, no one owes responsibility to him; however, he may acquire considerable power in various ways."

II. Specialist Staff

Whereas the general staff serves one manager, the specialist staff relates to a number of managers and departments, including other staff units. Thus a Purchasing Department not only purchases for a number of line units, but for other staff units as well.

As Davis notes: "Specialist staffs contribute advanced expertness in a narrow area of activity. Other persons look to them for leadership because of their *expertise*. Specialist staffs, therefore, represent an *authority of ideas*, instead of line authority to issue orders."

Davis conceives such specialist staffs may have three types of relations with other organization units:

A. Advisory Staff

A specialist staff which is advisory, Davis explains, acts as counsel to management by its own request in order to help "prepare plans, study problems, and reach decisions." The manager is not compelled to seek the services of advisory staff, nor is he required by formal structure to respect their services.

Davis concludes that advisory staff is "the least obnoxious of all" for the manager. However, he notes that the relation may be wearing on the staff unit. "It feels insecure," he notes, "because it knows it can be 'put out of business' unless it can convince people to use it. Since it cannot force others to seek its advice, it tries hard to 'sell' its services, sometimes to such an extent that it becomes a nuisance. It feels, properly so, that it must justify its existence."

B. Service Staff

The service staff does just that, performing for the manager

---

[29]Keith Davis, *Human Relations At Work* (New York: McGraw-Hill, 1962), pp. 208-12. See also William R. Spriegel and Joseph K. Bailey, "The Staff Function in Organization," *Advanced Management*, XVII (March, 1952), 2-6.

activities which are necessary to run the latter's program. The Purchasing Department illustrates a service staff.

Davis observes that this service role implies significant difficulties: "It is apparent that service staff relationships are likely to cause more human relations problems than advisory relationships, because the service staff restricts the scope of a manager's actions."

C. Control Staff

The control staff exercises control outside of its chain of command. Of course, every staff chief has line command over his own subordinates.

Davis considers the control staff to be particularly important because of its potential for line-staff conflict. It gives rise to the complaint about staff units which have all of the authority but no responsibility.

Davis isolates four types of staff control:

     1. functional control, which gives the staff the right to issue orders concerning some aspect of a manager's job and to take action if compliance does not result;

     2. agency control, which gives the staff the right to issue orders in the name of the line manager but not otherwise;

     3. policy control, which gives the staff the right to observe adherence to managerial policy, and to take appropriate action; and

     4. procedural control, which gives the staff the right to monitor procedures and to exercise review and approval of line decisions.

This taxonomy serves several purposes. Notice that Davis is careful to describe the kinds of tensions which develop between the line and the various types of staff. The influence of the NII concept also is reflected since at least part of the line reaction derives from the theoretical assignment of inferior status to staff. The NII concept also encourages certain extreme behaviors, especially by the advisory staff. Outlining the several kinds of staff, most important, pays its own way by implying a limit on the analysis to come. Davis alludes to the point when he notes that each type demands a different pattern of relations: "One of the reasons that specialist staffs have so much difficulty in business is that they do not understand these different relationships and consequently do not vary their action to fit the situation." Directly, the model of line-staff relations developed here seems most appropriate for what Davis calls control staff and for the control aspects of the work of other types of staff units.

The incidence, importance, and difficulties facing control staff in organizations preoccupy this analysis. This does not mean other types of staff are neglected. For they also face, if in reduced degree, the problems encountered by control staffs, a fact that further supports the design of a structure for the toughest problems that will be encountered. Indeed, any large staff unit is likely to reflect aspects of advice, service, and control. Therefore, the emphasis here can be pardoned in the sense that control is a significant feature of the activities of almost any staff unit. However, for activities with a very strong advisory and voluntary flavor — as employee counseling on personal problems — this analysis might be quite inappropriate. Indeed, such services often are best provided by an outsider — a consultant, physician, professor, or the like — in whom the employee can confide with reasonable assurance that matters revealed in confidence will not be used against him when promotions or pay increases are at issue.[30]

Organization as a System of Power: A Neglected Emphasis

The line-staff conflict spotlighted by Davis reflects human and social power that is not harnessed to organization purposes by the orthodox structural design. Contemporary treatments of power tend toward elegant formulations, but let us resist temptation. The very general concept here is of power as simply manifest or latent ability to control the environment. Any collective activity is thus a system of power whose major components are vectors of power that facilitate task performance or that inhibit it. The challenge to structural design is to increase the former and decrease the latter over the long-run.

Traditional organization theory acknowledges little or no substance in this challenge. That is, organizing often has been looked upon as purely a technical matter. There is no need to assemble the evidence. The point should be plain even to the casual reader of the literatures of business administration or public administration. In its most unadulterated form, this technical concept encourages a view of organization as simply a drawing-board task, a matter of assigning responsibilities, of allocating jobs or functions and mechanically coordinating them. Gulick clearly represents this

---

[30]When such services are provided by an "insider," relevantly, the temptation to use the information sometimes becomes irresistible. The struggles of the line to gain access to relevant files and of the counselor to protect their inviolability may disrupt working relations, encourage the staff to "improve" its position with its information, or compromise the service program. See Nigel Walker, *Morale in the Civil Service: A Study of the Desk Worker* (Edinburgh: Edinburgh Univ. Press, 1961), pp. 15-26.

emphasis when he argues in the influential *Papers on the Science of Administration* that "organizing" is essentially a "planning process." It is: "interrelating the subdivisions of work by allotting them to men who are placed in a structure of authority, so that the work may be coordinated by orders of superiors to subordinates, reaching from the top to the bottom of the entire enterprise."[31] In this view, organization has order and form, but no "life." More exuberant exponents of this view often lapse into mechanistic metaphor. Thus organizing becomes a meshing of gears and wheels in a "smoothly running machine." Such metaphors are merely explicit evidence of a technicist bias.

One Price of the Technical Bias:
The Traditional Line-Staff Concept

This technical emphasis is valid up to a point, but that point is usually overdone. For you do not process papers or build an automobile by letting the work be done willy-nilly. And, certainly, the work to be done will influence structure. One can make too much of a good thing, however, and the traditional theory of organization does just this. Mark these two emphases well, then — the studied neglect of power in the traditional theory of organization and the traditional line-staff distinction — for they are both warp and woof of this analysis. Literally, one emphasis cannot be touched here without disturbing the other.

One dominant theme of this study, that is to say, tells the tale of how and why the neglect of power phenomena built into traditional thought about organizing causes more problems than it alleviates. The traditional theory of organization has misemployed power so as to heighten the problems of creating unity in organizations, and this by setting sub-organization units against other units with which close cooperation is necessary to achieve organizational purposes.

The NII model awkwardly dances to the technical tune and thereby plays a crucial role in a pulling at organizational cross-purposes. It exalts the tendencies toward fragmentation encouraged by the traditional theory of organization; indeed, the model extends them into a major rule for organizing cooperative effort. Thus the NII model reflects in particularly interesting ways the artificiality of the neglect of power phenomena. At the same time, it

[31]Luther Gulick, "Notes on the Theory of Organization," *Papers on the Science of Administration*, eds., Luther Gulick and Lyndall Urwick (New York: Institute of Public Administration, Columbia Univ., 1937), p. 6.

strikingly illustrates the price of this artificiality in heightening the problems of integrating an organization's several component units. Indeed, the traditional staff concept rests upon a purported technical differentiation of work as that of the "specialist" *vs.* that of the "generalist," with authority (and, by implication, power) in the hands of the latter.

If they once permitted advances in the science and art of organizing, in summary preview, the traditional theory of organization and the NII model are fast approaching the structural equivalent of the point of grossly diminishing returns.

This is a tale old enough, and often told, not even enlightening if its moral is missed. A second dominant theme of this analysis seeks to avoid this sorry end. It stresses how a useful recognition of power phenomena can be built into a model for line-staff relations and into a broader theory of organization as well, and this with happy consequences.

Nothing is lost by the focus on staff, then. Indeed, the focus compels a wide-ranging investigation and requires handling problems that other foci might not disturb. In sum, the emphasis upon staff spotlights power phenomena explicitly and attempts to control them organizationally so that they contribute to organization unity rather than compromise it. At the same time, in order to get all the way around the problems of line-staff relations, it will prove necessary to redesign a new model of broad organizational relations. Directing attention to these two levels of analysis is about as much mileage as one can expect of any subject for study.

Toward a New Line-Staff Design:
Some Compulsions and Some Constraints

To build on the snowballing organizational research, to recognize power explicitly, and to take on the neglected problem of designing a suitable model of line-staff relations—these efforts are at once compelled and constrained by a variety of factors. Thus there is motivation aplenty for emphasis upon the staff concept. Although one must look sceptically at claims that such-and-such is *the* crucial problem of organization, one need not attempt to create a market for analysis of the staff concept.

On the broadest level, there seems every reason to build an awareness of power phenomena into all structural arrangements. Indeed, the husbanding of power may be *the* characteristically human preoccupation. The drive for power—that is, the ability to

control the environment—seems the major difference between humans and animals. Bertrand Russell makes the point sharply: A python, he notes, will gorge himself perhaps twice a year. And that is that. He will not kill simply to demonstrate his power. Indeed, the python can be forced to ingest food in the interim only with the greatest difficulty. Man has a continuing hunger for power in matters great and small, in contrast. For many practical purposes, this hunger seems insatiable. Much that is glorious, and a plentitude of the inglorious, derives from this characteristic of man. The point is hardly a novel one. The framers of the American Constitution, for example, were singularly insistent in denying man's "universal rectitude" as well as man's "universal venality" in their attempt to organize. Their point was not a quibble. For were human behavior both good and rational there would be no problem in designing an "ideal" structure, and this dilemma (expressed by Lincoln) would not exist: "Must a government, of necessity, be too strong for the liberties of its people, or too weak to maintain its own existence?" But human behavior is not so disciplined. As Adams emphasized, "human passions are insatiable." Adams was willing to "allow benevolence and generous affections to exist in the human breast." Yet he insisted that ". . . the selfish passions in the generality of men [are] the strongest." Some few individuals may love the public above themselves; and all individuals may act selflessly from time to time, but, Adams concluded, "Self-interest, private avidity, ambition, and avarice will exist in every state of society and under every form of government."[32]

The organizer of cooperative effort cannot neglect these potent human capacities. Indeed, his only reasonable alternative is to attempt to guide man's yearning for power through controlling his environment to make it work *for* organization purposes, on balance, rather than *against* them. In this sense, organization theory is akin to jiujitsu. This recognition of autonomous forces that must be served, however, has come hard to the social analyst. It is simpler to define them out of existence. Even the authors of the *Federalist Papers* yearned for the "perfect" govermental structure, simple and symmetric, that might be developed "if men were angels." Fortunately, they did take on the more complex task of designing a realistic and untidy structure for men as they are. This analysis follows the lead of these pioneers in the studied design of a structure that is "good enough."

---

[32]John Adams, *A Defense of the Constitution of the Government of the United States of America,* in *The Life and Works of John Adams,* ed. Charles Francis Adams (Boston: Little, Brown, 1851), Vol. IV.

Most students of productive organization have not absorbed such a lesson. Rather, they have indulged themselves in the quest for *the* perfect structure, albeit perfect only in terms of their own biases and goals and of a technology that is fast disappearing. The consequences are many and significant. Note here only one cost. As ample evidence will demonstrate, preoccupation with the perfect commonly leads to results that are not good enough or not as good as they might be. This is but one of the apparent paradoxes which studs this analysis.

The *Federalist Papers* also serve as a model for the organizer in another sense. The act of organizing, the *Papers* reflect, must be guided by a design that helps achieve a working consensus among members while it meets technical requirements. The traditional theory of organization does a rather poor job with regard to the latter feature of the double-barreled task of organizing. Fortunately, research to be reviewed in due course suggests that we need not sacrifice consensus for technical efficiency.[33] The word fortunately is used advisedly. Neither consensus nor technical performance can be sacrificed over the longer run, and particularly at advanced technological levels. Thus the stakes are high in the game which this analysis proposes to play.

Further, six straightforward emphases make the specific significance of an analysis of line-staff relations more clear. First, staff is there. Indeed, staff services loom increasingly large in determining an organization's profitability or efficiency. For example, staff personnel may outnumber the line.[34] If these be extreme cases, the normal state of affairs is no less impressive an argument for detailed consideration of the staff concept. A 1954 study of the Bureau of Business Research of The Ohio State University, for example, surveyed 211 manfacturing establishments in the Bureau's home state. On the average, each manufacturing concern employed seventy-five "indirect workers" for each one hundred employees who were directly involved in production.[35] Indirect workers tend to fit within the common meaning of staff. In contrast, the line is involved in production. To the same point, overall costs of admin-

---

[33]Generally, see Robert T. Golembiewski, *Men, Management, and Morality* (New York: McGraw-Hill, 1965).

[34]H. G. Lykken, "Finance: How Staff Departments Serve Line Management," *Line-Staff Relationships in Production, op. cit.*, p. 73.

[35]Alton W. Baker and Ralph C. Davis, *Ratios of Staff to Line Employees and Stages of Differentiation of Staff Function* (Columbus: Bureau of Business Research, Ohio State Univ., 1954), esp. p. 15. To a similar point, see Bruce E. DeSpelder, *Ratios of Staff to Line Personnel* (Columbus: Bureau of Business Research, Ohio State Univ., 1962), esp. p. 18.

istrative overhead (selling, general and administrative expenses, and so on) nearly doubled during the period 1950-1957. Meanwhile, sales increased by approximately 60 per cent.[36] Much of this increase reflects the growth of staff activities. There seems no escape from the trends which these data reflect.[37]

Second, common practice and prescription in organizing direct and indirect contributions are either very correct or very wrong. Either way, analysis is in order. For the NII model has all but preempted the field. In the case of personnel departments, for example, over 92 per cent in one large sample were formally organized in terms of the traditional concept.[38] The bias might not be so overwhelming in other samples, but neither is it likely to be very much less.

Third, staff relations become increasingly critical as organizations achieve some size. This means, in the context of contemporary trends, that the relations will become critical indeed. This is not to say that size is the only, or crucial, consideration. The degree of diversification also is a significant factor.[39] Whatever the critical mix of size and diversification that causes the greatest line-staff tension, however, the history of the present industrial giants clearly reflects the importance of line-staff relations in their growth.[40] And it seems likely that such firms as DuPont, General Motors, Standard Oil of New Jersey, and Sears, Roebuck achieved their present sizes in significant measure because of their innovative solutions to line-staff relations.

Fourth, the staff concept is of no mean consequence. Many inglorious chapters in the histories of organizations may be written in terms of the inadequacy of line-staff relations.[41] From another point of view, any staff concept must be significant because of what it must do. Consider these exalted purposes underlying the line-staff distinction: ". . . to increase the effectiveness of the chief

---

[36]*Nation's Business*, XLVII (April, 1959), 54-55.
[37]The data are not all that one would desire, but preliminary longitudinal studies clearly reflect sharp increases in staff aid over wide ranges of organizational growth. Mason Haire, "Biological Models and Empirical Histories in the Growth of Organizations," in *Modern Organization Theory*, ed. Mason Haire (New York: Wiley, 1959), pp. 290ff.
[38]Dalton E. McFarland, *Cooperation and Conflict in Personnel Administration* (New York: American Foundation for Management Research, 1963), p. 73.
[39]Alfred D. Chandler, Jr., *Strategy and Structure: Chapters in the History of the Industrial Enterprise* (Cambridge: Massachusetts Institute of Technology Press, 1962), p. 301.
[40]See *ibid.*, pp. 154-56, 179-80, and *passim.*
[41]Thomas A. Boyd, *Professional Amateur: The Biography of Charles Franklin Kettering* (New York: Dutton, 1957), pp. 119-23.

executive through a larger and abler staff of assistants to reduce the load, making it possible for him to devote himself to broader issues and closer contact with his men and with others."[42]

These perspectives on significance permit safe summary. There is no denigrating the role the staff model has played and was designed to play in organizations. The concept is one of the linch-pins in the efforts of man to live with size in organizations.

Fifth, the confusion surrounding the staff concept supports the most intense of inquiries. The resort to and the condemnation of the NII model paradoxically both go on apace while proponent and opponent often lack a common vocabulary. "Staff" has meant that many things to scholars and administrators. Moreover, this seman-tic confusion is compounded because the traditional and simplistic distinction has the unhappy faculty of encouraging a synthetic complexity which hinders more than it helps understanding. The following statement will be allowed to make the point:

> Just as there can be line within staff, so there can be staff within line. And, to further indicate the elaborate re-quirements to which the line-staff concept is sometimes subject, a line function within a staff group may in turn be supported by its own staff services.[43]

The ersatz complexity suggests there must be a more convenient concept.

Sixth, the experiences of organizations with line-staff relations seem generally unsatisfactory. In a recent survey, for example, only one of twelve companies appeared to have reasonably satisfactory relations between its line and staff agencies.[44] Restraint must gov-ern the interpretation of such results, given the lack of satisfactory empirical studies. But the slim empirical literature gets strong support from virtually all observers. For example, Koontz and O'Donnell note without flinching that "There is probably no other single area of management which in practice causes more difficul-ties, more friction, and more loss of time and effectiveness."[45] This is a powerful indictment and, slim empirical literature or not, does not inspire great confidence in the usual pattern of organizing line-staff relations.

---

[42]*Line-Staff Relationships in Production*, op. cit., pp. 7-8.
[43]*Ibid.*, p. 9.
[44]Edmund P. Learned, David N. Ulrich, and Donald R. Booz, *Executive Action* (Boston: Division of Research, Graduate School of Business Administration, Harvard Univ., 1951), p. 155.
[45]Harold Koontz and Cyril O'Donnell, *Principles of Management* (New York: McGraw-Hill, 1959), p. 135.

Granted that an analysis of line-staff relations is necessary, there are still very real constraints on this effort toward new structural design. Basically, this analysis must struggle against the common opinion that there must be one way to organize and that, therefore, one must utterly destroy traditional notions and replace them with another set. This is a self-inhibiting strategy. The more delicate position here is that many organizations are changing in ways that seriously reduce the applicability of traditional notions about organizing. Specifically, the NII model is still useful under certain conditions, but it falls farther and farther short of that universal applicability often attributed to it.

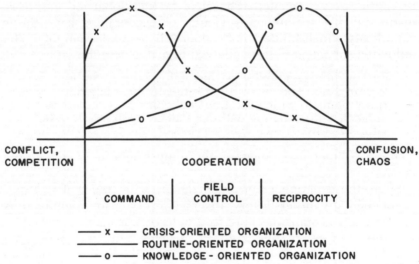

FIGURE 1. Three Patterns for Securing Collaboration in Organizations of Three Broad Types. From Waino W. Suojanen, "The Tactics of Jungle Warfare: Clarification," **Journal of the Academy of Management,** VII (September, 1964), 229-30.

There are many ways of supporting the point. For example, Suojanen[46] has argued within a military frame of reference that there are three basic patterns for securing collaboration in organizations: through command by officers at the top of an organization's hierarchy, through various degrees of "field control" by officers at lower levels of an organization within broad policy boundaries, and through reciprocal problem-solving by both high levels and low. Suojanen relied on the contributions of many academic disciplines

---

[46]Waino W. Suojanen, "The Tactics of Jungle Warfare: Clarification," *Journal of the Academy of Management*, VII (September, 1964), 229-30.

Conceptualizing Line-Staff Relations:

in developing his model[47] which can support a complex analysis. The strategy here develops one analytical aspect of the model for our limited purposes, while recognizing that specific kinds of organizations will differ in how much use they make of the three patterns. Figure 1 conveys the point visually. Thus a crisis-oriented organization, like our Strategic Air Command (SAC), must rely very heavily on command, and knowledge-oriented organizations, like our Air Force Systems Command (AFSC), must rely basically on reciprocity. To anticipate our analysis a little, traditional notions about organizing would be relatively appropriate for SAC but far less so for AFSC. Moreover, as will be shown, massive forces increasingly compel many organizations to recognize and emphasize "reciprocity" as a basic organizational pattern. The NII model and the broader traditional theory of organization are ill-suited to this new need.

Moderate interpretations of the following argument also are required because much relevant data is not available.[48] Every effort will be made to support this analysis with empirical data. But we must be satisfied with much hypothetical argument since the alternative model developed rests upon a host of propositions that must be subjected to close empirical scrutiny. The aim of such empirical testing, of course, is the development of an increasingly sophisticated and useful model. Consequently, the product here is not a new dogma but a new point of departure. A range of studies testing this approach, indeed, is in process.

Other constraints also are of some significance. Deliberately, the presentation to follow will avoid the detail required for any particular application of the colleague model. Only the general outline of a new organization theory, including a provision for new line-staff relations, will be presented. This is more than a convenient choice. For the model of relations developed here will be applicable to a

---

[47]Robert R. Blake and Jane S. Mouton, *Group Dynamics — Key to Decision Making* (Houston, Tex.: Gulf, 1961), pp. 27-38; Robert A. Dahl and Charles E. Lindblom, *Politics, Economics, and Welfare* (New York: Harper, 1953), pp. 93-126; and Herbert A. Shepard, "Superiors and Subordinates In Research," *Journal of Business*, XXIX (October, 1956), 261-67.

[48]Note, however, that some pilot studies of comparisons of various aspects of the NII *vs.* Colleague models have supported this analysis in complex ways. Some of this preliminary research is summarized in Robert T. Golembiewski, "The Orthodox Role of Personnel Administration: Logic Triumphs Over Purpose," *The Personnel Administrator* (in press). A more formal research report is Robert T. Golembiewski, Clinton Brown, and John Lanzano, "Personality and Organization Structure: Staff Models and Behavioral Patterns," *Journal of the Academy of Management*, IX (September, 1966), 217-32.

wide range of conditions, each requiring the tailor-fitting of work patterns to the requirements of the model and of the task. Several illustrations will outline what such tailor-fitting will involve in practice. But in the main the analysis will be restricted to the ample complexity of the general properties of an unorthodox staff model.

This approach has its costs, but emphasizing the pure model and its properties also serves three significant purposes. First, a more uncluttered analysis is possible. Second, the analysis need not run the risk of losing sight of the model's general applicability in the mass of detail necessary to bring off a particular application. Third, since the model requires the support of empirical testing, there is a real danger in embroidering the general model with burdensome detail. This might only hinder modifications of the model that may be dictated by empirical testing. Elaboration of detail, that is, might become an investment to protect. What is sought here, rather, is a model to provoke and permit testing.

Chapter 2

Pressures Toward Unorthodoxy, I: Changing Organizational Worlds

The literature critical of the NII model suggests great pressures toward unorthodoxy. But one cannot simply wait on the inexorable reshaping of organization theory, and every sign indicates that changes in the staff concept will come dearly. The point will be supported in three ways. First, the insensitivity to environmental change built into traditional thought about organizing will be introduced. Second, the massive contemporary environmental changes acting upon organizations will be sketched and the incredible practical significance of the insensitivity to these changes will be stressed. Third, the critical literature will be sampled so as to suggest the problems that structural redesign must meet.

Handling Environmental Change:
Insensitivity as a Methodology

One can be justifiably pessimistic about some congenial invisible hand adjusting organization theory to the new environmental realities. The usual pressures to resist change are complemented by subtle methodological inelegancies for one thing. Thus the method underlying the traditional theory of organization protected it from even the most extreme evidence of its own inadequacies.[1]

The explanation of the NII model's immunity to what exists lies in a subtle theoretical point. Thus we can test certain types of theories. For example, one can determine what is very likely to

---

[1] Robert T. Golembiewski, "Toward the New Organization Theories: Some Notes on 'Staff,'" *Midwest Journal of Political Science*, V (August, 1961), 237-59.

happen to a flower pot dropped from a fourth-floor window, and we would be foolish to neglect the import of such testing. Certain other kinds of theories cannot lose for winning. Line-staff theory illustrates this latter type, which at once tells us how things are and how things ought to be. One can have it both ways with the type of theory underlying the traditional staff model. Thus if one observes the relations provided for, that observation can be said to support the theory. And if the relations called for do not exist, well, they ought to. This has proved a considerable consolation to some. No similar consolation exists for the experimenter who predicts that he will fall up after he steps out of that fourth-story window. The inadequacy of the theory will soon be brought to his attention, as well as to the attention of observers who have a less direct stake in the outcome.

This methodological myopia of the traditional theory has enormous significance. Thus whenever a problem arises, the path of solution in organization theory is through its own underlying propositions and assumptions rather than through an analysis of the empirical world. This umbilicus-to-be-contemplated contains both explicit propositions as well as implicit assumptions. The explicit givens—the so-called principles of organization theory—include propositions such as the following:

1. Administrative efficiency is increased by specialization and routinization of the work process.

2. Administrative efficiency is increased when organization members are arranged in a definite hierarchy of authority from top to bottom and of responsibility from bottom to top, with a single head at the apex and a broad base at the bottom.

3. Administrative efficiency is increased if the unity of command is preserved, that is, if each organization member reports to but one superior.

4. Administrative efficiency is increased if the span of control is limited, that is, if only a few subordinates (usually less than 10) report to any single superior.

5. Administrative efficiency is increased if work is closely supervised, that is, if threat (or pressure) is high.

In addition, at least the following implicit assumptions underlie the principles:

Definition: "Organization" is defined in formal terms of positions and lines of authority and responsibility.

Axiom: The human organism for all practical purposes can be considered an isolated being with essentially physiological, or mechanical, properties.

Axiom: Management at all levels is supervisory rather than policy-making.

Axiom: Authority is formal, or legal, and is reflected only in organization charts, rules and regulations, and the like.

These assumptions are not treated explicitly in the many lists of principles but, for example, the principles logically imply that the individual is (or should be) an isolated being. For a cross-pressure condition exists if it is acknowledged that the individual has social identifications of a pervasive kind. Thus a small group may vie with the formal organization for the control of the behavior of a mutual member. One-line authority avoids the complexity of a cross-pressure condition, but only by implying socially isolated man.

The NII model also seems a product of logical derivation from the principles. Although coincidence may explain it, the Neutral and Inferior Instrument model of line-staff relations is most consistent with the principles of traditional organization theory.[2] All three ideal concepts of staff seem to respect the principle of specialization and little wonder, given its unhappy vagueness. However, only the NII concept is consistent with the *reductio ad absurdum* of specialization, the separation of "thinking" from "doing." This procrustean separation is at the heart of the traditional staff model. The principles of one-line authority and unity of command, moreover, could be logically at home only with the Neutral and Inferior Instrument concept of staff defined as "purely advisory" and "outside the lines of command." No other concept of staff could have avoided so completely any challenge to traditional organization theory.

This approach to the NII model also suggests a major reason for its persistence. The NII model can ride out critical storms, as it were, tethered to the broad organization theory from which it is derived. For, even if one of the offshoots of such an underlying theory is expertly nipped, the theory still remains.[3] And no doubt it will induce a similar derivation in time. The narrow analytical strategy of the critical literature on staff, then, credibly explains the failure to generate lasting changes in the NII concept.

Proceeding through the principles and their assumptions has a vital weakness. This "method," tersely, neglects changes in environmental conditions which require changes in the underlying propositions. Those who developed the principles were not sensi-

---

[2]*Ibid.*, pp. 242-46.

[3]Perhaps the most expert nipping of the traditional concept was contributed by Herbert A. Simon, Donald V. Smithburg, and Victor Thompson, *Public Administration* (New York: Knopf, 1956), esp. pp. 280-91.

tive to this simple datum. Indeed, the theory usually was represented as universal and applicable always-and-everywhere. That is, mere oversight does not explain the lack of sensitivity. Rather, proponents of the principles raised the neglect of environmental changes to the dignity of a methodological rule. This proved fatal.

The Changing Environment: Two Perspectives

History has been unkind to the basic weakness of the principles. Extreme environmental changes have made hollow shells of the propositions underlying the traditional theory of organization and thus of the NII model derived from those propositions. The division of effort establishing the point will be simple. First, the effects of environmental changes on the concept of authority will be outlined. Second, the ways in which major environmental changes have undercut the NII model will be analyzed.

Students and practitioners are increasingly aware that the NII model has outlived much of its usefulness. Major dimensions of this growing awareness are detailed here as one step toward structural redesign.

Authority and the Changing Environment

"Authority" clearly reflects the impact of the changing organizational environment. That is, the principles had as a basic purpose the reinforcement of a concept of authority rooted in ownership. Consequently, the structure generated by the principles stresses the parcelling out of the authority of the owner or the board of directors, through the chief executive, and eventually to the operatives. Hence the principles of one-line authority, close supervision, limited span of control, and all the rest. As Haire concludes of the line officials in such a scheme, then: "When such a man says, 'Do this,' he means, 'Do it because I say. I own the place, or at least represent the owner. If you don't do it, get off my (their) property.' This is the caricatured idea of managerial authority flowing from ownership."[4]

The NII concept fits very nicely with this ownership concept of authority. Indeed, it is difficult to conceive of any other model of staff, given this concept. To rely on Haire again:

---

[4]Mason Haire (ed.), *Organization Theory in Industrial Practice* (New York: Wiley, 1962), p. 5.

Pressures Toward Unorthodoxy, I:

The staff man ... with a special *expertise* in some phase of the process, understands not only what should be done but why it is appropriate. He says ... "If we want such and such an outcome, oughtn't we to take such and such a step now?" This again, in caricature, is what we often mean by the staff man's persuasion, indirection, and advice.[5]

The line man, then, *has authority* because of who he is. The staff man may *advise authority* because of what he knows.

Fallible men need not despise a convenient crutch, but leaning upon these two caricatures does not avoid all problems. In sum, the authority concept underlying the principles – and the NII model of staff – has been subjected to massive changes in technology, basic knowledge, and culture. To begin, the increasingly complex technology in all areas reduces the efficacy of prescriptions of threat-oriented authority. Conveniently, the point has been illustrated by dramatic developments in the study of human behavior. To illustrate, "learning theory" experiments demonstrate that subjects may learn simple tasks more effectively under conditions of threat. But the learning of more complex tasks is generally inhibited by the same condition.[6] These methodological developments have great significance. They point up inadequacies in the traditional theory which always existed, but which are heightened by environmental changes. Thus learning theory experiments demonstrate that the propositions underlying the mother theory do not adequately describe reality. For the individuals in these experiments patently reflect dynamics more complex than those implied by the principles. Moreover, these experiments demonstrate that when the conditions prescribed by the traditional organization theory do exist – high threat in this case – the anticipated consequences often are not forthcoming. A considerable and growing literature – of which but a single fragment has just been cited – supports this double-barreled inadequacy of traditional organization theory.[7]

Massive cultural changes complement these developments in technology and basic knowledge. Profound cultural changes under-

---

[5]*Ibid.*, p. 5. Emphasis in original.
[6]H. J. Eysenck, *Uses and Abuses of Psychology* (Baltimore: Penguin Books, 1953), pp. 27-28. Specifying personality characteristics permits finer predictions.
[7]Many studies demonstrate that when the conditions prescribed by the principles do exist (e.g., close supervision and high threat) administrative efficiency commonly is low. Similarly, factors like pride in work unit, which are not compatible with the principles, often are associated with higher output. See Robert L. Kahn and Daniel Katz, "Leadership Practices in Relation to Productivity and Morale," in *Group Dynamics: Research and Theory,* ed. Dorwin Cartwright and Alvin Zander (Evanston, Ill.: Row, Peterson, 1953), pp. 612-28.

cut the ownership concept of authority, for example, by acting directly on the role of the manager. The divorce of ownership from control has been the usual proof of the point, and it implies profound psychological changes in the attitudes of management and employee alike. These attitudinal changes affect the kinds of orders superiors expect to be obeyed and the kinds of orders which subordinates expect to receive. Perhaps the most dramatic demonstration of this point occurred during the nationalization of private British hospitals.[8]

Cumulatively, the effects of such environmental changes on the traditional authority concept are marked and clear. Janowitz' path-finding study of the military spotlights the trend in all sectors. He sees massive forces inducing the emergence of a new concept of authority. "As social demands and organization forms have grown more complex," Janowitz observes, "bureacratic authority has become generally less direct, arbitrary, and authoritarian." The basic change has been from an authoritative system based on domination to one based on manipulation. The change is not whimsical: It is "brought about by new weapons, the automation of warfare, the demands of technical expertise, and the emphasis upon individual initiative attending changes in warfare."[9] Failure to adjust to the new environment implies large costs. Changes in the traditional authority concept can be avoided only at great peril, then.

These environmental changes contrast sharply with the low-level bias of the principles and the concept of authority consistent with that bias. As compared to earlier times, a higher proportion of administrators operate in highly complex situations. Indeed, a similar effect operates quite far down the organization hierarchy. The technology encourages a kind of "middle-class organization" with increasingly greater numbers of trained specialists in comparison to low-level operatives. Instead of the pyramidal hierarchies with which we are most familiar in organizations, many organizations are developing personnel bulges at the middle levels. This tendency is perhaps most sharply illustrated in the military, where, for example, it forced the creation of the several specialist grades to reward and retain the low-level specialists. Other business and government agencies feel similar pressures, if they may be more moderate.

Perforce, therefore, administrators must adapt their action to cues

[8]Acton Society Trust, *Hospitals and the State* (London: Author, 1956), I, 17, II, 20-21.
[9]Morris Janowitz, "Changing Patterns of Organizational Authority: The Military Establishment," *Administrative Science Quarterly,* III (March, 1959), 473.

from many sources — including the burgeoning specialists — as well as from a single superior who is recognized as having authority.[10] Relatedly, a higher proportion of administrators and operatives are working under conditions in which creativity and self-reliance — and their concomitant, independence — are more necessary than the ability to execute specific instructions. As a major consequence, help and consultation become increasingly appropriate activities for supervisors, and authoritative order-giving becomes less common. These trends tend to be more marked at upper management levels, but even the foreman on the assembly line has been required to make substantial adjustments. Thus, characteristically, the foreman on the assembly line tends to respond to requests from below as opposed to initiating commands, and these requests tend to be for help, advice, or fire-fighting services from the supervisor.[11] McGregor concludes bluntly: "The distinctions between line and staff are being blurred."[12]

Such challenges to the ownership concept of authority imply the decreased usefulness of the NII concept. At one time, that is, the Neutral and Inferior Instrument model meshed nicely with the ownership concept of authority. Moreover, that model also did not conflict as sharply as it does today with the ways in which line and staff must behave in order to get the job done effectively. Today the pressure of events forces behavior patently inconsistent with the NII model. Whether or not administrative officials sin boldly against the traditional concept, and even if they suffer when they do and when they do not, therefore, this conclusion seems accurate: "The authority of the line man is becoming more like the staff man's every day.... He influences and persuades, and his force comes from an expertise based on an understanding of the process."[13] This demolishes the major simplistic crutches of the NII concept that the line official has authority because of who he is and that the staff official may advise authority because of what he knows.

There are those, then, who have had it with the NII concept of staff. Haire, for example, is willing to give the traditional concept

---

[10]The strongest available case emphasizing the new "specialist" role is made by Victor Thompson, *Modern Organization* (New York: Knopf, 1961). See also Douglas McGregor, "The Role of Staff in Modern Industry," in *Management Organization and the Computer,* ed. George P. Shultz and Thomas L. Whisler (Glencoe, Ill.: Free Press, 1960), p. 155.

[11]Peter M. Blau and W. Richard Scott, *Formal Organizations* (San Francisco: Chandler, 1962), pp. 173, 177.

[12]McGregor, *op. cit.*, p. 115.

[13]Haire, *op, cit.*, pp. 5-6.

"back to the military ... where its use often seems equally dubi-
ous."[14] He has influential support. E. F. Scoutten, Vice-President of
Personnel of the Maytag Corporation, for example, raises this
disharmony with traditional organization theory and its derivative
NII concept of staff:

> We believe that the only truly effective authority which
> one man asserts over others springs from competence.
> We believe that mere rank, as such, carries essentially no
> intrinsic authority. Finally, we believe that authority is
> granted by the subordinates to the superior, and that such
> granting of authority comes only because of demon-
> strated competence on the part of the superior. . . .
> We suggest that the real authority of the staff is identi-
> cal with the real authority of the line: It must be, and is,
> earned.[15]

Scoutten very clearly rejects the ownership concept of authority,
that of "authority [as a] commodity which, basically and originally,
is in the exclusive possession of the chief executive of the
company." Indeed, he stands the ownership concept on its head, as
it were. Scoutten's authority is granted "upwards." This destroys
much of the basis of the NII model.

Given the clear implication that influence upward and across the
organization is as significant as authority downward, any adequate
staff model must have several properties. Likert's insights conveniently suggest them. The NII model, he notes, becomes increasingly inappropriate as technical processes and other problems
become more complex. Serious conflict often results. Rather than
assigning authority to the line and advice to the staff, then, Likert
recommends building "an effective interaction-influence system
involving multiple overlapping groups through which communication, decision-making, and influence processes would occur. . . .
The contributions of line and staff would vary with the problem
and with the resources each possessed."[16] Likert's general directions serve to orient the following attempt to design a more satisfactory staff model. But much more detail is necessary before this
development can be attempted seriously.

---

[14]*Ibid.*, p. 6.
[15]*Ibid.*, pp. 79, 84.
[16]Rensis Likert, *New Patterns of Management* (New York: McGraw-Hill, 1961),
p.186. To a similar point, others have advocated "integrating departments" or
"cross-functional committees." See Jay W. Lorsch, "The Diagnosis of Organizational Problems" (Unpublished manuscript, 1965).

Three Components of the Changing Environment

The influence of environmental conditions on the NII concept also may be illuminated by considering three specific and related properties of the "change syndrome" which characterizes the recent history of organizations: the growth in the *size* of organizations and of staff units, the advancing *level of technology*, and the rapid *pace of technological change*. These changes reduce the descriptive usefulness of the "principles" and relegate to the pedantic level the question of the prescriptive usefulness of the principles and their staff derivative. For the administrative world has changed in ways which make it increasingly unlikely that the conditions implied by the principles can be approximated closely.

Increasing Size and the Change Syndrome. The inability of the NII model to cope with large size may be illustrated directly by considering *the* major structural way of compensating for, and adapting to, large size. The focus is upon decentralization. Decentralization refers to the delegation of very substantial powers to the component units of an organization with overhead control in terms of major policies but with great latitude for the component units in precisely how they go about meeting overall policies. Commonly, individual plants or product lines of a corporate giant will be organized as "independent profit centers," responsible for profit and adherence to broad corporate policies. In General Electric, to be specific, there are over one hundred Operating Departments. The General Manager of each of them could make commitments for capital expenditures up to $500,000 on his own.[17]

Decentralization poses very substantial challenges to the NII model of line-staff relations. Indeed, this seems too mild. The two are mutual organizational poison. The point will be supported in two ways.

Companies which have decentralized have been forced to experiment with their staff relations — to indirectly suggest the inappropriateness of the NII model — as in the "consultant" type of staff developed by Humble. The appropriate role is not well defined in a positive sense, but what the consultant is *not* supposed to do conveys the sense of the desired role of the staff man as one who reports directly to the head of the decentralized unit and (it would seem to follow) reports no specific information concerning irregular-

---

[17]Ralph J. Cordiner, *New Frontiers for Professional Managers* (New York: McGraw-Hill, 1956), p. 61.

ities to headquarters even if the head of the decentralized unit decides to disregard such information. Thus behaviors considered *inappropriate* for the consultant role at Humble "may constitute telling the local managers what they may or should not do. [Inappropriate staff behavior] involves utilizing the influence of headquarters management in order to constitute pressure on field units to get them to do what the staff man feels they should do."[18]

Humble's definition of the consultant role, then, strives to meet two demands of decentralization. On the one hand, decentralization does not mean that headquarters abandons the decentralized units. This might prove fatal. However, neither does decentralization mean that headquarters will help these units as under a centralized structure. This would be the death of benefits attributed to decentralization: the training of lower-level managers in making and implementing decisions, the flexibility of adapting to local situations, and the speed of decision-making which avoids waiting for the tail of headquarters to wag the corporate body. Consequently, the consultant is supposed to act in certain prescribed ways which put him on tap without encouraging him into an informer's role.

That the NII concept could hardly be tailored to the twin requirements of decentralization also may be established more directly. Thus staff traditionally has been considered an extension of the personality of the chief executive, and this bit of intentional symbolism has not been wasted on line or staff. Perhaps crudely, the NII concept defines a role that is investigative and potentially punitive. Recall that the staff man reports up rather than across. Not too subtly, then, the NII role is oriented toward getting the goods on the lower-line so that the upper-line can exercise close and direct control. One executive illustrated the point in arguing for a new model of line-staff relations between headquarters and the decentralized units. He noted that bringing in line officials from the field to a headquarters staff department and asking them to discuss the types of help they wanted, charitable intentions and all, was not likely to prove rewarding. The reason: "The headquarters man is normally seen as being in a controlling role rather than a consulting one. He sits in judgment. He has an inherent power of recommendation and communication to the headquarters line management." If those in the field in his firm ever did seek eagerly for help, according to this executive, only a few experiences with staff's

---

[18]Harry D. Kolb, "The Headquarters Staff Man in the Role of a Consultant," in Haire, *op. cit.*, p. 145.

Pressures Toward Unorthodoxy, I:

punitive aspects were enough to restrain the field official from asking for more of the same. The headquarters man, we are told, "has often failed to measure up to the expectations of those in the field who may have looked to him for help."[19]

Some observers of organizations sense a way out of the challenges thrown up by decentralization to the principles and the NII concept. The development of computers augurs for some the coming of a new centralization. That is, one of the major motivators of decentralization has been the inadequacy of the "information technology"—the gathering, assembling, and digesting of data being necessarily parceled out to constituent field units because of complexity. Computers reduce this motivation for decentralization in many cases, providing great range and speed for calculations at headquarters.

Computers can be used to spur the new centralization, but they also can strengthen decentralization. Thus one of Sylvania Corporation's officials acknowledged that electronic data processing implied significant changes in top management thinking. But this did not mean that the firm's decision to build a data-processing center required a reversal of a long-standing commitment to a philosophy of decentralization. "Our answer at Sylvania is that we expect the new tool to strengthen our belief in decentralization," the official concludes. "Our definition of decentralization has always been decentralization of authority and responsibility with centralization of control."[20]

That is, decentralization does not presume a root, hog, or die philosophy of the relations between headquarters and decentralized units. Performance must be monitored and appraised by headquarters, and direct intervention may be necessary. The computer will help in such tasks to make decentralization more viable. And, of course, other motivations of decentralization—e.g., the involvement of individuals in their work—still provide support for that approach to organizing.

Technological Level and the Change Syndrome. Second, the level of technology (admittedly a somewhat slippery notion) also affects the traditional concept of staff and the organization theory from which it derives. The persistence of the Neutral and Inferior Instrument concept is wonderful in the same sense that the aristocrats of Chekhov's *The Cherry Orchard* are wonderful. Technology has simply moved out from beneath the concept.

---

[19]*Ibid.*, pp. 143-44.
[20]Don G. Mitchell, *Proceedings of the American Management Association's Special Electronic Conference* (New York: March, 1955).

The point may be made more prosaically. Directly, a simple technology inspired the subordination of the staff to the line. Thus when Gustavus Adolphus separated combat from supply, transport, and finance (as line and staff, respectively) there was *some* reason to emphasize the combatant versus the noncombatant nature of the functions and to assign precedence to the former. This may seem a fragile foundation for so durable a concept, but others have come to a similar conclusion. Haire recounts that he once heard an executive say: "Such and such a department used to be staff, but it has become so important that it's now a line function." Haire originally marked the observation as ridiculous, but he is not so certain in retrospect: "More and more I begin to feel that this may have the heart of the distinction in it, after all."[21]

There always have been proponents of the thesis that "an army marches on its stomach," that is, on the contributions of staff. But the point is unavoidable under conditions of a complex technology. To explain within the military frame of reference, both the combatant and the noncombatant activities are functional differentiations. Both functions are delegated powers from the commander and both are coordinated by him with other functional specialties. Moreover, assigning precedence to one of these functional specialties is arbitrary. For their contributions differ basically in terms of time only, and the relative importance of the functions is not determined by which function follows or precedes the other. Under present technological conditions, for example, future wars will be won (or lost) more and more in the laboratory, on the proving ground, and on the training field. Indeed, future wars may be prevented by staff activities. Similarly, business success can hinge upon the contributions of such staff activities as finance and marketing. The point has a growing popular currency. Commentators have argued that the 1960's are the "Age of Marketing," for example, and interesting jingoistic efforts are being made by marketing specialists to avoid the stigma of the NII model while they preserve the NII model.[22] The instincts of such commentators are sharp, but their strategy is awkward.

Despite resistance, practice in organizations increasingly emphasizes the importance of staff and stresses its participation in command functions. Both emphases are patent in the resume of a recently held panel on "Staff: To Advise or Control?" "There is much complaining about the staff concept today because the use of

---

[21]Haire, *op. cit.*, p. 5.
[22]Hector Lazo and Arnold Corbin, *Management in Marketing* (New York: McGraw-Hill, 1961), esp. pp. 23-24.

staff is intimately connected with management's growing difficulties in controlling its program," went the dominant theme of the panel. Some managements have acted. Thus the Internal Revenue Service has been led to divide its staff personal, one set being purely advisory and the other being empowered to issue directives.[23]

These general comments may be given some body by two kinds of evidence showing that organization structure must vary with technological conditions. First, the automated factory — undoubtedly the dominant technology of the future — does not seem very congenial to the traditional pattern of line-staff relations. The NII model evolved out of the job-lot and assembly-line technology that is being left behind and is ill-suited to the rapid communication required in the automated factory. Moreover, the pressure for action in the automated factory at once requires the Colleague-like participation in command by the various specialists while it leaves no room for the competitiveness and rigidity encouraged by the Neutral and Inferior Instrument concept. Buckingham's careful study of automation summarizes the pressures on the orthodox staff concept in these terms:

> As automation changes productive processes and factory layouts, the problem of determining managerial responsibility changes. Formerly discontinuous, specialized functions are frequently tied together in a continuous flow process. For example, the design and manufacture of products need to be more closely integrated under automation. Technical departments [e.g., staff] should therefore have a more effective voice in management. . . . The specialists who are needed for automated plants will require more direct control over their operations. . . . The widely used "Line and Staff" principle grew out of the needs of mass production technology. This principle may have to be reexamined in the light of automation.[24]

Nor need the firm be automated to profit from unorthodox staff relations. "Project managers" in the aircraft industry were developed because the NII model made it difficult to integrate the various activities required for a long list of complex end items.[25] Organizing around projects moves toward the Colleague model, as subsequent analysis will show.

---

[23]American Society for Public Administration, *Public Administration News* (Winter, 1960), p. 2.
[24]Walter Buckingham, *Automation* (New York: Harper, 1961), pp. 56-57.
[25]Adolph Vlcek, Jr., "Minimizing Line-Staff Friction at Martin-Baltimore," in *Line-Staff Relationships in Production* (New York: American Management Association, 1957), p. 41.

Second, the effects of different degrees of technological development on organization structure also may be illustrated by a study of
British firms. One hundred manufacturing firms were classified
according to their technological development, the end points of the
continuum being the small, job-order shop and the large, automated
factory. One of the organizational characteristics which varied with
technological complexity is of particular interest.[26] The traditional
staff pattern was most highly developed in firms falling in the
middle ranges of the continuum. This is consistent with the previous analysis. The NII concept tends to appear—because it is the
conventional thing—when the enterprise can no longer be run out
of the back pocket of the owner or manager. But convention is no
long-run substitute for effectiveness, which plausibly accounts for
the absence of the traditional pattern of organizing line-staff relations in the large, automated factory.

These considerations imply straightforward conclusions. Choice
of a staff model cannot be divorced from the technology, and the
assignment of staff to a subordinate position has no obvious support
under conditions of a complex technology.

Pace of Change and the Change Syndrome. The orientation
toward change also has an important effect on the Neutral and
Inferior Instrument concept of staff. If adaptation is valued, there is
ample reason why staff should not be relegated to an inferior role in
organization theory. For line-staff parity may act as a stimulus to
adaptive behavior. That is, line and staff operatives tend to have
responsibilities that encourage different orientations toward action
and change. "The factory supervisors' outlook on things is different," one budget officer noted in illustrating the point. "They
emphasize today. Yes, they're looking at only the short run. We

---

[26]Joan Woodward, "The Effects of Technical Innovations on Management Administration," in *International Conference on Economic and Social Aspects of Automation* (Namur, Belgium: International Associates for Cybernetics, 1958). Although
the available data leave much to be desired, to extend the point, Woodward's
distinctions between levels of technological sophistication seem to correspond to
sharply-different ranges of the percentages of plant-force performing administrative,
maintenance, and technical specialties. "Craft" technology seems to require fewest
of these specialties; "large batch" technology seems intermediate in its demands
for staff services; and "continuous processes" seem to require the highest percentage of these specialties. For some data, see Elmer H. Burack, *Industrial
Technology Project, 1964-65* (Chicago: Illinois Institute of Technology, 1965);
Robert H. Guest, *Organizational Change* (Homewood, Ill.: Irwin and Dorsey,
1962), p. 15; and Richard A. Beaumont and Roy B. Helfgott, *Management, Automation, and People* (New York: Industrial Relations Counselors, Inc., 1964), pp. 41-44.
That "continuous process" technology requires two or three times more such specialists than "crafts" suggests the more complex problems of line-staff relations
associated with technological progress.

have to look at things in the long run. We have to see the whole unit. They worry about their individual departments."[27]

The NII model gives staff units little formal leverage for this global action orientation. This seems awkward. For staff units are more likely to perceive, and to monitor solutions of, problems which are long-run and organization-wide. The more limited action perspective common among line officials, in contrast, compromises their effectiveness in that increasingly important task facing organized life, the perception and solution of interunit, long-run problems. Admiral Rickover's battles with line officers over the atomic submarine in the United States Navy, for example, provide ready illustration of the point. In addition, Rickover's experience reflects the important influence of the massive assumption of the superiority of the line officers over the segregated EDO (Engineering Duty Only).[28]

Some balance between the line and staff orientations toward action seems desirable under all conditions, in short, save a technological stagnancy at an early stage of development. Most desirably, the balance should be an easily shifting one. No doubt this is far too happy a solution to expect in any power situation. In any case, the traditional staff concept, imposed under conditions which do not correspond to the low-level, static technology implicit in the concept, legitimates a lack of balance and makes organization adaptation sticky.

Since the pace of technological change in the past twenty years has been unparalleled, the NII model is that much more undesirable as a model for line-staff relations. The pace of technological change sets a stiff standard for a corresponding change in thinking about staff.

Environmental Changes in Retrospect

These factors suggest that Fisch's conclusion is accurate: "Line-Staff is Obsolete." The NII concept developed when American industry faced limited problems. Product lines were relatively fixed and homogeneous; the factory was the focus of operations; and technical improvements in manufacturing and processing techniques were the keys to efficiency and success. Time, therefore,

---

[27]Chris Argyris, *The Impact of Budgets on People* (New York: Controllership Foundation, Inc., 1952), p. 7.
[28]Clay Blair, Jr., *The Atomic Submarine and Admiral Rickover* (New York: Holt, 1954).

was not a particularly crucial factor. Indeed, many practitioners—including Henry Ford and F. W. Taylor—thought that once a work process had been perfected, it would continue to produce items ad infinitum. Hence Ford's dictum that consumers could have any color car they desired, providing it was black, and his resistance to changes in design. These leisurely requirements suited the NII concept. For speed and smooth functioning—as later chapters will document—do not rank high among the roster of consequences of the NII model.

Things have changed, and radically so. "Whereas the hub of corporate life used to be in a single factory," Fisch observes, "today it is in the product and service mix. . . ." The datum implies an organizational revolution. "The product line, of course," Fisch explains, "is created by research, development, and engineering, or by acquisition or mergers studied by the finance department." History, that is to say, has far outrun the once-reasonable assignment by the NII model of superiority to the line.

The dead hand of the past still has a relatively firm grip on thought about organizing, however. "These [staff] functions have become the very core of profit or loss opportunity," according to Fisch, but they are still "classified as staff or advisory functions" only. This being the case, the NII model is not sweet reasonableness. *"Surely there must be something wrong with a concept which treats as advisory or support groups those functions* that create the hub of today's manufacturing enterprises,"[29] Fisch concluded.

Villers' advice, then, seems apt: "No organization structure can ever be considered as final."[30] Supporters of the NII model neglect the point when they represent the traditional theory of organization as beyond environmental change, as a "one-best way."

The Growing Critical Literature:
Similarities and a Selection

If it has a prominent place in the literature, the Neutral and Inferior Instrument concept of staff also has become an increasingly common whipping boy. Certainly the enthusiasm for criticism implies nothing less than a clear perception of the environmental changes previously detailed. Students of both public administra-

---

[29]Gerald C. Fisch, "Line-Staff Is Obsolete," *Harvard Business Review*, XXXIX (September, 1961), 68.
[30]Raymond Villers, *Dynamic Management in Industry* (Englewood Cliffs, N. J.: Prentice-Hall, 1960), p. 159.

tion and business administration have joined in the critical analysis, reputations have been made by disagreeing with the NII concept, and the weight of polemics pro and especially con grows apace.

The striking similarities of the literature critical of the NII model deserve careful detailing. Thus the critical staff literature in both public and business administration was received with excitement.[31] This enthusiasm suggests that reliance on the NII concept is encouraged primarily by an inability to pull the literature out of the muck of the traditional simplism, rather than a lack of suspicion of the NII concept or a lack of willingness to contest it.

The literature critical of the orthodox staff model, in addition, also similarly stresses that organization is a system of power. Stahl thus writes of a "network of power" in which all units of an organization are represented. The traditional line-staff distinction does not recognize power, Stahl argues, and hence could hardly provide for its effective management. Other contributions to the critical literature on staff similarly stress "how things are done" in organizations, while emphasizing that the NII concept stresses "how they should be done." As the latter-day iconoclasts see it, the disregard of so elemental a fact of organizational reality does not encourage confidence in the traditional concept as a guide for behavior.

The NII model also comes in for substantial criticism because of its simplistic view of organization dynamics. The complexity of modern organization, goes the typical critical refrain, outstrips the NII model. Matters are too fluid, and the relative contributions of various activities are too variable over time and over different problems, to accord an organizational inferiority to any activity. Relatedly, there are many activities which require organization-wide adherence and yet are staff provinces. These activities perforce require some involvement by staff in the affairs of line officials

---

[31]Frank M. Stewart, "Purchasing of Highway Equipment in Texas," *American Political Science Review*, XXIX (May, 1930), 409-15; Willard Hogan, "A Dangerous Tendency in Government," *Public Administration Review*, VI (Autumn, 1946), 362-67; Douglas McGregor, "The Staff Function in Human Relations," *Journal of Social Issues*, IV (Summer, 1948), 6-23; Herbert A. Simon, Donald V. Smithburg, and Victor Thompson, *Public Administration* (New York: Knopf, 1950), esp. pp. 280-91; Peter F. Drucker, *The Practice of Management* (New York: Harper, 1954), pp. 241ff.; Edward C. Schleh, *Successful Executive Action* (Englewood Cliffs, N. J.: Prentice-Hall, 1955); Charles A. Myers and John G. Turnbull, "Line and Staff in Industrial Relations," *Harvard Business Review*, XXXIV (July-August, 1956), 113-24; J. Rich Johnson, "Line-Staff Revisited," *Advanced Management*, XXIII (May, 1958), esp. 17; Gerald C. Fisch, "Line-Staff Is Obsolete," *Harvard Business Review*, XXXIX (September-October, 1961), 67-69; O. Glenn Stahl, "The Network of Authority," *Public Administration Review*, XVIII (Winter, 1958), ii-lv; and Stahl, "More on the Network of Authority," *Public Administration Review*, XX (Winter, 1960), 35-37.

and some control over line operations. The NII model merely complicates these unavoidable dynamics, runs the citicial literature.

The critical literature also is at one in that it usually is just critical, and no more. Thus that literature has not gone deeply into the question of designing line-staff relations more sensitive to the facts of organizational life. This may seem curious. Having once been burned by an orthodoxy, perhaps, students are leery about designing another. But they most assuredly have avoided redesign.

These similarities permit the selection of a representative effort to illustrate the critical family. The critical literature will be sampled in depth here by reproducing major excerpts from two brief articles by O. Glenn Stahl, presently the director of the Bureau of Programs and Standards of the United States Civil Service Commission. Stahl's position is argued cogently and concisely, and his experience in the staff agency monitoring personnel activities in the administrative colossus that is the federal government urges careful consideration of his views of line-staff relations.

Stahl's attack on the NII model is two-pronged, stressing that the traditional concept does not often accurately describe behavior in organizations and that, in any case, it would not be particularly conducive to effective performance if it did guide behavior. He abandons the traditional line-staff distinction in favor of a distinction between "program" and "sustaining" units acting within a network of power. The argument does not aim at designing a more suitable structure. The Colleague model of relations is implied, however.

Stahl's "The Network of Authority": Major Excerpts

In the environment of "the organization man" every workday produces classic examples of worshipful observance of the sacrosanct division between "line" and "staff." The observance is more often than not in ritual rather than in substance.

In both public and private enterprise care is taken to couch directives so that they accord with the "line of command." It is common, too, for concern to be expressed when power and directional authority do not fit the proper preconceptions, when leadership does not appear to come from the "right" sources. Many an administrative decision (including errors and excuses) is the product of this genuine conviction that "line is line and staff is staff and ne'er the twain shall meet."

It is ironical that such determinations are usually made on behalf of a chief executive by assistants who are themselves "staff" but who actually wield great power. The virtues of simplicity and good communication are frequently sacrificed on the altar of an unverified definition of administrative authority.

I find more realistic a contrary theory—that "line" and "staff" are hardly distinguishable as *indicators of power status;* that the terms are merely convenient for identifying (1) those functions of an organization that are direct subdivisions of its program purposes and (2) those that are oriented principally to its inner form, its sustenance, and its methods; that it is more useful to view these two types of specialization as intersecting lines of authority than as primary versus incidental functions, especially in the public service.

There are a number of considerations that lead to this conclusion:

1. The conventional criteria of the line function or "operations" appear to be: (a) supervisory command—giving orders and instructions; (b) decision-making on "cases"; (c) producing a product or a service; (d) dealing with clientele groups in connection with any of the first three. The conventional criteria of the staff function appear to be: (a) planning; (b) research; (c) advice; (d) the absence of "command." How many organizational entities can be found that exemplify one of these sets of criteria to the exclusion of the others? The "pure" staff unit, according to the above measures, is so rare as to be almost nonexistent. It is simply a fact of administrative behavior that executives come to lean on staff units to exercise assigned portions of their "command" authority. Often this is done by clear and unequivocal delegation.

The classicists will say: "Ah yes, but this kind of staff exercise of command is appealable by the 'line'; it won't necessarily stick." But how is this distinguishable from a decision (even under a delegation) by a so-called "line" official. Is it not reversible upon appeal by *other segments of the line?* Furthermore, is not the authority of "staff" realistically effective when practicality dictates that the "line" *not* appeal *its* determination?

The command function exercised by staff units—even by some that give the most lip service to the sharp distinction between line and staff—is genuinely effective authority when it makes sense to do it this way, when it saves an executive's time, and when it is accepted by the operating divisions. Line operators who are the most vigorous in their denunciation of power exercised by staff units commonly use their own staff units in the same manner.

2. The breakdown of distinction between line and staff

is further illustrated by various activities in which there is an inescapable need for organizationwide adherence. Subordinate echelons in an enterprise cannot be allowed to go their own way on such matters as budgeting, pay, or career planning. Career planning, for example, by its very nature must embrace standard policies and methods for in-hiring, mobility or even planned rotation in assignment, training that spans divisional lines, and promotion systems that imply movement and release of people. The concept of the individual line supervisor being the basic locus of the personnel function or the budget function is satisfactory up to a point but utterly unrealistic when one considers many organizationwide features of personnel and budget objectives. . . .

I am not precluding that methods of a staff unit, in arriving at decisions, should embrace extensive consultation with and participation of other organizational segments. The only point at issue here is power status.

3. Because a staff activity has a particular specialization as a trademark it is no less an "operation." So-called line activities are simply *specialized segments* of the end-purpose functions of the enterprise. They are just as susceptible to provincialism, to organizational myopia, as are the so-called staff activities. Indeed, the staff activity is often the more likely one to have the Olympian point of view, to see the forest as a whole. On top of this consideration, every staff unit that achieves any size comes to have an internal operating task of its own. Its relationships with other staff units and many features of its behavior and orientation are identical to those of a program subdivision of the organization. When one gets down to the core of the subject he is likely to find that "all God's chillun" are operators.

4. Staff functions usually have more to do with *how* something is done than *what* is done. They customarily represent the framework and the boundaries within which program operators may perform. This has special significance in the public service, because the manner in which governmental functions are administered is frequently as important as the functions themselves. . . .

It is futile to pontificate that every operator must have *authority commensurate with his responsibility* so that he can be held accountable. This is usually interpreted as freedom from restraints and limitations of various sorts; yet these very restraints and limitations are *part of the responsibility*, not something extraneous to it. . . .

In conclusion, then, would it not make sense to divest ourselves of the abracadabra that divides "line" and "staff" into incongruous kinds of activity and to recognize that *all* such activities are simply specialized subdivisions of an organization's work? Because some of them,

Pressures Toward Unorthodoxy, I:

called staff functions, develop only by virtue of the existence of the organization and operate to sustain it does not detract from their necessity or their importance. They may be no more incidental to end purpose than individual program subdivisions themselves, for there may be end purposes as to *means* that override single immediate program objectives. This is neither to be deplored nor applauded; it is simply a fact of organizational life that is inescapable, and peculiarly so in the public service. When specialists of program and sustaining activities are equals, there is more incentive to reconcile conflicts at low levels and less disposition to push decisions up the hierarchy.

I find it convenient to think of the work of an enterprise as a network, a grid, or a checkerboard in which vertical program subdivisions are interlaced with horizontal sustaining activities. The chief executive sits in a position at a top corner from which he holds both the vertical and the horizontal lines. They are all lines; for controls are exercised in both directions at once. Where they intersect there is potentiality for conflict or at least the necessity for reconciliation, but such a conception breeds the settlement of issues where they are first detected. This constitutes half the dynamics of running an organization.

No purpose is served in fighting this phenomenon in the name of confining staff and line to their respective hypothetical roles. Let's relax and enjoy it! It at least saves us from guilt complexes, makes everyone's behavior more open and above board, lubricates communication channels, and facilitates decision-making at a given point in the hierarchy on the common-sense basis of a combination of the requisite information and capacity, without preoccupying us with who has the right to do what to whom.[32]

Stahl's "More on the Network of Authority": Major Excerpts

In a brief statement which appeared two years ago in this journal . . . I advanced the thesis that "line" and "staff" are hardly distinguishable as indicators of power status. I observed:
1. that so-called staff units usually do and must necessarily carry out functions of command;
2. that there are some activities for which there is an inescapable need for organizationwide adherence;
3. that a staff activity is no more a restricted, special-

---

[32]Stahl, "The Network of Authority," *op. cit.*

ized function than are individual line segments of an enterprise;

4. that staff functions, having to do with *how* things are done more than *what* is done, assume a special importance in the public service;

5. that it is convenient to think of line and staff as "program" functions and "sustaining" functions, respectively, which interlace with each other in a *network;* that the chief executive controls an organization by means of both the vertical "program" channels and the horizontal "sustaining" channels;

6. that this approach avoids awkward and unrealistic actions or assumptions on the grounds that decision-making can occur only in certain offices in an organization which have been blessed with the label "line"; and that conflicts are reconciled and communication facilitated at lower levels in the organization when there is no presumption of unvarying command superiority of line over staff.

What Was Not Meant

Apparently this statement has provoked a good deal of discussion and reappraisal of some ancient and hallowed concepts. To some extent, however, the objective I had in mind may have been misconstrued. It may be well therefore to make clear what I was *not* saying:

1. I did not say that the staff or sustaining functions consist *entirely* of command-type activities.

2. I did not mean to discount the valuable and important *advisory and leadership functions* of these sustaining activities.

The main thing I was cavilling at was the purist approach that staff must be wholly advisory and wholly subordinate to all levels of the line. I was concerned that program supervisors down the line are too prone to interpret the activities of the sustaining or staff arms of their chief executives as having no real sanction so far as control over *them* is concerned. I was contending that this not only *should not* be the case but *is not and never has been* the case; that it is impossible to expect a generalist executive to get organizationwide coherence on such matters as budget planning, personnel standards, career development, and public relations policy without depending upon his sustaining units to *apply* some policy judgments for him, to exercise some portion of command authority.

None of this line of reasoning detracts in the slightest from the importance of the advisory function and the "authority of influence." Sustaining units, of necessity, have many areas of activity in which they can only cajole or persuade. This is as it should be. Staff units should not interpret my remarks as providing them with a theoretical basis for abandoning the "selling" technique and to operate smugly on the assumption that they can tell program directors "where to get off" at any time. These are complementary and supplementary roles, not antithetical ones.

Neither should program officers hide behind my thesis to mask abandonment of their responsibility for a heavy amount of decision-making on their own. Each supervisor is his own personnel man and budget man — up to a point. That there is such a point is what is important. Some conditions must be established organization-wide which set boundaries on supervisory decision-making. Management specialists inevitably become the interpreters and, to a considerable extent, the real enforcers of these limits. But this does not preclude the large discretion ordinarily left in such matters to program supervision.

Incidentally, even if a staff function consisted mainly of a control-type activity, I would still advocate heavy dependence on persuasive techniques. But so would I advocate such an approach for program or line managers in directing their own subordinates.

The Real Villain: Narrow Specialization

In my judgment, the most serious fault in organization life is not the much overworked "interference by staff with the line" but the curse of specialization. I submit that the preoccupation of any specialist, whether line or staff, with the trivia of his profession and his tendency to relate all that goes on about him to the particular orbit of his work assignment, causes more trouble than anything else. The difficulty is *at least* as much a characteristic of program operators as it is of staff specialists. In fact, it can often be more so.

One of the things that has contributed to this has been the overemphasis on subordination of staff to line. Program managers rationalize degrees of autonomy and independence from other activities in the organization on the grounds that necessary efforts at cohesion and coordination constitute "staff interference." My point is that the independent success of a specialized phase of an organization objective is not always as important as the intermeshing of programs into the whole purpose — and sustaining activities, with adequate control measures, may contribute a great deal more to this over-all objective than any individual segment of *program* operations....

Where program leadership and management specialists *are* compatible in tempo and depth, the probability of the manager using such assistants to make *some* decisions and to interpret and apply general policy is all the more likely. Here, then, is the central thesis again—that there is an inevitability, an inexorable character to the exercise of command authority by the sustaining units of an organization. . . .

In other words, it is idle to rationalize all of our organization structure and behavior on the theory that the sustaining management activities are invariably and forever subordinate to the initial program objectives of the organization, particularly when it is a governmental organization. It is a mistake to maintain the sanctity of any single program objective *at all costs*. Doing so creates false illusions on the part of some program operators, develops frustrations when they are told to view management activities as legitimate only when they serve as *aids* rather than *inhibitors*, leaves staff specialists dismayed when they cannot help being inhibitors at times, promotes provincialism and a magnified sense of importance of a field of specialization when it happens to be a program specialization, and generally detracts from the maintenance of cohesion and coordination in the government service.

This is not to say that the judgments made in the name of organization-wide sustaining policy are always right, nor that they should be made without regard to the interests and objectives of program administration. . . .

Whatever conflict must occur between program objectives and sustaining objectives—and there will always be some—should be reconciled on the basis of practicality and a weighing of relative values in the light of total public interest, the law, and all that goes therewith, not on the basis of subordination of one set of aims to another. The problem is not that we really fail to do it this way. It's just that we cause so much misery by constantly insisting that we shouldn't.[33]

Some Guides for Theoretical Responses to Change and Criticism

Environmental changes and the critical literature exemplified by the excerpts from Stahl provide multiple directions toward the goal of this volume, structural redesign. Let us sharpen two particularly important classes of such directions. One of these classes provides a general guide for further work, the other details specific challenges that face such analysis. Environmental change and criticism both imply, first, that line-staff relations must be tailored to the demands that organizations face today. We shall try our hand at developing

[33]Stahl, "More on the Network of Authority," *op. cit.*

the point and its implications. Second, the preceding sections also generate a set of specific constraints that subsequent analysis must respect. They will be detailed in due time.

One convenient way of distinguishing the structural demands facing organizations focuses on basic strategies. In sum, the structure of any enterprise must be patterned to suit the basic strategies which an enterprise is pursuing, first, whether these strategies are conscious and well-articulated or whether they were blundered into. The point also patently holds for a staff concept. Second, the NII model ill suits the kinds of strategies that more and more guide the enterprise, whether its executives are sensitive or oblivious to these strategies. No reasonable reconciliation of power phenomena may be expected under the circumstances.

The relations of strategy and structure may be illustrated by considering Chandler's four basic strategies for growth: expansion of volume, geographical dispersion, vertical integration, and diversification.[34] The strategy of expansion of volume does not imply great structural subtlety, since it requires only the creation of an administrative office to oversee one or a few closely related products or activities in one local area. This strategy implies a rather low ceiling on growth, however, although a Henry Ford making a black Model T can build a River Rouge plant.

Further growth will require such another strategy as geographical dispersion. But this strategy makes greater demands on a structure. Thus headquarters must be organized to supervise the field units and, commonly, this means developing a departmental structure to supervise each of the several functions performed by each field unit. In sum, structure had to be designed to combat not only distance, but also to meet the diverse problems of the several field units within uniform policies, as well as to help mold consensus about programs both at headquarters and in the field. Comparatively, organizing for the expansion of volume was child's play.

Other strategies are even more demanding. Thus vertical integration refers to growth accomplished by adding new functions, such as setting up a department to handle the advertising of our hypothetical single product, which work once had been entrusted to an advertising agency. Vertical integration thereby exaggerates such pressures on structure as those outlined above.

---

[34]Alfred D. Chandler, Jr., *Strategy and Structure: Chapters in the History of the Industrial Enterprise* (Cambridge: Massachusetts Institute of Technology Press, 1962), p. 14. Be it noted, however, that this author sometimes makes different use of these strategies than does Chandler, and he might not agree with the present interpretation.

The strategy of diversification—of developing new products and expanding into national or international markets—requires the greatest organizational touch. Crudely, the structural problems of geographical dispersion and vertical integration are complicated by the often inconsistent demands of the several products and, particularly, by the problems of developing new products. The magnitude of these difficulties is suggested by the experience of the Ford Motor Co. Ford had been geared to the strategy of the expansion of volume, reflecting the massive and monolithic influence of its founder. Not unrelatedly, Ford had little luck in diversifying, even though it attempted to do so with high-quality agricultural equipment and aircraft.[35] And Ford also sustained more than $200,000,000 in losses on its Edsel, a record which in no small part may be attributed to organizationally based negative attitudes of many Ford executives that developed from their identifications with existing operations and products, resistance to the "borrowing" of their technical and managerial personnel to develop the new auto, plus the novel (for Ford) and revolutionary significance given marketing research on the Edsel. Avoiding such awkward reactions generally has required this major structural innovation: organizing around products (as opposed to functions),[36] of which ante-Edsel Ford attempted too little, too late.

The four growth strategies imply these propositions: Contemporary organizations require strategies of great and increasing structural subtlety, and the NII model therefore becomes increasingly inappropriate. The whole of this analysis demonstrates the fullness of the point, but note here that the NII model is most suitable for meeting the problems of geographical dispersion. That is, any organization with field units must face the question: To whom is a personnel official in a field unit directly responsible, to the manager of the field unit or to personnel officials at headquarters?[37] The NII model takes care of this problem by definition, by ascribing organizational inferiority to staff. The strategy of diversification, in contrast, which requires developing new products and new markets, does not permit even this tainted comfort. The NII model does not provide staff with organizational support for playing its vital required role in such a strategy, and " . . . there must be

[35]Cyrus McCormick, III, *Century of the Reaper* (Boston: Houghton-Mifflin, 1931), p. 198.
[36]See Ernest Dale, "Du Pont: Pioneer in Systematic Management," *Administrative Science Quarterly*, II (June, 1957), 35-40.
[37]Chandler, *op. cit.*, for example, time and again stresses the prominence of this question and its deleterious consequences for performance in the four giant firms he studied. See his pp. 183-90 for the experience at Standard Oil of New Jersey.

something wrong with a concept which treats as advisory or support those functions that create the hub of today's manufacturing enterprise."[38]

Finally, and still broadly, our administrative and industrial giants have felt the inadequacies of the NII model most sharply, but smaller organizations can profit from the extreme cases in point and modify their structure in appropriate ways. This must be classified as a matter of personal belief, but it is at worst a harmless belief.

The preceding analysis also is amenable to more delicate brush-strokes than the bolder analytical splashes just completed. First, changes in the traditional concept of staff depend upon the development of organization theories of greater specificity than the principles. The tail is attached to a very big dog, as it were. Subsequent analysis must respect this fact.

The methodological directions for such an effort, fortunately, need not be developed from scratch. The new watchwords will be those of empirical theory and of the concepts and operations that constitute its vitals. These watchwords are tentativeness and testing, neither of which characterized traditional organization theory. Nor is it necessary to wait until tomorrow for applications of the methodology to provide grist for the mills of theory. Indeed, the natural-science approach to organization phenomena already has yielded findings that wait to be built into any satisfactory theory of organization. These findings will be employed on succeeding pages to guide the design of a suitable structure for the Colleague concept.

Second, the Neutral and Inferior Instrument concept is inadequate from a number of points of view. Primarily, the concept is a derivative from an inadequate base. The concept does not stand on any substantial proof either of its prescriptive usefulness or of the degree to which it describes organization relations. Indeed, there is substantial evidence of the mischief of adhering to the concept, as in the matter of adaptation to change. Finally, the traditional concept seems patently out of tune with the modern environment of administration. These considerations demand the root-and-branch redesign of the staff concept.

Third, the evidence suggests the usefulness of a Colleague concept in many situations, both in *describing* line-staff behavior and in *prescribing* the behavior which best serves organization purposes. Subsequent analysis will reinforce this suggestion.

Fourth, this analysis implies the need for substantial research of a

---

[38]Fisch, *op. cit.*, p. 68.

comparative sort. For example, the relations of various staff models to effectiveness, satisfaction, and similar variables should be studied. Many knotty research problems must be surmounted. But the choice of a staff model by logical derivation from an organization theory is a convenience incompatible with a sophisticated theory of organization.

Fifth, the persistence of the NII model implies a loss of realism. Perhaps administrators have been more sensible in practice than the concept requires. But progress on the theoretical level has been at a snail's pace. This is not the fault of lack of awareness pure and simple. Thus Gulick proposed many years ago that, since the principles prescribed a course of action, wisdom required that staff be designed so as to reconcile the diverse demands of unity of command and specialization.[39] The NII model, in contrast, was logically molded to the unity of command. This gives the impression that unity of command and specialization are neatly compatible always and ever. Matters thus were simplified, but at significant cost. Matters have remained simplified, essentially. The loss of realism also remains.

Specialization and unity of command still represent unreconciled strains of traditional organization theory. Simon's classic paper still applies. "What is needed to decide the issue is a principle of administration that would enable one to weigh the relative advantages of the two courses of action." Neither specialization nor the unity of command settles matters. "They merely contradict each other without indicating any procedure for resolving the contradiction."[40]

The failure to reconcile specialization and unity of command poses no mere logical difficulty: In short, the ghost does not allow the foul deed to be forgotten. Witness the conflict between the principle of specialization (as reflected in the provision of auxiliary staff services) and the principle of unity of command and of one-line authority (which imply the control of the means necessary to perform program functions). As Willard Hogan articulates the conflict between the two principles:

> One of the principal tenets of the practitioners of modern management methods ... is the centralization of authority. ... Yet the development of efficient manage-

---

[39]Luther Gulick and Lyndall Urwick (eds.), *Papers on the Science of Administration* (New York: Institute of Public Administration, Columbia Univ., 1937), p. 24.
[40]Herbert A. Simon, "The Proverbs of Administration," *Public Administration Review*, VI (Winter, 1946), 55.

ment methods and their application ... are resulting in a
new division of authority and responsibility with resul-
tant cross purposes, and other evils which management
methods are designed to eliminate.[41]

The NII model not only flies in the face of organizational realities,
then. It may also leave a legacy of guilt when that model must be
violated in the interests of effectiveness. This is an unfortunate
combination.

----

[41]Willard W. Hogan, "A Dangerous Tendency in Government," *Public Administration Review*, VI (Summer, 1946), 235.

Chapter 3
Pressures Toward Unorthodoxy, II: Problems of Orthodox Staff in Operation

This analysis must move consciously toward the design of structural arrangements for staff that specifically provide for power phenomena. Thus Chapter I establishes that organization is loaded with power phenomena, while that chapter also demonstrates that the NII model is not up to the task of containing the dynamics of power. Chapter II shows why this could not be otherwise. For the methodology underlying the traditional staff model is not adequate to handle such empirically rooted phenomena as power. Moreover, the properties of a staff concept consciously grounded in power phenomena clearly violate the Neutral and Inferior Instrument model, as Stahl's argument shows.

This chapter extends the variegated demonstration of the need to discipline power in line-staff relations. The approach is microscopic and emphasizes the specific problems that the NII model aggravates or creates. This is a necessary prelude to specific structural redesign more sensitive to power phenomena.

For those involved in the serious effort to work rigorously with the concept "power," the present rudimentary definition here as control of the environment may be unsatisfactory. These students may be more comfortable with an equivalent statement of what this volume seeks. To explain, ample evidence testifies that the prevailing model of line-staff relations does not engage a significant part of the efforts of members in organizational goals. Indeed, that model encourages and perhaps requires that employees exercise power—that is, that they control their environment—in ways that complicate attaining common objectives and that also impede the development of consensus as to what the common objectives are. Simply, the present goal is dual: to reduce the volume of human efforts that "get away" in organizations while serving human needs in the process.

Tensions Between Program and Sustaining Activities: Nine Common Sources

The analysis here is straightforward in design, if it is somewhat involved in execution. A first phase develops from this central question: What sources of tension are likely to develop between program and sustaining activities? Answering this question will permit the comparative analysis of the two extreme models outlined on pp. 7 to 14 — the NII and the Colleague models — to determine whether they ease or inflame these sources of tension. Nine such tensions will be stressed.

I. *"Control" is the other side of the coin of "service."* That is, tension will exist inherently between program and sustaining activities as both strive to do their job effectively. "Service" often will have "control" overtones that can effect the performance of program activities. There simply is no getting around it. This source of tension inherent in the service-control dualism was introduced earlier as a limit on the generality of the principle of unity of command. Therefore, the point may be handled here with some dispatch.

The ineluctable blend of service and control is an organizational universal. Consider "personnel" as a sustaining activity. It may be noted that a personnel department merely does the preliminary screening of potential employees and ministerially forwards to line supervisors a list of candidates for a particular job from which the line man makes his choice. However, determining who gets on the list patently constitutes control over the head of the program unit as well as service. Final choice does not change this fact. Thus Whyte asked the presidents and personnel directors of major enterprises to choose between two types of applicants for a job: the man "with strong personal convictions who is not shy about making unorthodox decisions that will unsettle tested procedures," and "the adaptable administrator schooled in managerial skills and concerned primarily with human relations and the techniques of making the corporation a smooth-working team." The presidents split their choices; but 70 per cent of the personnel directors choose the "adaptable administrator."[1] Service becomes control in the long

---

[1] William H. Whyte, Jr., *The Organization Man* (Garden City, N. Y.: Doubleday Anchor Books, 1956), pp. 148-49.

run in such a case when the trainees chosen by the directors (and, more often than not, reflecting the director's preferences) rise to positions of influence.

The control aspects of service can be more obvious, of course. Thus sustaining units can utilize a wide variety of tactics to make their control a matter of fact as well as their service a matter of help, the NII model notwithstanding. Illustratively, Ernest Dale argues that sustaining officials have at least these five major sources of leverage for exerting influence or for "participating in command":

1. command through superior articulation, since communicative skills and opportunities probably are more common in staff jobs;
2. command through technical competence;
3. command through status, since line officials commonly deal with higher-level staff officers;
4. command through sanctions, which range from (apparently) occasional formal power to various non-formal sources of influence, as "having the ear" of some high-level line official; and
5. command by default of line officials.[2]

All of this, indeed, may make too much of a point that has a firm place in common shoptalk about organized effort. Figure 2 can be relied upon to demonstrate the common recognition that service and control often are not separable. This will be the case whatever the model of relations between program and sustaining officials. The only relevent consideration is whether the model recognizes this comingling or neglects it.

II. *Sustaining activities allocate scarce resources.* The point holds whether one is considering office space, the delivery of mail, information, or professional advice and services. Often a question of priority is involved, not because anyone wants it that way, but because that is the way things are. Not everyone can get everything he wants when he wants it. Scarce resources are valuable to the heads of program units, and so the problem of priorities must imply tension between sustaining and program units.

Elemental acquaintance with life in organizations provides ample supporting evidence. The records of a maintenance department often reflect the effects of such bargaining, for example, since both maintenance and its costs are important to program heads. The informal determination of priorities may be reflected in many backorders for some program units and few for others. Or mainte-

---

[2]Ernest Dale, *Planning and Developing the Company Organization Structure* (New York: American Management Association, 1952), pp. 100-104.

Pressures Toward Unorthodoxy, II:

nance costs may differ for similar jobs for different units.[3] Prompt service and low charges (or their absence) imply control over the program chief's ability to get the job done.

NII model or no, the sustaining official may be moved to just such attempts at control by some power-oriented facts of life in organiza-

"Hah! Accounting tried to walk all over me!"
FIGURE 2. Is It Service or Control? Reproduced from **Manage Magazine** (June, 1955), p. 9.

tions. For favored program units might feel obliged to provide support for the generous sustaining unit in the inevitable contests for other scarce resources, such as the scuffles for budget. Certainly, there are delicate and crude ways by which sustaining officials might encourage respect for their interests from program officials. Illustratively, Strauss and Sayles describe this strategy of a Ship's Stores sustaining unit on a large vessel stemming from the fact that

---

[3]Melville Dalton, *Men Who Manage* (New York: Wiley, 1959), pp. 32, 24.

. . . certain groups were always demanding rapid service on complicated requisitions. The Ship's Stores workers, moving with speed and efficiency, merely announced that these offending groups would have to fill out in perfect detail the multi-copy, excessively complicated formal requisition sheets that were required by an official, but rarely observed, rule.[4]

These pressuring units, in addition, were denied their share of other goods and services (such as ice cream) that were distributed by Ship's Stores.

The allocation of scarce resources, then, is a source of power to be husbanded carefully. Overplaying one's resources may be catastrophic; underplaying them may invite scorn or the impositions of colleagues. Again, one cannot wish away the problem of scarcity in organizations. It underlies the informal resolutions-by-power of the many issues that have no strictly technical answer, if any issues permit value-free solutions.

Organizational gamesmanship has broad structural implications. Any line-staff structure can only be more or less useful in providing an arena for the inevitable byplay out of which organizational success or failure evolves. A structure which neglects such dynamics is not likely to provide a congenial ballpark for the organizational game that will be played. If sustaining officials must resort to stratagems to force recognition of their importance, however, performance is not likely to be facilitated over the generality of cases.

III. *Program and sustaining activities have different time orientations.* To simplify only a little, job pressures encourage program officials to be today-oriented, while personnel in sustaining units experience pressures that are by-and-by-oriented. Patently, being more or less out-of-phase encourages tension between program and sustaining units and officials. Indeed, personality differences apparently reinforce and complicate these differing time orientations.[5] Further, matters are gravely aggravated by complementary differences in the difficulty of measuring results. Many program activities have a relatively short lead time in evaluating results. The positive or negative payoffs of a training program, in contrast,

[4]George Strauss and Leonard R. Sayles, *Personnel: The Human Problems of Management* (Englewood Cliffs, N. J.: Prentice-Hall, 1960), p. 365. See also Ralph H. Turner, "The Navy Disbursing Officer as Bureaucrat," *American Sociological Review,* XII (June, 1947), 342-48.
[5]Behavioral Research Service, General Electric Company, *Motive Patterns of Managers and Specialists* (New York: General Electric Company, 1960); Lyman W. Porter and Mildred M. Henry, "Job Attitudes in Management: VI. Perceptions of the Importance of Certain Personality Traits As A Function of Line versus Staff Type of Job," *Journal of Applied Psychology,* XLVIII (October, 1964), 305-9.

may not show up for a decade or more. Thus for there to be any training at all, program heads must be convinced that it is sensible to take men out of work which has short-run returns and put them on work with a very long-run return, if any at all.

Such differing temporal orientations imply some interesting dynamics that structural arrangements must contain. Consider but a single point. The longer-run payoffs characteristic of sustaining activities often leave staff agencies and individuals disadvantaged in such matters as the allocation of the budget although management opinion may offset this disadvantage to varying degrees.[6] Sustaining units or officials can be expected to compensate for any bargaining weakness by taking advantage of the complementarity of service/control. A staff model must recognize this datum-of-power and provide for its effective resolution in organizations.

IV. *Performers of sustaining activities, for a variety of reasons, are encouraged to play the role of informant.* There is no dearth of notices that sustaining units and officials perform the "fink function." And compelling factors support such behavior. Sustaining activities were designed to augment the senses of the manager or owner in an organization grown too large for his own faculties. The picturesque analogies expressing this point of view were unhappy caricatures, but they were all the more influential for it. Thus one commentator explained that the growth of large-scale organization required that a substitute be found for the "proprietor's personal 'sense' faculties ... when he ran the business himself." The substitute was found in sustaining activities. "Now for smell, taste and touch there is a central testing laboratory; now for eyes and ears there are inspectors of various kinds and specializations; now for collecting and coordinating information and presenting it [there is a private staff]."[7] This reads curiously today. But the general notions underlying this point of view have not been without influence, casting sustaining units in the roles of informants or glorified prosthetic devices for management.

This may make too much of a crude organismic metaphor. At the very least, the sustaining official often is privy to much information — often of an interunit nature — which could help overhead program heads. This information is a source of power for sustaining units or

---

[6]James N. Mosel, "Why Training Programs Fail to Carry Over," in *Modifications in Manpower Management* (Urbana: Univ. of Illinois, 1958), pp. 17-25.

[7]See F. W. Lawe, "Staff Organization," *The Human Factor,* VII (January, 1933), 1-10. Such reflections of a gross "organic" concept of "organization" are not rare. As a matter of fact, the concept has captivated students in this country since the late 1800's. For a discussion of the broad dimensions of the organic approach, see Dwight Waldo, *The Administrative State* (New York: Ronald, 1948), pp. 100-104.

officials as well as a source of tension between them and program units or officials. The advantage of sustaining personnel in being "all over" an administrative unit can be striking. For example, one enterprising staff unit in the Pentagon made extraordinary use of its access to all administrative units. While delivering office supplies via carrier bicycle in the mammoth Pentagon Building, members of the sustaining unit also took "numbers." Their weekly handle was $100,000. Similar access of persons, places, and information can be put to like if less blatant uses.

Such advantages of access often held by sustaining officials can lead to tension with program personnel, whether the information is merely a casual but choice tidbit or the product of a regular audit. The range of feelings triggered is nicely illustrated by the case of F. Haupt from Industrial Engineering at Dalton's "Milo" factory. One of Haupt's roving subordinates learned that one shop was using substitute materials. Haupt informed Tirpitz, a program head from another division, although the matter was none of Haupt's official concern. Dalton suggests that the "leak" was inspired by Haupt's difficulties with T. Kuester—the general foreman of the shop using the substitute materials—over one of Haupt's pet projects. That is, sustaining officials can make their advice difficult to disregard. But such dynamics have broader and subtler motivations as well. Dalton explains the consequences of Haupt's tip in terms of this significant chain of events:

> Tirpitz had ordered that the makeshift material never again be used because of processing difficulties in his own department. According to Haupt, Tirpitz immediately called both Kuester and Kuester's chief... "and bawled hell out of them. Tirpitz was so damn glad to learn what was going on that he invited me to have lunch with him." In Milo's executive dining room Tirpitz and Haupt sat at different tables, but this day they lunched together in Tirpitz' home, the better to cement the developing commitment to mutual aid. One of Haupt's intimates reported that he spent an hour in his office that afternoon "crowing about how Kuester had caught hell without knowing who had peeped." Later at parties, Haupt's wife boasted of the "new contact" her husband had made and what a "swell guy" Tirpitz was.[8]

Thus may higher-level program and sustaining officials be drawn together, by accident or by design.

Any staff model must contain such dynamics. Given their delicateness, the usefulness of any model will in significant measure be

---

[8]Melville Dalton, *Men Who Manage* (New York: Wiley, 1959), p. 75.

Pressures Toward Unorthodoxy, II:

determined by its success in restricting these too human tendencies within some reasonable bounds.

V. *Can performers of sustaining activities "look the paymaster in the eye"?* This source of tension derives from several features of sustaining activities, among them being the size and growth of staff services and the relatively high rate of failure that characterizes many sustaining activities. Both sources of tension are particularly significant because of the difficulty of evaluating the performance of staff activities.

As for the size and growth of staff services, what may be called the staff "bulge" is common in organizations. Parkinson exaggerated the point when he pontificated that staff will increase whether the work load increases, stays the same, or decreases. As with many folk tales, Parkinson's has some substance. Many organizations experience rapid growth of their sustaining activities after passing some minimal organization size. In a general way, one can appreciate why this is so. Given a small organization, single individuals may handle both program and sustaining activities. Witness the small entrepreneur who hires, fires, sets his own budgets, and so on. Given even moderate organization growth, it soon becomes possible and often necessary to spin off some of these activities. And, for a while, sustaining activities seem to grow very rapidly. Haire's study of a small number of firms supports this intuitive explanation. He reported that in the early years of an organization's history, staff grows exponentially as the line grows linearly. Later, the rates tend to equalize. To give some approximate orders of magnitude to this growth history, the first doubling of the line saw a sixfold increase in staff. With the next two doublings of the size of the line, staff increased about five times and then threefold. Beyond this point, both line and staff grew at similar rates.[9]

Many organizations have such a history. It can be a source of substantial tension between program and sustaining units. For the heart of administration is scarcity, and what the sustaining units take must come out of the kitty from which the program activities also draw. Given the differing time orientations of the two types of activities plus the differences in the measurability of results, the taunt of "can you look the paymaster in the eye?" can be a sharp one when directed at sustaining officials.

To a similar end, program officials often have much evidence of "money spent on blunders" or, at the very least, of money spent for

---

[9]Mason Haire, "Biological Model and Empirical Histories of the Growth of Organizations," in *Modern Organization Theory*, ed. Mason Haire (New York: Wiley, 1959), p. 292.

purposes whose contribution to performance is difficult or impossible to assess. Program officials will have ample opportunity to make bold use of such charges, given the emphasis upon change in sustaining activities (which is a source of tension in its own right). Change and development can be costly and uncertain of success, and even slightly sour program-sustaining relations can make the worst of these data. Sustaining officials might react very emotionally to criticisms for "just doing their job," a job which includes a great margin for error and also poses uncommon difficulties for measuring performance.

The argument here must not be extended in extremis, but little qualification is necessary. There are cases in which the value of sustaining services may be calculated closely. For example, Helmer presents data on the "net worth" of a five-day retraining project for workers on an assembly conveyor that very handsomely support the project's value.[10] Similar opportunities for measuring performance, however, seem relatively rare.[11] Thus if labor turnover is high, inept selection by the personnel department and/or inadequate supervision may be at fault. How are such charges to be allocated? In general, both program and sustaining officials are anxious to take full credit for the successes and no responsibility for the failures. Compelling factors discourage a comely modesty in scuffling over such matters. As one staff officer explained the facts of life with respect to promotion in his company:

> The higher you get, the more your advancement depends on impressions that your supervisors have of you. And these impressions are based on almost no real evidence [of technical accomplishment]. If a high staff officer . . . were asked what he'd done for the company during the last year he'd have a hell of a time pulling up anything concrete. When you're in a position like that you know all the time that other people want your job and are trying to get it—and you know that impressions are constantly being formed of you . . . the higher you went the more you got involved in politics.[12]

This point of view gets very strong support from a variety of observers and practitioners placed both high and low in organizations.[13] But more of this later.

---

[10]H. J. Helmer, "You Can Measure the Results of Production Training," *Factory Management and Maintenance,* CX (March, 1952), 128-30.
[11]American Management Association, *Measuring Results of Personnel Functions* (New York: Author, 1947).
[12]Dalton, *op. cit.,* pp. 156-57.
[13]See the interesting observations of high-level executives in Eli Ginzberg (ed.), *What Makes an Executive?* (New York: Columbia Univ. Press, 1953), pp. 67-74.

The two features particularly encouraging tension from source V —the growth and size of sustaining services and the difficulty of measuring their performance—set a dual task for any satisfactory model of staff relations. The model must tend to reduce requirements for sustaining personnel as compared to alternative models. In practice, this means that a satisfactory model must reduce the number of lower- and middle-level paper manipulating jobs. A satisfactory model also must permit relatively facile measurement of performance which, in turn, will reduce the need for staff aid.

There is a considerable practical urgency for resolving such problems endemic to sustaining activities. Straightforwardly, if we must admit to some exaggeration, staff commonly is the last to be hired and the first to be fired. No incontrovertible evidence on the point exists. However, limited personal observation supports our conclusion as a useful rule-of-thumb for many staff activities. Consistently, one chronicler of the fate of departments of personnel observed that, with the business setbacks of 1949 and 1954, some curtailing of personnel activities occurred. A small number of firms discontinued employee publications, many reduced the workforce of personnel departments, and a few concerns eliminated these departments.[14] Consequently, an awkward staff model might well encourage sustaining officials to develop power, NII model or no, the better to withstand economic ups and downs. This mode of adaptation is likely to increase line-staff tension while it strives to reduce it. Or an awkward model might heighten the level of frustration among staff officials, a circumstance likely to goad performance over the long haul only under limited conditions. Worse still, staff personnel may turn to the perpetual pursuit of gimmicks or to overly strident demands for line adherence to procedures as the means of proclaiming their value to the enterprise.

VI. *Sustaining units specialize in change and reorganization; program units specialize in a stable technology.* Argyris' study of the budget process reflects these sources of tension sharply. Thus a sustaining officer articulated a fundamental bias toward change when he noted that "We guard the fields. The budget department has to constantly strive to improve the goods and make the plant better. There is always room to make things better." In contrast, a program official saw this persistent orientation toward change as a threat to the stability of operations. "They are not fully acquainted with ... production problems," one program supervisor com-

---

[14]Richard P. Calhoon, "The Eventuation of Personnel Administration," *The Personnel Administrator,* I (April, 1947), 32-33.

plained of the budget people. "They don't realize our troubles and our difficulties. The best thing to do is to bring them down and see our problems."[15]

The tension between change and stability can be sharp. The forces supporting stability are great, including as they do the inertia of habit, the fear of the strange, and the suspicion of the untried. Moreover, long-run considerations often run afoul of short-run convenience, the consequence being an organizational equivalent of Gresham's rule-of-thumb that bad money drives out the good. Finally, individuals often have deep personality commitments for or against change. The choice between stability and change, therefore, is not always decided on technical grounds. The organizational stakes are too high, and patterns of behavior are too deeply entrenched.

Consequently, the records of organizations abound with evidence that the staff's crackling was the line's calories, and vice versa. Thus in the General Motors of the 1920's, developmental work on a radically new engine was abandoned after millions of dollars had been spent. The engine was lighter, more powerful, used less fuel, and was not subject to overheating or freezing. Whether or not it was feasible or practical no one really knew at that time. Perhaps the question can be settled in retrospect today, perhaps not. In any case, GM program officials did not appreciate the potential of the new engine as much as they feared the production problems its adoption would certainly bring.[16] Being human, they succumbed to the temptation to settle for the problems of the known rather than face the new and unsettling. It was relatively easy to do, for we are told that the innovating staff men were considered "interfering outsiders and theorists."[17]

The bases of tension often are consciously recognized, fortunately.[18] But if it helps to know why you are going to hell in a wheelbarrow, it does not hurt much less if matters end there. That is, consciousness is only the first step toward a structural design that acknowledges such differences and permits some consistantly reasonable adjustment of the long-run to the short.

---

[15]Chris Argyris, *The Impact of Budgets on People* (New York: Controllership Foundation, Inc., 1952), p. 14.
[16]Thomas A. Boyd, *Professional Amateur: The Biography of Charles Franklin Kettering* (New York: Dutton, 1957), pp. 119-23.
[17]Alfred D. Chandler, Jr., *Strategy and Structure: Chapters in the History of the Industrial Enterprise* (Cambridge: Massachusetts Institute of Technology Press, 1962), p. 154.
[18]Argyris, *op. cit.*, p. 7. Emphasis in original.

Pressures Toward Unorthodoxy, II:

VII. *There often are substantial differences between the "cultures" of program and sustaining units.* The concept "culture" refers to the sum total of the ways of living that are developed by a group of humans. Considerable forces tend to encourage the development of two such "total ways of living" in program and sustaining units that do not always blend easily, particularly at lower and middle levels of organization.

These cultural differences are not contrived; they develop from a number of potent factors that are associated with the performance of program and sustaining activities. The two activities are not monolithic opposites, to be sure. However, such factors as the greater possibility in program activities of measuring results directly and easily contribute to the sense of "being on the firing line." Sustaining activities commonly permit somewhat more detachment.

Moreover, the careers of program and sustaining officials often differ significantly.[19] Program officials are far more likely to have worked their way up through their present organization and to have done so on the basis of experience and knowledge of particular jobs or operations rather than on the basis of formal training. These factors suggest that program officials may be designated, for rough classificatory purposes, as "locals." In contrast, sustaining officials often are appointed directly to their present job from outside, they often have had considerable formal training, and they commonly have outside professional interests. These characteristics suggest that sustaining officials are "cosmopolitans." These differing orientations provide reason aplenty for tension, as when sustaining officials argue for a policy as the only one acceptable to them professionally, and when program officials insist that such frills may be acceptable in theory but one can hardly expect them to work *in their company.*[20]

These comments may draw a more definite picture than existing

---

[19]Melville Dalton, "Conflicts Between Staff and Line Officers," *American Sociological Review,* XV (June, 1950), 342-51.

[20]The phenomenon of professionalism is too little analyzed. Certainly, however, neither the traditional theory of organization nor the NII model makes provision for the control of behavior by professional ties. The analysis of professionalization has long preoccupied public administration. For an influential pro and con, respectively, see Carl J. Friedrich and Taylor Cole, *Responsible Bureaucracy: A Study of the Swiss Civil Service* (Cambridge: Harvard Univ. Press, 1932); Herman Finer, "Administrative Responsibility in Democratic Government," *Public Administration Review,* I (Summer, 1941), esp. 335. More recently, a wide range of social scientists have focused on the phenomenon of specialization as it affects participation in organizations. Conveniently, see Peter M. Blau and W. Richard Scott, *Formal Organizations* (San Francisco: Chandler, 1962); *Administrative Science Quarterly,* X (June, 1965), entire issue.

research permits, but the slim available data do support the gross contrasts already mentioned. Thus sustaining activities normally draw people with substantially more education than do program activities.[21] Whyte, indeed, complains that the "bright young men" coming out of business schools commonly do not consider any alternative as being acceptable.[22] Moreover, sustaining activities tend to draw younger men. Length of service also tends to be significantly longer in the program activities.[23] Such factors imply and reinforce the differences previously sketched. For example, their shorter length of average service suggests that sustaining officials identify more strongly with their training or profession than with their organization.

The cumulative impact of such factors encourages profound and lasting cultural differences in the performance of the two types of activities. Dress and language often obviously reflect these differences. For example, Dalton explains the failure by heads of lower-level program units to use a cafeteria for management, to which they had been invited, in terms of cultural differences. He cites one program official as explaining:

> Most of the [people in sustaining units] that eat there are stuck up.... They don't go into the cafeteria to eat and relax while they talk over their problems. They go in there to look around and see how somebody is dressed or to talk over the hot party they had last night. Well, that kind of damn stuff don't go with me.[24]

The tension could not be expressed more poignantly, if some obvious improvements in the grammar might be made. Such feelings are more likely to be characteristic of middle- and lower-level program officials, in addition, for lower-level staff are most likely to "put on the dog" to distinguish themselves sharply from the line by stressing the advantages of their work (such as being able to wear a white shirt and tie). This makes matters seriously worse. For it is at these levels, if anywhere, that healthy program-sustaining relations must exist.

A provisional conclusion, therefore, seems in order. Any staff model that does not promise to reduce cultural differences has little to support it. Certainly, any staff model that aggravates such differences must have extraordinary compensating features. For cultural

---

[21]Dalton, *Men Who Manage, op. cit.*, pp. 87-88.
[22]Whyte, *op. cit.*, pp. 81-84.
[23]Dalton, *Men Who Manage, op. cit.*, pp. 89-91, 95-97.
[24]*Ibid.*, p. 94.

differences provide an organizational humus in which the several sources of tension can flower splendidly. More plainly, communication is encumbered by cultural differentiae. And this lifeline of cooperative effort is difficult enough to sustain, given such features as the different temporal orientations of program and sustaining activities.

VIII. *Sustaining activities seem to induce a high degree of frustration in the personnel performing them.* This datum seems of profound significance although it is difficult to predict the consequences of frustration. For mild degrees of frustration may improve performance, or they may inhibit it. It is an educated guess, made for considerations which cannot be detailed here, that frustration can seldom be managed so as to have mostly favorable consequences for performance.[25] On balance, the frustration implied in sustaining activities will charge the work situation emotionally and often will prove an unproductive source of tension between agencies or individuals performing sustaining activities and those in program activities.

The frustration associated with sustaining activities derives from a number of sources. Sources of tension III, IV, and VII, particularly, encourage high degrees of frustration. The short promotion ladders common in sustaining units have the same effect. Thus an organization in which there are ten levels in the program units may have three or so levels on the sustaining side. Hence one avenue for alleviating frustration — upward mobility in organizations — is not as available to sustaining personnel as to those in program units.

Frustration of staff looms large in organization practice, both directly and by inference. Thus observers often stress this datum of life in organizations. More impersonal data also suggest the point, even if one must rely on an inferential chain. The turnover differences in Table 1 are consistent with the hypothesis of greater frustration of staff officials, for example. The differences, however, also reflect other factors characteristic of staff such as the greater commitment to profession than to an organization.

The high frustration potential sets a stern task for any structure. No structural arrangements can eliminate this potential, and it is probably undesirable to attempt to do so. However, a structure which encourages frustration should have very substantial advantages in other respects. If nothing else, the high costs of labor turnover demand such extreme compensating features.

---

[25]Robert T. Golembiewski, *Behavior and Organization* (Chicago: Rand McNally, 1962), pp. 127-48.

TABLE 1. TURNOVER OF PROGRAM AND
SUSTAINING PERSONNEL IN ONE FACTORY

Year	Percentage Turnover[a]	
	Program Units	Sustaining Units
19__	24.2	78.9
19__	28.3	88.0
19__	31.7	88.0
19__	31.5	81.5

From Melville Dalton, **Men Who Manage** (New York: Wiley, 1959), p. 96.
[a]Calculated by dividing the average number of employees into accessions or separations, whichever was smaller. Only nonsupervisory employees are considered.

IX. *The integration of sustaining activities is a problem of great magnitude.* The problem of integration bedevils any organization, and the problem has a particular urgency for sustaining activities in today's organizations. "Integration" here refers to the smooth bringing together of all activities—whether line or staff—required for performing some task. In some organizations with parallel activities, therefore, little or no integration in our sense is required. But complex interdependence of activities is increasingly the order of the day, and here integration is vital. Such integration may be accomplished in two ways: either by departmentalizing so as to include all or most necessary activities in the same organization units at the lowest levels and/or by establishing effective relations between several monofunctional organization units. The NII model rejects the first approach and complicates the second.

More specifically, integrative problems in organizations derive from three major sources in today's organizations. The contemporary proliferation of sustaining specialties has been wondrous, first. Most sizeable organizations house a formidable array of such specialties, ranging from operations research to cost control to human relations. This very proliferation, of course, implies significant integrative problems.

Integrative problems are heightened, second, by the torturous (and sometimes manufactured) complexity of the several sustaining activities. At times, as in operations research, a good deal of the complexity is inherent in the activity. Not infrequently, however, one suspects complexity for its own sake or for the edification of fellow professionals. In either case, the problems of communication between (let alone the integration of) sustaining specialties become pressing.

The problems of integrating sustaining activities, third, seem to increase in direct proportion to the size of the sustaining units

Pressures Toward Unorthodoxy, II:

involved. Given the history of the substantial growth of sustaining units common in organizations of even moderate size,[26] this is a matter of great significance. Muller-Thym describes the tendency toward increased fragmentation with growth in size in these terms:

> In companies where groups of staff or specialized personnel have been consistently organized into management pyramids of their own, there has been a tendency to separate the "thinking" or "planning" parts of the organization from the "pushing" or "doing" parts. The effective working contacts of staff and specialized groups have been made primarily with people at the top of the organization. The "thinking, planning, controlling, problem-solving" people transmit their skills to the point of action through a long supervisory chain.[27]

These considerations challenge any staff model. The separation of "thinking" from "doing," the working contacts of staff with top management, the transmission of skills through long supervisory chains—these imply serious roadblocks to integrative effort that must be met in larger organizations. A useful staff model must struggle toward integration against this tide of separatism. A model offering little hope of counterbalancing the pervasive pressures toward fragmentation has little to recommend it.

Indeed, this puts matters too mildly. Integrative problems can only increase. The adequacy of any staff model in meeting the problems of integration has both a great and a growing significance.

Can the NII Model Handle Program-Sustaining Tensions?: The Sketch of a Negative View

This brief review of nine sources of tension sets the stage for a complex analysis. Thus the nine sources of tension will exist between program and sustaining units, whatever the prescribed relations between the two types of units. The task, then, is to determine which pattern of relations between program and sustaining units makes the best of these tensions. The effort is not totally presumptuous. Certainly much research will be necessary to determine the precise conditions under which a particular pattern of relations will be most well-suited. But it will be instructive to see how far existing work can take us.

---

[26]Haire, *op. cit.*, p. 290.
[27]Robert C. Sampson, *The Staff Role in Management* (New York: Harper, 1955), p. 193.

The Marginal Hypothesis

Let one particular note of caution be posted. Much of the discussion to follow will center on the consistency of the NII model with what is known, based on generalizations drawn from many episodic descriptions of "critical incidents" that give but little attention to the methodological canons of empirical research. This reflects, simply, the general state of the literature.

Necessity also has independent virtues in this case. Thus critical incidents — like the physical testing of materials — do demonstrate how structural relations affect behavior under stress. And this is certainly valuable information even though 95 per cent of life in organizations is not like that. Moreover, critical incidents have an impact upon organizational behavior enormously out of proportion to their occurrence. Indeed, in many senses an organization is the product of the ways in which its critical incidents have been handled. Hence the working hypothesis that the essential facts of life in organizations are at least more clear at the margins.

Such factors barely legitimate the approach here. Fortunately, this feeble outline of the "marginal hypothesis" can lean upon more sophisticated and extended developments of the point.[28]

The Test of the NII Model

Let us chart the immediate course of the analysis. The nine sources of tension permit a comparison of the NII and the Colleague models of program-sustaining relations, the two sharply opposed models that were sketched in Chapter II. This question will be put to each model for each of the nine sources of tension: Does the model effectively handle this source of tension common in program-sustaining relations, or does the model heighten the tension from this source?

The Neutral and Inferior Instrument concept can be put to the test first. In sum, the NII concept tends to heighten the normal tensions between program and sustaining units. But it is necessary to flesh out this skeletal answer in five major areas.

The NII concept will serve to aggravate program-sustaining tensions, first, because it is oblivious to significant forces that must be controlled to achieve effective performance. In short, the NII

---

[28]Harold Stein, "On Public Administration and Public Administration Cases," in *Public Administration and Policy Development: A Case Book*, ed. Harold Stein (New York: Harcourt, Brace, 1952), pp. ix-xiv.

TABLE 2. NORMAL SOURCES OF TENSION BETWEEN PROGRAM AND
SUSTAINING ACTIVITIES AS AFFECTED BY THE NII MODEL

"Normal" Sources of Tension	Neutral and Inferior Instrument Concept
I. "Control" is the correlate of "service."	heightens tension
II. Sustaining activities handle scarce resources.	heightens tension
III. Program and sustaining activities have differing time orientations.	heightens tension
IV. Sustaining units or officials: (a) are ordered to play, or (b) face a greater temptation to play, the role of the informant.	heightens tension
V. This may be a potent taunt to sustaining officials: "Can you look the paymaster in the eye?"	heightens tension
VI. Sustaining units and officials are oriented toward change and program units and officials toward stability.	heightens tension
VII. Cultural differences exist between program and sustaining activities and officials.	heightens tension
VIII. Sustaining activities induce high levels of frustration.	heightens tension
IX. The integration of sustaining activities often is a major problem.	heightens tension

concept flies in the face of reality. This is true in many senses. Consider only sources I and II in Table 2. Thus the Neutral and Inferior Instrument concept denies that "control" is a correlate of "service" (source of tension I). The denial does nothing to change the way things often are: Service and control are subtly but inextricably intertwined. Similarly, the concept implies that sustaining units will not take advantage of the political influences their handling of scarce resources makes possible (source of tension II). This gives too much to often-fragile human nature. Indeed, the inferior status prescribed by the Neutral and Inferior Instrument concept actually might encourage sustaining units to get informally what the formal organization denies them. Organizational survival is harsh enough to make this outcome highly probable.

Sustaining officials are not above the bargaining that characterizes all human effort, if only because sustaining officials will be but partly successful in winning the support of top-level program officials and concealing friction with program officials at lower levels. Patches of compromise prevent embarrassing news of friction from escaping to levels that are important for career development. Hence Dalton found that sustaining officials commonly bought the cooperation of lower-level program officials in suppressing evidence of friction with such quid pro quo:

1. toleration by sustaining officials of minor rule-breaking by program officials;
2. delay in implementing decisions already made by top management for changes affecting program units; and
3. transfer to program accounts of funds earmarked for sustaining units (e.g., research).[29]

These alternatives are not unique to situations in which the NII concept governs program-sustaining relations, but the Neutral and Inferior Instrument concept encourages staff to seek the cooperation of program officials. As Dalton explains: "... the line *is* the firm. It is established and brings in the staff groups. It demands that staff prove themselves, and it decides issues between staffs and itself." In addition, the line appoints and promotes all members of management, with the information percolating up from the middle and lower line being of great influence. "Hence every staff member knows that if he aspires to higher office the weightiest part of his record must be a reputation for 'understanding' line problems and getting along with line people."[30] Relegated to a subordinate status by the NII concept, that is, sustaining officials are encouraged to scramble for support for themselves and for their programs. If anything, the sustaining official will tend to overreach himself, either by pushing too hard for recognition of his contributions (which runs the risk of censure) or by "cooperating" too eagerly (which may affect performance adversely).

To complicate matters, this cooperation cannot be condemned simply and roundly. Selfishness inadequately explains such behavior, although such cooperation may ill serve the needs of the entire organization. The effectiveness of one's organizational subunit may be at stake, and this transcends selfish personal interests while it includes them. Moreover, since sustaining officials under the NII concept are "not responsible for performance," such compromises may be easy for them to rationalize in terms of their subordinate status. Indeed, finally, such give-and-take is the lubricant that allows the machinery of organization to work in many cases. For effort in organizations is a subtle composite of technical and social demands, and the effectiveness of filling the latter will affect technical performance.

The NII model is inflexibly indiscriminate. It commonly forces an illegitimate resolution of forces deriving from the demands of effective performance as well as from man's weaknesses. The illegitimacy of the necessary adaptive behavior merely adds

---

[29]Dalton, *Men Who Manage, op. cit.*, pp. 104-5.
[30]*Ibid.*, p. 99.

another significant source of tension for those who accept the traditional theory and makes deeper cynics of the sceptical. This describes a psychologically unhealthy situation.

Consequently, Table 2 assigns the designation "heightens tensions" to sources of tension I and II when the NII model prescribes the structural relations between program and sustaining activities.

The Neutral and Inferior Instrument concept, second, heightens the tension that derives from the differing time orientations of program and sustaining activities (source III in Table 2). That is, compelling day-to-day pressures make it difficult to give due weight to longer-run needs. This is the case, for example, in training. If anything, organization units with more futuristic time orientations should be given an advantage, the pressures of the present being so difficult to overreach. The NII model does precisely the contrary.

Saddling sustaining activities—which are most likely to provide the longer-run view—with an organizational inferiority often will have a wide range of unfortunate consequences. Thus it may increase the tension between program and sustaining units, as the latter strain mightily toward tomorrow while program officials defend today with the support of their superior organization role. Or sustaining units may exact a stiff price for their subordinate status, as by obstinate adherence to procedure under all conditions or by administrative slowdowns to demonstrate staff's importance. Or sustaining officials may become docile and neglect long-run considerations. The catalog of alternatives is unattractive. Moreover, the NII model provides a constant excuse for the program official to spurn the contributions of sustaining officials, as well as a constant temptation for sustaining officials to develop informally the power that they lack formally. Strauss and Sayles put the matter in typically penetrating terms:

> To understand the antipathy that often crackles between staff and line managers, we must also take into account personal jealousies. This is an example of the struggle between the specialist and the [self-avowed] generalist —the man of ideas and the man of action. The line official, who has over-all responsibility for some activity, feels that the specialist can't really understand his problems because he is interested in only a narrow area. Over and over again the protests and suggestions of personnel men are greeted by a "Yeah, but you don't have to get out the production."[31]

---

[31]George Strauss and Leonard R. Sayles, *Personnel: The Human Problems of Management* (Englewood Cliffs, N. J.: Prentice-Hall, 1960), p. 405.

Such a position is a self-fulfilling one. For the program official has responsibility for some activity, but he also must control the several contributions to that activity. When he stresses that sustaining officials do not share that responsibility, the program official encourages behavior by sustaining officials which is likely to reduce the program official's control over the several contributions to the activity for which he is responsible. Sustaining officials can respond to this common refrain by acting as if they had no responsibility for production.

For such reasons, source of tension III in Table 2 carries the legend "heightens tension." No structure of program-sustaining relations can eliminate the tension between the pressures of today and tomorrow. But the NII model makes matters worse. It does not encourage that delicate balance of the long-run and the short-run which must characterize effective performance over time. Docile submission or passionate empire-building by sustaining officials become all too likely. Something more positive must be expected of any structural model.

The NII model, third, heightens the tensions in what may be called one-upmanship in organizations, that area covered by the sources of tension numbered IV, V, and VI in Table 2. To deal with tension source IV, the NII model increases tension between program and sustaining officials by placing the latter in the role of an organizational outsider, if not in the role of an informant. Consider a budgeting officer who observes an irregularity in a program unit. If he behaves in the strictly advisory role prescribed by the NII model, his observation will take this long route: up the staff hierarchy one or more levels, across (or up to) an appropriate line official, and then down the line hierarchy one or more levels to the line official with supervisory responsibility for the program unit in which the irregularity was observed. No matter how pure the intentions of the budget officer, the psychological climate induced is a punitive one. And individuals tend to reject punitive actors and conditions. The NII model pays a stiff price, then.

The broader consequences of behavior consistent with the NII model are no more favorable. Thus the program supervisor would tend to react unfavorably to the report of the budget officer going through the supervisor's chief. The supervisor would be more discrete about future irregularities, although such duplicity would do little to create favorable program-sustaining relations. Moreover, at the very least, time is lost; as frequently happens, the opportunity for corrective action may pass; unnecessary paperwork is generated; and the primary contact with the supervisor is to be made by the program chief, who may not understand the budget officer's point fully and thus is hardly in a favorable position to facilitate corrective action. Possibly, in addition, the program chief may be miffed because he or his immediate subordinates did not catch the irregularity themselves. Nor does this exhaust the Pandora's box of potential problems.

There are other inducements for sustaining officials to play the informant's role (source of tension IV), even beyond the requirements of their formally designated duties. The orientation of sustaining units toward change (tension source VI), plus the taunt concerning the contributions to performance of sustaining activities (tension source V), unless carefully shepherded by a suitable structure, can induce sustaining officials to play the role of informant over a wide field. The goal might be to develop the political support necessary to counterbalance the formal inferiority of a staff unit, thereby contributing to its success in selling its program. The technique of informing also could be an effective individual ploy, the quid pro quo being the support of upper-level program officials. Drawing such attention to one's self is an understandable desire on the part of talented and/or ambitious sustaining officials. However, the technique for drawing attention is well-designed to fragment program and sustaining officials and units and to complicate their working relations.

How does the NII model handle such powerful inducements to informally playing the informant's role? Not only does the NII model do little to save sustaining officials from temptation, as it were, it forces them into the occasion of organizational sin. For example, the NII model provides only naively or not at all for the conflicting orientations of line and staff toward change and stability (source of tension IV). The model's provision is at least naive in its assumptions concerning the conditions under which creativity will emerge,[32] the apparent philosophy being that the more inhospitable the conditions, the better. Only the zealot is likely to rise to such bait consistently, and many (perhaps most) zealots are more troublesome than they are helpful. Mild frustration may encourage adaptive problem-solving, but the NII model makes too much of a good thing.

The NII model also rests upon major assumptions that overlook the cross-pressures toward change and toward stability (tension source IV) that are one of the "objective dilemmas" of cooperative

---

[32]Frederic D. Randall, "Stimulate Your Executives to Think Creatively," *Harvard Business Review,* XXXIII (July-August, 1955), 121-28, for example, presents a contrary and more useful view.

effort. One of these assumptions is the still-influential notion that once an enterprise is going correctly, little or no intervention is necessary or, at the very least, intervention is not necessary in any great hurry. Hence the organizational inferiority of the NII model merely accords the staff innovator his just deserts. This position receives support from a most unlikely source, the delicate efforts of the academic followers of the study of bureaucracy according to Max Weber. Among other characteristics, the approach yields an "ideal type" structure. This ideal type was explored in some detail by Weber with more[33] or less[34] full consciousness that he was elaborating an educated guess of where the extreme logical extension of certain trends he observed in organizations in a limited sector of his own German society would lead. Commonly, his interpreters have been less careful. They confuse the rational with the existing.[35] Thus Thompson notes that " . . . most behavior *in bureaucratic organizations* is programmed. . . . Only rarely are new programs or innovations needed."[36] Such interpretations are correct, however, only within the narrow confines of Weberian definition. They are wide of the mark as descriptions of actual organizations. Such interpretations of Weber—who *was* in vogue among academic students of organizations[37]—encouraged many to assign organizational change agents to a second-class role. Indeed, even Weber could not resist the drift of his own argument,[38] although in many other matters he had the good sense to rise above his speculative work.

Naivete about, or neglect of, the conflict of change and stability amount to pretty much the same thing. They encourage the staff official to develop extralegal support for his contributions, for he is after all in an organization to contribute something, or at least to create that impression. Protecting his job, and perhaps his self-respect and professional identifications, often will goad the staff

---

[33]Max Weber, *The Methodology of the Social Sciences*, trans. and ed. Edward A. Shils and Henry A. Finch (Glencoe, Ill.: Free Press, 1949), p. 90, notes clearly that "In its conceptual purity, this mental construct cannot be found empirically anywhere in reality. It is a utopia."

[34]Talcott Parsons, *The Structure of Social Action* (2nd ed.; Glencoe, Ill.: Free Press, 1949), p. 605, emphasizes that Weber at times shifted his analytical ground.

[35]Alfred Diamant, "The Bureaucratic Model: Max Weber Rejected, Rediscovered, Reformed," paper presented at the Annual Meeting of the American Political Science Association, September 8, 1961, pp. 10-21.

[36]Victor A. Thompson, *Modern Organization: A General Theory* (New York: Knopf, 1961), p. 84. This author's emphasis.

[37]See the increasingly common use of Weber as a stalking horse, as in Peter M. Blau, *The Dynamics of Bureaucracy* (Chicago: Univ. of Chicago Press, 1955).

[38]Diamant, *op. cit.*, p. 7.

official to compensate for the neglect by the NII model of a vital dimension of his organizational life.

Whatever the inducements to play the informant's role, finally, the NII concept of line-staff relations provides a degree of protection for the sustaining official, even if he does not have the tacit or active support of the upper line. As Davis explains, the staff man commonly is in a separate chain of command. This inhibits the lower-level line official when conflicts develop, for it requires that a line official be "willing to appeal all the way to the top to a mutual supervisor of the two departments."[39] There are many constraints on such behavior. This competitive advantage is not likely to be overlooked by either the program or the sustaining official. No wonder, then, that the game of cat-and-mouse often characterizes the relationships of program and sustaining officials. The flow of information upward is thereby impeded, sustaining officials may feel thwarted and thus press to unearth data, and in the process little occurs that helps the program official do his job.

Hence sources of tension IV, V, and VI do not seem ameliorated by the NII model, as the designation "heightens tension" in Table 2 reflects. Awkward adaptations may be anticipated, therefore. Thus staff officials reasonably might be expected to develop defenses against tension, more or less independent of their implications for cooperative effort. This probability suggests the self-defeating tendencies of the NII model. Or staff officials might become extraordinarily sensitive concerning adherence to, or acceptance of, policies originated and supported by themselves. This rigidity implies substantial drains on the reservoir of cooperative effort that successful enterprises require. Or staff might follow what seems a more neutral course, an intense and persistent preoccupation with gimmicks and gadgetry that is intended to create an impression of sincere and substantial contributions to performance. Indeed, this ploy is so common that it creates a deep suspicion of the perversity of the relations prescribed by the NII model. Consider this ultimate of staff-inspired gadgetry as an evidence of the incredible industry thus expended. An automated suggestion box, we are told, has been developed. The device not only senses an approaching employee, but plays a stimulating march and then delivers a taped inspirational talk on the value of suggestions. Finally, miracle of miracles, the employee is given a free shoeshine.[40]

---

[39]Keith Davis, *Human Relations At Work* (New York: McGraw-Hill, 1962), pp. 215-16.
[40]*Industrial Relations News*, March 7, 1959.

The unfortunate effects of the NII model on source of tension V may be demonstrated from a different angle, and this with profit. In the grossest introductory summary, many undesirable features of sustaining activities seem linked to the Neutral and Inferior Instrument concept. Moreover, the specific features considered undesirable by specific authors commonly seem linked to the very NII model which these authors support.

Consider Drucker's well-known pessimistic reply to this provocative query: "Is Personnel Management Bankrupt?"[41] Repeating McGregor,[42] Drucker brings three charges against Personnel Administration. First, he notes, both its students and practitioners believe that people do not want to work and do so only so that they can afford to get satisfaction elsewhere. This belief has the awkward consequence of placing "emphasis on satisfaction outside and beyond the work," an emphasis reflected in the high and growing percentage of the total wage bill now going into "indirect wage payments" such as pensions or insurance[43] or into enterprise-provided services such as employee recreation programs. Drucker's point, simply, is that the emphasis is beside the point. Such rewards are not tied directly to work or performance and, therefore, need not increase either the employee's satisfaction at work or his efficiency. Existing research suggests that the probability of such a dual abort is high.[44] Second, Personnel Administration is grounded in the perverse belief that personnel management is the province of the personnel specialist rather than of the line supervisor. The programs of a Personnel Department largely are "thought up, established and operated by the department," a bias that charges the relations of line and the personnel staff with a high potential for conflict. Third, Personnel Administration emphasizes "fire-fighting." The problem is that such a focus discourages the effective management of work, even if it does not give Personnel a dangerous stake in the continued existence of "problems" or "headaches."

Though causal relations cannot be determined with certainty, these three charges against Personnel Administration may be interpreted as three consequences of the NII model. Drucker supports

[41]Peter F. Drucker, *The Practice of Management* (New York: Harper, 1954), pp. 273-88.
[42]Douglas McGregor, *Line Management's Responsibility for Human Relations* (New York: American Management Association, 1953).
[43]"Fringe Benefits: Some Neglected Considerations," *Personnel*, XXXIII (January, 1957), 337-46.
[44]Rensis Likert, *Motivation: The Core of Management* (New York: American Management Association, 1953), pp. 3-4.

the sense of that model while, with all justice and acuteness, he belabors Personnel Administration. You cannot have both, however. For example, the "emphasis on satisfactions *outside and beyond the work,*" given the supremacy of the line *within work* prescribed by the NII model, seems a reasonable emphasis indeed for a specialty seeking a place for itself under the organizational sun. The emphasis upon Personnel Administration as the province of the specialist, moreover, also seems a reasonable adaptation to these dual forces: the denial of status inherent in the NII model and the exigencies of developing and maintaining power in organizations, of becoming more than advisory, and of attempting to demonstrate one's worth to the organization. The stake of Personnel Administration in fire-fighting, in addition, also seems a derivative of the NII model. Such a role is not a desirable one, but what other role is there for the nonline under the NII model? The line can be expected to slough off the "messy" aspects of administration, such as the employee's cafeteria and grievances, but little else. And Personnel Administration can be pardoned for its variation on that old folk theme: "When I can't be near to the one I hold dear, I'm dear to the one I'm near." Sometimes, no doubt, this was done for very shortsighted reasons. At least today, however, many personnel specialists consciously play such a game in order to get an adequate program in other areas. And others call for specific criteria to determine the activities that should be given an organizational home in departments of personnel.[45]

The present point may be put directly, then. The NII model may not have directed the development of Personnel Administration, but the NII model will contribute little to the development of the function in ways that will cancel Drucker's objections. Indeed, personnel administrators must reject both the traditional staff concept and the principles underlying them, and their failure to do so helps explain the widespread acknowledgement of Drucker's acuteness while so little has been done in Personnel Administration about meeting his criticisms.[46]

The Neutral and Inferior Instrument model, fourth, reinforces rather than reduces the cultural differences between sustaining and program units (see tension source VII in Table 2). The model

---

[45]Dalton E. McFarland, "The Scope of the Industrial Relations Function," *Personnel,* XXXVI (January-February, 1949), 42-51. To the same point, see Edmund P. Learned and Audrey T. Sproat, *Organization Theory and Policy: Notes for Analysis* (Homewood, Ill.: Irwin, 1966), pp. 44-47.
[46]Robert T. Golembiewski, "Is Personnel Management Bankrupt?: Theories and Practice," *The Personnel Administrator,* VIII (March-April, 1963), 15-21.

provides yet another potent reason for the social and psychological isolation of units performing the two types of activities. Matters are not aided by the fact that the self-evaluations of sustaining officials often will not square with the NII concept. For example, the latter's type of work and greater education are among the factors which consciously or unconsciously could be used to impute values to line activities that conflict with the values implicit in the NII model.

Too little attention has been paid to the enormous impact of cultural differences on performance. For example, communication becomes more of a problem to the degree that such differences exist. Even if vocabularies are equivalent, communication under the stress of cultural differences easily can lead to misunderstanding the message or misperceiving the subtle verbal and facial cues that carry so much meaning. Protests by program officials that sustaining officials "do not understand our problems" (or vice versa) often reflect such communicative difficulties. "If they only came down here to see our problems" goes the usual remedy. However, psychological as well as physical proximity are required to really understand. The NII model does not encourage either type of closeness. Major factors contributing to psychological distance spot the previous analysis. Geographically, the NII model is congenial to locating staff at a central site away from the line, as in "the front office" or at headquarters. Geography can support and reinforce psychological and social fragmentation with significant consequences.[47]

Given these dual shortcomings of the NII model, it is reasonable that the tension implicit in source VII is increased by following the traditional model.

The greater frustration associated with the performance of sustaining activities, fifth, probably would be increased by the NII model of relations between program and sustaining units (see source of tension VIII). Consider the young graduate of a business school who has internalized the NII model, an all-too-likely consequence, given the model's convenient simplicity. His initial brushes with organizational reality may demonstrate that the approach is an unrealistic guide for behavior. The failure of the

[47]Experimental work on locus as a significant variable has only begun. But physical location no doubt has significant effects on communication, liking, and other crucial features of social life that in general can be expected to exaggerate cultural differences between line and staff. For some of the early experimental work on locus, see R. Sommer, "Leadership and Group Geometry," *Sociometry,* XXIV (March, 1961), 94-100. For interesting insights into the consequences of social and physical "closeness," see William Erbe, "Gregariousness, Group Membership and the Flow of Information," *American Journal of Sociology,* LXVII (March, 1962), 502-16.

images by which we live is no trifling matter, particularly when success comes to those who know when and how to violate these ideals.

Assigning the costs of the NII model in this regard to naivete, however, certainly puts matters too simply. Thus playing the role of the neutral advisor seems difficult for most people, particularly for individuals who have strong commitments to professional standards or to suborganization programs. And this is the role prescribed by the NII model *in all cases.* Various adaptations to the implied frustrating condition, in addition, tend to be unsatisfactory regulators. For example, sustaining officials may feed ideas to program officials who later "think of them" and proffer them as their own. This may seem a harmless approach, but the cynicism common among such sustaining officials seems a high price to pay. Only under conditions of very careful management would working relations avoid being polluted.

The problem of the integration of sustaining activities, finally, also is heightened by the NII approach. This model presumes that the line official will perform the integration. The diversity and complexity of sustaining activities, however, makes this a pious hope rather than a probability. The NII concept, consequently, does not imply either great ingenuity or great effectiveness in its solution of the problem of integrating sustaining specialties.

Approaches to the integration of sustaining specialties in practice may take a variety of paths. Only two possible (and perhaps probable) paths will be considered here. A program official may throw up his hands and (formally or informally) give powers of command to a sustaining unit. This approach has a number of consequences, none of which particularly encourage the integration of sustaining activities. Thus other sustaining units may press for similar justice. Or the heads of program units may be cut off from their program superior. This is not a trifling circumstance. For example, the program superior has the official say in the promotion or salary increases of the heads of subordinate program units. Such are the circumstances that induce cabals to "get the ear of" a program executive. Program and sustaining officials are naturally cast as antagonists in this quest. This hardly encourages smooth operations.

Alternately, the diversity and complexity of sustaining activities may encourage its practitioners to do things on their own "for the good of the organization" which are beyond the grasp of the poor program head. This condescension is common, but its likely consequences are not all favorable. The job of integrating sustaining activities, primarily, will not become any simpler. Indeed, the integration often will go begging to the extent that the program official is in the dark. He alone, remember, has the responsibility for integration under the NII concept. Each sustaining unit, moreover, reasonably may have to "take charge" or lose political influence in the organization. When sustaining personnel are solicitous of the chief's inadequacies, also, lower-level officials will soon be wise as to who has influence. Consequently, the chief program official may find himself increasingly deprived of valuable information. The common response—to add more staff to unearth the required data—may simply overlook if not actually intensify the tussle between sustaining units and lower-level program units.

A specific case will handily illustrate some of the inadequacies of the NII model in the complex integration of sustaining specialties. Many factors help make this integration a hot issue: the implicit threat to the program head who accepts the NII model of line-staff relations; the difficulty of measuring staff contributions coupled with the program official's monopoly of responsibility for performance; the desire of sustaining officials to have their contributions recognized, if not by the organization structure, then by their ability to influence program officials; and the clash of little feudalities with suborganization identifications (of which more will be written presently) whose development is encouraged by the traditional theory of organization. All of these factors appear in one attempt to put a new item into production. The program supervisor complained bitterly of the integrative problems he faced:

> It is up to me to get the Amicon tube section rolling. I am the production foreman; the job of the industrial engineers is to help me get set up for production. Instead, the engineers deny my authority as foreman. More than that they make it clear that I do not exist for them personally. They do not care that I am on the spot. Now I have to prove my ideas are as good as theirs.[48]

The program official's difficulties, patently, are in large part a function of his do-or-die acceptance of the NII model. His social and psychological estrangement from those with whom he must interact in a flow of work is implied by the constant I-they juxtaposition.

Such fragmentation can easily pollute a wide range of work relations. And not only program officials suffer. One industrial

---

[48]Harriet O. Ronken and Paul R. Lawrence, *Administering Changes* (Cambridge: Harvard Univ. Press, 1952), p. 123.

engineer caught up in these integrative battles was at odds not only with the program head but with the development engineers as well. He reflected sadly that the NII structure may only intensify the problems of integration:

> I have never worked in such a mixed-up place. It seems impossible for any two people to cooperate around here. Everybody tries to tear down everybody else's ideas. It would seem to me to be more constructive to try to find something good in what new ideas come along instead of trying to find something wrong with them.[49]

Such fault-finding was a reasonable reaction of sustaining officials to the implied failure of the program head to accord them what they considered an appropriate appreciation of their contributions. Those staff men would not accept the secondary status of the NII model which the program head attempted to enforce.

All in all, then, the NII concept does not help solve the tough problem of the integration of sustaining activities. Hence this entry appears in Table 2 opposite source of tension IX: "heightens tension."

---

[49]*Ibid.*, p. 129.

Chapter 4
Pressures Toward Unorthodoxy, III:
The NII Model and Vertical Fragmentation

"Vertical fragmentation" summarizes many of the forces generated by the NII model that reduce effectiveness in organizations. Crudely, the principles and the traditional staff model encourage identifications "within" the individual activities and "upwards" in the organization rather than "across." Hence work suffers in such a structure, for the flow of work in organizations requires significant "horizontal integration," that is, cooperation "across" the organization.

Vertical fragmentation also refers to the development of sub-agency identifications that approach the organizational common goal from a number of directions, and sometimes conflicting ones. The importance of sub-organization identifications cannot be over-emphasized, even though the traditional theory does not provide for them. These informal patterns often determine what things get done, by whom they are done, and how they are done. Thus a perceptive student headed one of the sections of an important recent book in this revealing way: "Cliques As Fountainheads of Action."[1]

Although sub-organization identifications cannot be eliminated, pessimism is not in order. Rather, the subtle trick in organizing is to arrange matters so that such identifications contribute to the flow of work rather than disrupt it.

Vertical Fragmentation:
Three Sources Inhering in Organization

This chapter documents and analyzes sub-organization development, thus laying the groundwork for later attempts to discipline it

[1]Melville Dalton, *Men Who Manage* (New York: Wiley, 1959), pp. 52-57.

to the purposes of the organization. The emphasis will be threefold: First, the very act of organizing implies strong pressures toward the fragmentation of organization units, whatever the basis of subdivision. Any staff model must reckon with these pressures. Second, again whatever the basis of subdivision, strong forces tend to focus identifications within an organization unit and vertically with overhead counterpart units or officials. Third, the principles of the traditional theory of organization make the worst of these tendencies by prescribing functions and processes as the basis of subdivision. The effect is to vertically fragment units contributing different activities to common flows of work, as opposed to the horizontal integration of these activities. The NII model reinforces this effect, which is awkward.

The Act of Organizing and Vertical Fragmentation

Paradoxically, first, the very act of organizing generates fragmenting tendencies. Consider the anticipated and the unanticipated consequences of attempting to achieve greater control over some factor in an organization's environment. Figure 3 sketches some examples of these divergent consequences that exist whatever the guiding model of relations. Interpretively, any large-scale activity requires delegation. It is the primal act of organizing. And effective delegation presupposes training which, to the degree that it is successful, will have the anticipated consequence of meeting the demand for control. But unanticipated consequences also are implied. Thus both delegation and training encourage the development of particularistic interests which test management's ability to coordinate. For example, a budget department is not a mere creature of management; its members have their own interests to protect as well. These sub-organization interests are powerful, in part, because individuals develop an internalized "conscience" about them which guides their behavior.

These fragmenting tendencies are not ephemeral. Sub-organization "consciences" are reflected in such significant processes as decision-making, for example, with self-supporting consequences. Illustratively, a certain public agency has a clear formal policy about reporting bribe offers immediately to superiors. The policy, patently, aims at greater control of the administrative environment. And its observance must be delegated to field agents, who are the ones who will be propositioned. So much for the anticipated consequences. However, the agents feel that any "good man" will never let matters go so far that a bribe is offered. Consequently, actual

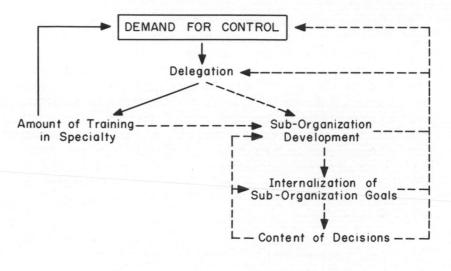

DEMAND FOR CONTROL

Delegation

Amount of Training
in Specialty

Sub-Organization
Development

Internalization of
Sub-Organization Goals

Content of Decisions

⟶ designates anticipated consequences

⤏ designates unanticipated consequences

FIGURE 3. Fragmenting Tendencies Implicit in the Act of Organizing. Based upon James G. March and Herbert A. Simon. **Organizations** (New York: Wiley, 1958), p. 43.

offers go unreported. For the very report implies that one is not a good agent. The dynamics do not end here. In turn, the "spotless" record on bribe offers encourages greater delegation by top management, a probability well designed to further inhibit reporting.[2]

These fragmenting tendencies inherent in the primordial act of delegation will exist whatever the pattern of formal relations underlying the structure of an organization, but the NII model significantly aggravates them. The NII model does this by the very differentiation of line and staff units as superior and inferior, respectively. In this elemental sense the concept merely supplies another substantial reason for separating sub-organizations geographically, socially, and psychologically. More subtly, increased staff aid is a normal prescription for top management's desire for greater control. Thus inherent fragmenting tendencies imply a vital need for staff services. Yet, paradoxically, the NII model brings its own legacy of fragmenting tendencies and not only in the sense of differential status of line and staff. For effective staff work implies delegation, with consequences such as those illustrated in Figure 3.

The process, to give the long and short of it, is a nasty circular one.

---

[2]Peter M. Blau, *The Dynamics of Bureaucracy* (Chicago: Univ. of Chicago Press, 1955), pp. 99-115.

Sub-Organizations and Vertical Ties

Second, strong pressures channel the development of sub-organizations into vertical paths. This gives direction to the forces implicit in the act of delegation. The NII model complements these forces, as Figure 4 helps demonstrate. To explain, A tends to identify with his immediate work unit or with cliques including members of his counterpart unit above him. The pressures of work encourage this.

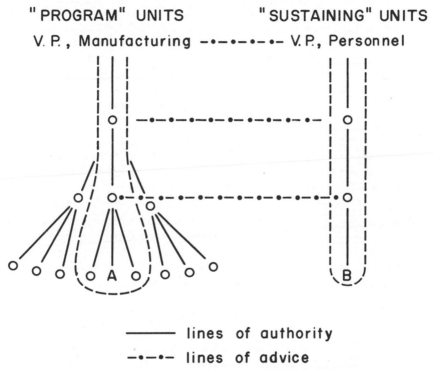

FIGURE 4.   Skeletal Structure Patterned After the NII Model.

For example, a unit in an organization which cannot muster the loyalty of its members hardly can fare well in the scrimmaging for scarce resources (e.g., budgets, promotions, pay increases) endemic in organizations. Failure reduces the effectiveness of the work unit. Hence the definite tendency for identifications to cluster along a vertical axis. Consequently, A and B may perform activities which contribute to the same task. However, they are not likely to be identified psychologically or socially. Or if they do identify, and this is crucial, the principles of organization deserve no credit.

The Neutral and Inferior Instrument concept heightens this

separatism. Thus *A* (a program official) may dislike the fact that *B* (from Personnel) reports deviations "up and over" to *A*'s superior (as the NII concept requires). A program official may be pardoned for seeking protection among the colleagues in his particular program activity. This separatism increases the problems of communication and creates a tense atmosphere within which cooperation is difficult. The isolation of *A* and *B* thus is supported by the NII model. Such isolation is probable under the best of circumstances and requires no encouragement. For example, the movement of personnel between program and sustaining units often seems slight. Experience in one plant, although it does not necessarily reflect a universal condition, supports the point of line-staff isolation. There were few transfers between the two activities, and these few were concentrated in movement from sustaining to program activities. The NII concept — which was the guiding model in the plant in question — helps account for the direction of the transfers since positions in program units had "more income, authority, and prestige . . . at any level."[3]

The NII model plays a dangerous game in this regard, for vertical relations are common enough without any help. Dalton's recent work,[4] particularly, points up the incidence and pervasiveness of vertical relations. His descriptive reports are supported by some experimental evidence from other researchers which reveals that very strong socioemotional forces, in addition, reinforce the vertical demands of the hierarchical role as defined by the principles of traditional organization theory.[5] Dalton's observations will be relied upon here. He isolates these basic types of "cliques" in an industrial plant:

1. Vertical cliques. This type of clique is based upon an exchange of services. For example, a supervisor may aid and protect his subordinates, in return for which they keep him posted concerning conditions at work or threats to the supervisor's position, and so on.

Dalton concludes of the main kind of vertical clique — the "symbiotic" — that it "is the *most common and enduring* clique in large structures . . . the real power [center which] is essential for a given department *to* compete on a par with other departments for favors from higherups and to set up workable arrangements with other departments."

---

[3] Dalton, *op. cit.*, p. 98.
[4] *Ibid.*, pp. 58-64.
[5] Herman Turk and Theresa Turk, "Personal Sentiments in a Hierarchy," *Social Forces*, XL (December, 1961), 134-40.

2. Horizontal cliques. Horizontal cliques may be "defensive" or "aggressive." These cliques cut across departments, in contrast to the vertical cliques. Defensive cliques are usually formed in response to threat or crisis, e.g., reorganization, which affects several functions. Aggressive cliques are interested in bringing off a change rather than resisting it.

Horizontal cliques, of course, reduce interdepartmental and interfunction tension and they ameliorate the particularism of vertical cliques in serving as a mutual-aid bloc for the several departments or functions.

However, horizontal cliques are strong only as long as the threat or crisis exists. Consequently, they disturb the primacy of the vertical cliques only temporarily, disappearing as a particular crisis or threat abates.

3. Random cliques. The random clique is based upon friendship and social satisfaction. This differentiates it from the other types of cliques, in which (according to Dalton) "Friendship is not [the] end and may be hardly present."

In comparison to the vertical or horizontal cliques, random clique's members "may come from any part of the personnel, managers and managed, [and] do not anticipate important consequences of their association."

Although random cliques may be long-lived, various factors limit their incidence, persistence, and influence in organizations. Primarily, they lack in many organizations continuing and compelling support. In contrast, vertical cliques receive such support from the NII concept and the strong tendency to organize by major function or process, as prescribed by the "principles."

Vertical informal relations, then, seem the major axis of organization behavior. The NII model and the principles reinforce this vertical bias and with unfortunate consequences.

The Principles and Vertical Fragmentation

A third view of fragmentation requires some stage-setting. The previous two approaches to fragmentation may be thought of as independent of any specific structural relations. And although these fragmenting tendencies will usually exist, whether they are deleterious or not depends upon the broader organizational structure in which the NII model is imbedded.

Traditional organization theory prescribes that major functions (at high levels of organization) and processes (at low levels) should

be the basic foci for organizing, and this encourages vertical fragmentation. There are alternative ways of departmentalizing—such
as area and clientele served—but functional and processual departmentation are the traditional workhorses. Other modes of specializ-
ing take distinctly secondary roles in the usual list of principles.
And even casual thumbing-through the *Government Organization
Manual* or perusing company organization charts amply supports
the impact of the theoretical formulation on practice. Times are
changing, of course, and due attention will be given to the implications for line-staff relations of the new guidelines for organizing.

But let us do justice to the commonplace emphasis on functions
and processes. Consider the organization of individuals performing
the activities *A*, *B*, and *C* whose integration constitutes a product or
service. The traditional theory generates the structure of formal
authority depicted in Figure 5, with a manager (M) and three
supervisors (S). Such a structure implies significant tendencies
toward the vertical fragmentation of activities that must be integrated into a common flow of work. Relatedly, horizontal relations
are given (at best) inadequate attention in the literature.

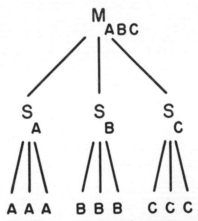

FIGURE 5. Simplified Formal Structure Generated by the Traditional
Theory of Organization.

The principles run counter to the flow of work, which has major
horizontal components. For example, Table 3 shows that nearly 50
per cent of the total interaction time of the three levels of executives was spent in horizontal contacts with peers. Hence Dubin's
assertion—based on data like that in Table 3 for executives as well
as for lower-level operatives—that the sheer volume of horizontal

Pressures Toward Unorthodoxy, III:

interactions keeps the organization going. "Indeed," he concludes, "it is probably among organization equals that the real co-ordination of work flow and operations takes place. . . ."[6] Since the horizontal dimension is neglected by the NII model and by the "principles," horizontal relations are not facilitated by the traditional theory. The costs should be great.

TABLE 3. EXECUTIVE INTERACTIONS WITH
ORGANIZATION MEMBERS AT VARIOUS LEVELS

Rank of Persons with Whom Interaction Occurs	Percentages of Total Interaction Time		
	Three Executive Levels		
	Department Manager	His Senior Staff[a]	His Junior Staff[b]
Superiors	6	23	34
Peers	29	50	46
Subordinates	65	27	20

Data from Tom Burns, "The Direction of Activity and Communication in a Departmental Executive Group," **Human Relations,** VII (February, 1954), 9.
[a]Comparable to assistant departmental manager.
[b]Comparable to section manager with foremen under him.

Managing Vertical Fragmentation: Some Costs of the Traditional Theory

The preceding conclusion is a very mild one. The general point may be established more broadly. Worthy notes that "cooperation can no longer be achieved spontaneously" where the principles are respected. "After all," he explains, "each functional unit was set up as a distinct entity in order that it might achieve a more efficient system." Sub-organization needs consequently become preeminent and are zealously served, even where the needs of the larger organization must be compromised.[7] This increases management's problems of reconciling differences between organization units which, in turn, commonly encourages the development of staff aid.

The specific disabilities of the vertical bias of the NII model and the principles may be sketched usefully in terms of four kinds of costs: the increased pressure for the integration of activities and its

[6]Robert Dubin, "Business Behavior *Behaviorally* Viewed," in *Social Science Approaches to Business Behavior,* ed. George B. Strother (Homewood, Ill.: Dorsey Press and Irwin, 1962), pp. 14-15. As one goes down the hierarchy, however, interaction with superiors does tend to increase. See Q. D. Ponder, "The Effective Manufacturing Foreman," *Proceedings of the Tenth Annual Meeting, Industrial Relations Research Association* (Madison, Wis., IRRA Publication No. 20, 1963).
[7]James C. Worthy, "Factors Influencing Employee Morale," *Harvard Business Review,* XXVIII (January-February, 1950), 71.

consequences, the difficulties of measuring and motivating behavior, the unwieldy managerial units prescribed by the traditional theory, and the complications of the foreman's job induced by the principles and the NII model.

Increased Pressure and Its Consequences

Worthy's summary recommends detailed analysis of the costs of the orthodox structural arrangements. Thus to begin a selective survey with a patent observation, the horizontal integration of the several activities *A, B,* and *C* in Figure 5 is crucial. A breakdown at any one work station can affect the entire operation. The point holds most obviously for a three-step manufacturing operation when the machinery necessary for step 1 breaks down. Steps 2 and 3 are soon affected. The point also applies to the integration of broad activities such as sales, personnel, shipping, and the like. This possibility of breakdown encourages extreme precautions. Derivatively, the acute need for integration argues for a narrow span of control and close supervision. That is, any supervisor is enjoined to have but a few subordinates, with the usual rule of thumb putting the number at between three and seven or ten. In addition, the supervisory role is defined in terms of issuing detailed and frequent instructions, closely observing performance, and the like.

Even the ingenuity of the principles and the NII model does not avoid serious awkward consequences. As recent research shows, for example, close supervision is associated with low output far more often than with high output,[8] and particularly as the task depends on coordinated contributions of several actors. Most studies support this relation in six or seven of ten cases or more. And, at higher levels of organization particularly, a narrow span of control implies tremendous costs in the lack of training of subordinates and in the loss of more capable employees who require that work challenge and test them.[9] Both consequences will receive attention later. In addition, high pressure encourages representatives of the several activities to become adept at relocating responsibility for error, a

---

[8]Robert L. Kahn and Daniel Katz, "Leadership Practices in Relation to Productivity and Morale," in *Group Dynamics: Research and Theory,* ed. Dorwin Cartwright and Alvin Zander (Evanston, Ill.: Row, Peterson, 1960), pp. 559, 561.

[9]James C. Worthy from a report dealing with internal operations at Sears, Roebuck as abstracted in William F. Whyte, *Man and Organization* (Homewood, Ill.: Dorsey Press and Irwin, 1959), pp. 11-16. The original report is no longer available.

talent indelicately described as "throwing dead cats in the back-yards of others." Vertical fragmentation, of course, encourages this reaction to high pressure.

Difficulties of Measuring and Motivating Performance

The traditional theory of organization relatedly implies sub-stantial problems for the measurement and motivation of effort. This significant point requires detailed analysis of the ways in which measurement and motivation subtly interact, as well as analysis of the ways in which the principles tend to sour the mensural-motivational mix. The primary focus is upon the ways in which the principles encourage vertical fragmentation.

The general liabilities of the traditional theory of organization in measuring and motivating performance may be encapsuled in these terms if Figure 5 is kept in mind: Activities A, B, and C contribute to some discrete sub-assembly, but these contributions are "par-tial" rather than "total." That is, S_A is interested primarily in A; the welfare of B and C are of far less immediate concern. The super-visors are not perverse. Their direct responsibility is for A or B or C, not A and B and C. Moreover, the supervisors must worry primarily about their status in the eyes of their employees. It is no honor to be a patsy for other supervisors who are sharp operators when it comes to gaining praise or avoiding blame. Finally, the supervisors are behaving like human beings, that is, they tend to overvalue their specialty.[10] These particularisms can be avoided, but not easily.

Identifications with workmates or an organization unit can be both useful and satisfying, but the traditional theory of organization bungles the job. It orients these identifications to inhibit the flow of work—or at least not to facilitate it—and this by emphasizing particularistic functions. Schleh has done valuable thinking on the subject. He describes the difficulties inherent in traditional think-ing in this way:

> Many management men feel that if you define respon-sibilities by function . . . you will automatically lead to a blended result. This viewpoint, in our opinion, is a fundamental error throughout much organization plan-ning. People too often go in different directions unless you specify the results or objectives that you wish them

[10]DeWitt C. Dearborn and Herbert A. Simon, "Selective Perception: A Note on the Departmental Identification of Executives," *Sociometry*, XXI (June, 1958), 140-44.

to accomplish. The person in charge of a function too often yields to a human tendency: emphasis of certain phases of his function without regard to their proper relevancy to the over-all objectives of the enterprise.[11]

The trick in successfully managing identifications involves defining responsibilities in ways that encourage integration rather than fragmentation. It has been done. The Martin Company, for example, had great difficulties in integrating work when it was organized functionally—engineering, design, production, and the like. These problems largely abated when total tasks were emphasized, as in a "Vanguard Project" to which all required personnel were assigned and with which they tended to identify. In the latter case, responsibility for results was clear. In the former case, responsibility was very unclear. Work on the Vanguard was at that point only some small part of the workload of each of the many relevant departments whose efforts ought to have been very closely integrated but seldom were because of the problems of communication, time lags, the possibility of buck-passing, and the like.[12] The reorganization, in sum, centered on major results or objectives and permitted the straight forward allocation of responsibility for performance.

The liabilities of the traditional theory stand out prominently. The principles do not facilitate the specification of "results" or "objectives." Rather, they encourage attention to "partial" results or objectives. This complicates assigning responsibility for "total" performance. In fact, the mensural effort may be self-defeating. Thus the greater the precision with which partial results or objectives are specified and measured, the greater the probable emphasis on partial contributions. Consequently, an even greater disregard of responsibility for total performance may result. Bluntly, if one measures partial contributions with zest, one can rest assured that executives will labor to provide just what is being measured even if sharp dealing between units and competitiveness of the "zero-sum" kind is required.

Vertical fragmentation derives great impetus from the principles and the NII concept of program-sustaining relations, therefore. Schleh emphasizes the point. Since staff typically has the jobs of advising, consulting, or assisting, it also commonly has no accountability for "specific contributions to the final objectives of the enterprise." This view also encourages staff constantly to try to "sell"

---

[11]Edward D. Schleh, *The Results Approach to Organization* (New York: Society for the Advancement of Management, 1958), p. 7.
[12]Adolph Vlcek, Jr., "Minimizing Line-Staff Friction at Martin-Baltimore," in *Line-Staff Relationships in Production* (New York: American Management Association, 1957), pp. 29-53.

their activity or, alternatively, to wait until help is requested. Neither alternative is attractive. "In our opinion," Schleh concludes, "such a staff setup leads to fewer results from staff, a poorly blended result with line, and most frequently, a body of frustrated staff specialists."[13]

The manager bears the brunt of these structural difficulties. As in Figure 5, M_{ABC}, who alone controls enough components of work to do the integrating, often finds himself the victim of particularistic interests of the sub-organizations reporting to him. To make matters worse, M_{ABC} often acknowledges the legitimacy of the efforts of each supervisor to build a "high-morale" unit. Thus M_{ABC} may have to weigh action vs. inaction very carefully. In any case, M_{ABC} in Figure 5 is two levels away from the action level. In many larger organizations, real-life counterparts may be a half-dozen or more levels removed. There sits M_{ABC}, in either case, depending for crucial information upon parties to the controversy or upon staff units with their own interests. M_{ABC} must tread warily, or vent his anxiety (usually without improving matters) as a local bull of the woods. Other forms of adaptation are difficult to sustain.

Problems of Measuring Performance. These general liabilities of the traditional theory of organization have left their specific marks. For example, certain features of the history of accountancy have been induced and/or reinforced by the difficulties implicit in the traditional theory of organization. One point illustrates the general picture. After having begun with measures of macroscopic performance, accountants attempted to develop increasing sophistication concerning the performance of sub-organization units organized by functions (and, at lower levels, processes). This was apparently reasonable. However, performance in organizations, broadly speaking, is as pervasive a horizontal phenomenon as it is a vertical one. Consequently, enormous difficulties confronted accountants in assigning costs.

Some of the difficulties of costing may be sketched. Where a number of activities are involved in a flow of work, for example, how are the costs to be parcelled out when many complex factors may affect the efficiency of a particular operation even though its supervisor has no control over them? Moreover, given the vertical fragmentation encouraged by the principles, the avoidance of any costs by any means tends to become part of the accepted rules of the game. In addition, costs-in-contention are not usually black and white. That is, room aplenty usually remains for maneuvering by program units with a relatively clear conscience. Moreover, com-

---

[13]*Ibid.*, p. 12.

monly, one's organizational record is determined in just such marginal cases. Finally, what we know about personality types and how they influence behavior even under conditions of elaborate specification of rules and procedures[14] raises serious doubts about the validity and reliability of allocations in marginal cases. Bluntly, organization units with high power seem to do uncommonly well in such cases, a position understandable in terms of the repercussions for cost accounting staff if too many allocations go the wrong way.

These are not altogether pleasant features of administrative or industrial life. They do exist, however, and the supervisor must realistically prepare his defenses even if this means spending more time in arranging acceptable figures than in improving performance. After all, the supervisor will be judged in terms of these figures whatever their validity. Organizing by functions or processes motivates much behavior not designed to improve performance, then, and particularly since the various accounting fictions designed to patch over the gaps in assigning responsibility implicit in the principles have significant limitations. The effectiveness of an entire organization may be judged with tolerable precision, but where the organization is departmentalized by functions or processes no such "natural" standards of performance exist. Controls must be contrived, but, as Worthy explains, they "often become themselves a source of conflict. The individual supervisor or executive is under strong compulsion to operate in such a manner as to make a good showing in terms of the particular set of controls to which he is subject, and often he does so only at the expense of effective collaboration across divisional lines."[15] Such conflict will be most acute when two or more functions contributing to a common flow of work report up two or more different chains of command and operate under different standards and controls. The NII model, of course, sanctions just such separate chains of command for line and staff.

The traditional theory of organization formulates problems for the measurement of performance in awkward terms, then. Thus the principles imply a stern task for the cost accountant. The structure encourages ducking responsibility when a common problem

---

[14]Gabriel Almond and Harold D. Lasswell, "Aggressive Behavior by Clients Toward Public Relief Administrators," *American Political Science Review*, XXVIII (September, 1934), 643-55.
[15]James C. Worthy, "Some Aspects of Organization Structure in Relation to Pressure on Company Decision-Making," in *Proceedings of the Fifth Annual Meeting, Industrial Relations Research Association*, ed. L. Reed Tripp (Madison, Wis., IRRA Publication No. 10, 1953).

touches the particularistic interests of several supervisors. The dialogue of avoidance can take this form: Work difficulties can be marked down as "the other fellow's fault." Referring again to Figure 5, S_A might claim: "We just do A, and everything was O.K. there." S_B and S_C often can take similar refuge. But Product $_{ABC}$ may not be completed on time and an order may be lost.

That the possibility of such "dead cat throwing" does little to improve operations may be suggested by one experience, the allocation of charges for a $3,000 error. Several departments made "partial" contributions to the task in question, but no supervisor volunteered to take "total" responsibility and to have the error count against the record of his department. The great debate dragged on for two months, emotions ran so high that at least two supervisors vowed not to speak to each other again, and hundreds of man-hours were spent by supervisors on the matter. The resolution of the problem of allocating the charge suggests the common weakness of M_{ABC} in such cases. Thus Argyris reports that the division manager was necessarily embroiled in the controversy:

> The division manager was also in conflict. He had to make the decision. To charge any supervisor with such an error would certainly invite hostility from that supervisor. This hostility might have further effects in the future. . . .
>
> A meeting was held with the interested supervisors. The problem was discussed until just about everybody and everything that could be blamed, were blamed for the error. The division manager finally "gave in." He decided to place the error under "general factory loss." No department would be affected.[16]

That the actions of the supervisors were reasonable from the point of view of the division manager certainly contributed to his decision. For a supervisor who surrendered might thereby impair his effectiveness.

There are other alternatives. Thus M_{ABC} may push harder. In most cases, he would be well-advised to avoid a "get tough" policy where responsibility is not quite clear. For an M_{ABC} needs his subordinates: nothing so debillitates an organization as a superior who has lost the confidence of his subordinates. Sometimes this dependence is dramatically illustrated. Consider the new factory manager who wanted to establish who was boss, and quickly: He walked over to the union steward and delivered this message the

---

[16]Chris Argyris, *The Impact of Budgets on People* (New York: Controllership Foundation, Inc., 1952), p. 19.

first day on the job. The steward got *a* message, but not the intended one. The union steward waved his hand. Every machine in the room stopped. "So you run the place,"the steward said. "All right, go ahead and run it."[17] The case may be unusual, but the point is valid.

Problems of Motivating Performance. Problems of measuring performance imply motivational difficulties. Recall that the traditional theory prescribes grouping together those individuals who perform the same or similar functions or processes. This position seems naive if it has a transparent plausibility. Sayles' careful study of three hundred work units points up the dimensions of this naivete.[18] Sayles isolated four types of work groups which had distinct styles of behavior. Two of these types are of particular interest here:

1. *Strategic groups* were characterized by active participation in union matters and were centers of significant grievances, acting as shrewdly calculating interest groups which exercised great control and taxed both management and union officials, but which were "under control" because they acted predictably; and

2. *Erratic groups* were considered "most dangerous" by management, not only because they were unpredictable in the sense that there often was no relation between the seriousness of a grievance and the intensity of their protests, but also because such work groups were liable to sudden and extreme changes of behavior.

Sayles concludes that the critical variable in inducing various styles of behavior is the structure for organizing work. Different patterns of organization imply different degrees of "resonance," a concept which refers to the social amplification of the evaluations of individuals which the flow of work permits them to share. "Particularly in erratic and strategic groups," Chapple and Sayles explain, "a man who tells his mates of a job problem finds that they share it. With sympathetic repetition, the problem grows in importance." Employees thus can come to feel not only that someting should be done but that it also can be done.[19] The very structure of work, that is, can help induce strategic and erratic work teams by permitting high resonance.

The differences between the two types of work groups may be

---

[17]Douglas McGregor, *The Human Side of Enterprise* (New York: McGraw-Hill, 1960), p. 23.

[18]Leonard R. Sayles, *Behavior of Industrial Work Groups: Prediction and Control* (New York: Wiley, 1958).

[19]Eliot D. Chapple and Leonard R. Sayles, *The Measure of Management* (New York: Macmillan, 1961), p. 89.

traced to the same source as their similarities, the functional or processual organization of work. All of the erratic groups in Sayles' sample performed homogeneous, low-level processes. The loading of materials typified the identical jobs performed. The derived high resonance takes the path of erratic behavior in grievances because the traditional theory deprives workers of any substantial control over work while it organizes them so as to emphasize their sense of common purpose. This is a volatile combination. Strategic groups, similarly, were organized in terms of process or function. They thereby gained great social leverage. It was not employed erratically, however, and for good reasons. Thus many strategic groups are in a position to halt production. That is, their jobs are somehow crucial to the flow of work. Therefore strategic groups can utilize their organizational togetherness to pursue long-run objectives.

The general point here is further illustrated by a careful study of the records of wildcat strikes in electrical goods and rubber tires.[20] The tire industry has a strikingly higher incidence of wildcatting, a fact reasonably attributed to the fixed sequence of operations common in the technology. Electrical goods, in contrast, are characterized by reserve banks of parts and by discontinuous processing. Therefore, individual wildcatting work units in the electrical goods industry may be bypassed for considerable periods. This fact is well-designed to reduce zeal for wildcatting.

Paradoxically, the attempt to assure control via functional or processual specialization often will have the consequence of compounding the problems of control. The traditional theory is a double loser whether erratic or strategic groups are induced.

Prescribing Unwieldy Managerial Units

Effective performance also suffers from the strong bias of the traditional theory of organization to restrict delegation and to increase the size of the unit that any "integrative" supervisor must administer. Worthy frames the issue provocatively in discussing the "managerial unit." He explains that such a unit includes "that portion of the organization falling within the jurisdiction of an individual who controls enough elements of the total process to make effective decisions regarding the total process."[21] The administrative unit required by traditional organization theory is

[20]The study, by James Kuhn, is discussed in *ibid.*, pp. 92-93.
[21]James C. Worthy, *Big Business and Free Men* (New York: Harper, 1959), pp. 92-93.

bounded by the elliptical area in Figure 6. Notice that the illustration employs the simple set of tasks utilized in Figure 5.

The gross consequences of the large managerial unit required by the principles are significant. Primarily, M_{ABC} will find it difficult to delegate anything but the trivial. Thus M_{ABC} will be a busy man,

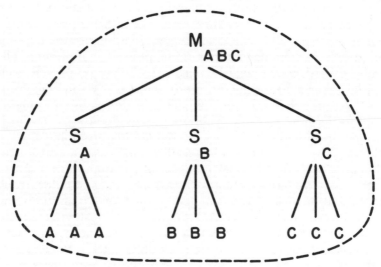

FIGURE 6.   Managerial Unit in a Formal Structure Generated by the Principles.

forced to concern himself directly with operations two levels below his own. The several Ss, in addition, will miss the training experience that delegation could have given them. Moreover, the position of the several superiors is delicate, for lack of delegation implies their low power, that is, the inability to control their environment in meaningful ways. The employees also pay a price. For example, the size of the managerial unit seems to affect employee attitudes[22] and absenteeism;[23] larger size is associated in general with unfavorable increases in such areas. "The evidence of our surveys," Worthy notes of the Sears experience, "demonstrates that there is probably no more important influence on attitudes and morale than sheer size of the organization (not necessarily size of the total company, but rather size of the individual operating branch)."[24]

The large administrative units prescribed by the principles also

[22]Sergio Talacchi, "Organization Size, Individual Attitudes and Behavior: An Empirical Study," *Administrative Science Quarterly*, IV (December, 1960), 410.
[23]Howard Baumgartel, "Organization Size and Absenteeism," *Kansas Business Review*, X (July, 1958), Sec. 2, 3.
[24]Worthy, "Factors Influencing Employee Morale," *op. cit.*, p. 69.

raise broader problems. Emphasis upon supervisory "power" will make the point. By way of introduction, research demonstrates that low-power supervisors tend to have low-output work units.[25] This is credible. For a supervisor with low power is not likely to inspire his workers. Indeed, he may be the butt of some indelicate joking if he must consistently clear matters with M_{ABC} before acting. If nothing else, the procedure is time-consuming. A supervisor, in short, cannot expect to control his men if he does not have the opportunity to control the work environment. Nor can the loyalty of the men be expected to depend on more fragile supports. Derivatively, then, any theory of organization should augment the power of lower-level supervisors.

The traditional theory of organization fails this test. It plays dangerous games with supervisory personnel. That theory places a great burden on M_{ABC} at least because of his administrative distance from operations. The development of sustaining units at the manager's level is the common remedy, but if the NII concept is respected the remedy is less than foolproof. At best, the time lag in decision making will be increased. Similarly, the remedy tends to weaken the position of any S who is close to the work and might respond quickly. The growth of a multiplicity of sustaining units — a common reaction to the pressures for integrating operations faced by the manager — further aggravates the supervisor's lack of power.

Complicating the Foreman's Job

The mischief of the principles and the NII model in encouraging vertical fragmentation and reducing supervisory power is revealed nowhere more clearly than in the job of the first-line foreman. Indeed, in contributing to (if not causing) the decline of the status of the foreman, the traditional approach to organizing has assisted very materially in tearing employees and management apart. This is particularly the case in what might be called "intermittent manufacturing," which characterizes much of our economy. Scott suggestively summarizes the massive historical forces that have tended to complicate the job of first-level supervisor in performing the critical linking function, as in Figure 7. The translation of policies into action patently is a crucial creative act. Any slippage, therefore, must be significant even if it is not easily measurable.

---

[25]Rensis Likert, *New Patterns of Management* (New York: McGraw-Hill, 1961), pp. 55-57.

Considerable slippage has occurred, in fact, and a great deal of it is due to the NII model. First, the NII concept has encouraged the vertical fragmentation of socioemotional specialists in foreman positions and subject-matter specialists in staff positions. Clark, for example, stressed the socioemotional role of the foreman as far back

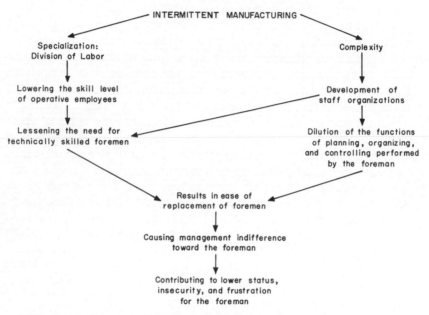

FIGURE 7. Decline of the Foreman's Status in Intermittent Manufacturing. Based upon William G. Scott, **Human Relations in Management** (Homewood, Ill.: Richard D. Irwin, 1962), p. 299.

as 1920: "The former most important qualifications for foremanship . . . are eclipsed by the modern requirement that a foreman must know how to handle men."[26] This emphasis probably could be made even more insistently today, although the growth of staff departments of personnel assures that the foreman has no monopoly on the socioemotional role. In any case, increasingly, significant activities — organizing, planning, and controlling — are being taken over by staff personnel, whatever the prevailing model of program-sustaining activities.

These trends suggest significant loss of supervisory power. For the principles still hold the foreman responsible for performance, while the growth of staff activities permits supervisors to complain of "authority without responsibility." Perhaps more significant,

---

[26]William G. Scott, *Human Relations in Management: A Behavioral Science Approach* (Homewood, Ill.: Irwin, 1962), p. 303.

Pressures Toward Unorthodoxy, III:

however, constant strain inheres in making livable in human terms technical procedures and policies developed with little or no consideration for the particular human problems of their specific on-site implementation. This tension, of course, always will exist to some degree. However, its intensity is greatest when one organizes separate units around socioemotional and technical roles as the NII model and the traditional theory of organization prescribe. The normal tension between people and policy then becomes exaggerrated.

Second, the NII model and the principles tend to reinforce the particularly sensitive problems facing the first-level supervisor. Consider Scott's list of five problem areas that bedevil first-line supervisors:

1. poor "downward" communications concerning policy;
2. little "upward" influence by the first-line supervisor in policy decisions;
3. disagreements regarding supervisory job responsibilities;
4. compensation of the first-line supervisor inadequate to sharply differentiate him from his employees, particularly given the advantage of employees through the collective bargaining of their unions, which foremen almost unanimously lack; and
5. poor training opportunities in foremanship.[27]

The NII model aggravates these problems. Thus compensation of foremen suffers because of the flight of activities to the staff, reducing the skills supervisors need and helping despoil foremanship of valuable training opportunities. Adding insult to injury, the NII concept encourages confusion about the degree to which a supervisor possesses power to act in any given case. In pointed contrast with the myth of line superiority preached by the NII model, supervisors and staff actually share many task responsibilities. "When" work is to be performed will be influenced or determined by production planning specialists, "how" work will be done is within the province of methods specialists, quality-control specialists will determine whether standards have been met and what they are, and employee relations specialists share many of the foreman's responsibilities.[28] A line supervisor accepting the NII model has reason to be confused. If he is "in authority" it is in a tiny area indeed.

---

[27]*Ibid.*, pp. 309-13.
[28]Herbert A. Meyer, "A Comparison of Foreman and General Foreman Conceptions of the Foreman's Job Responsibility," *Personnel Psychology*, XXII (Autumn, 1959), 445-52.

This predicament of the first-line supervisor has widespread effects. Being responsible, the line supervisor is constantly pressured by the general foreman for results over which the supervisor may have little control. The supervisor's power is thereby reduced. The high pressure helps no one's emotional state, moreover, let alone productivity and satisfaction. Guest beautifully describes the tragic picture of the first-line supervisor playing a game that is difficult to win by organizational rules which penalize him for moves he does not make and which he often cannot influence significantly.

> Foremen are always getting caught in this familiar vicious cycle. Material inspection, say, has failed to spot some faulty pieces. Something goes wrong at a welding operation. The general foreman is on the foreman's neck to "get it straightened out, or else!" The foreman drops everything to spend time on this new item. He cannot pay attention to the man he was breaking-in on a new job. He cannot check on the stock bin which the stock man forgot to replenish. He meant to warn an operator about a safety condition. He knew another man was down in the dumps about a personal problem. By the time he has cleared up the original trouble and satisfied the boss, something else has blown up and the general foreman is roaring down the aisle again.[29]

More's the pity, the general foreman may have no less grim alternative. For he must force the integration of operations that are impeded by the vertical fragmentation deriving from the principles and the NII model of the staff. The general foreman must do it or very likely it will not be done. Every breakdown in a "partial" contribution will set off a chain reaction in many other units organized in terms of other "partial" contributions. Roaring down the aisles is an understandable adaptation to the enormity of the situation.

Sustaining Officials Bridge the Gap:
Four Techniques for Horizontal and Diagonal Contacts

The sustaining official, whatever the model of his relations with program officials, cannot accept these tendencies toward vertical fragmentation with equanimity. He must make horizontal contacts with peers in other program or sustaining specialties as well as

---

[29]Robert H. Guest, "Of Time and the Foreman," *Personnel*, XXXIII (May-June, 1956), 484-85.

diagonal contacts with officials at higher levels. If sustaining officials can bring off such horizontal and diagonal contacts, fragmentation *might* be reduced. No doubt this will sometimes be the case. However, the NII model encourages the making of horizontal and diagonal contacts in ways that disrupt effective performance or in ways that are not relevant for performance. Relatedly, also, the NII concept discourages horizontal and diagonal contacts which would be less upsetting, e.g., "flashing" a deviation observed by a sustaining official directly across to the program official immediately concerned.

Several factors encourage aggressiveness by sustaining officials in cultivating horizontal and diagonal contacts. Getting a job done often requires such behavior, but sustaining officials have other motivations for developing horizontal and diagonal contacts. For example, program officials—as the NII model implies—will have a crucial say in appointing and promoting sustaining officials.

In developing such contacts, efficiency may come off a winner or a loser. Four techniques designed to bring off this double play for sustaining officials suggest the mixed results: (1) strenghthening ties with top line officials, (2) adhering to the traditional definition of the staff role and studiously avoiding any controversial matters which might cause unfavorable comments to percolate up to the top line officials, (3) compromising with line officials below the top level in order to keep in their good graces, and (4) developing firm working relations with line and staff officials based upon a mutual respect for their areas of expertise and for each other. These techniques are not mutually exclusive, and any sustaining official will employ more than one of the techniques over time. However, practice seems to emphasize the first three.

"Watch Me!"

The technique of attempting to win top-level line support seems reasonable, but its many variations can have profoundly disturbing consequences. The common complaint that staff officials "always gobble up everything you tell them and then take credit for it," for example, suggests one way of winning top-level line approval which is not evaluated kindly by the lower line. Organization politicking may have similar negative effects. The staff man is not out of the woods even if he has an insight which he can legitimately call his own. For if (as is only human) the staff man would like full credit, he may be able to get it only by "showing up"

the line. Life is difficult for the staff man reticent about hiding his lights under a cloak of anonymity.

These comments suggest a curious circular process. Thus staff is encouraged to develop top-level line support and to face hostile reactions of the lower line, which in turn encourages attempts to cultivate the top line, and so on. For example, the lower line commonly rejects staff advice until top line officials have given their approval. The line rationale is direct: any change represents instability and unpredictability. Such a reaction by the line has its unfavorable consequences. Many good ideas perish on the parched earth of resistance, and working relations tend to be stiff and the personnel not predisposed to view the difficulties of others with charity. NII model or no, realistically, the staff man might conclude that his only course of action is to work for top-level support. The relatively self-less staff official might be willing to give up his best ideas to the line official to foster good relations while hoping for just credit or remaining content with a job well done. The author has seen just this happen. Few people behave this way consistently, however. We tend instead to seek credit for what we cannot justly or clearly claim as our own.

The "watch me" technique has its drawbacks, then, not the least of which is that it attracts an audience for what may be a colossal flop. Perhaps only the most able (and most fortunate) can make a go of developing favorable relations with top-level program officials in this way.

With A Smile, But Is It Service?

If the first approach to nonvertical contacts is narrow, lonely, and dangerous, the timid sustaining official need not despair of developing support from program officials. Indeed, avoiding the hint of trouble, if diametrically opposed to the "watch me" technique, similarly may be used to attempt to develop and maintain favorable relations with line officials. The rationale is straightforward. Lack of dissension, if it does not always mean earnest cooperation, may be a tolerable substitute for overt tension between sustaining officials and the lower program officials. This cautious approach may be enough to develop satisfactory relations with line officials near the top of the hierarchy.

There are many variations on this theme, some of which attempt to gain the support of the upper line as protection against lower-line officials. Thus many observers have commented upon the tendency

of staff officials to preserve a "good appearance." Dalton provides a striking case in point. A staff official explains to his subordinates the facts of life concerning relations with the line and particularly with line official C. Kother. The lecture was occasioned by an opening for which the staff official was a candidate. "Some of you may be in line for promotion," he noted. "If you are, you want everything to be in your favor. Well, one of the best things anybody can do for himself is to make a good impression." The impression they had been creating was something less than good. Did they realize, he asked, "that when you have coffee and rolls out there in the room it looks as though you're having breakfast?" The staff official also was aware of positive ways of creating a good impression. "And if you're going to have coffee on tap," he advised, "don't be surprised if you see me carrying in a cup to [program superior] Kother. . . ."[30]

Other sharp differences between program and sustaining officials at lower levels also stem from this desire to create a good impression. The pronounced cultural differences already mentioned, for example, are consistent with the interest of the staff in preserving appearances in ways acceptable to upper-level line officials. Similarly, the often-observed differences between staff and the lower line in attire, education, and vocabulary support the position here, although other reasons for the differences also exist.

Creating a good impression may or may not have favorable consequences for the organization. Carried far enough, the implicit obsequiousness hardly would support staff in doing its work. Indeed, staff initiative might be dormant except in those cases in which it became imperative to act to preserve a "good impression." Frenetic effort then would be expended, as it were, to stand still. There is no reason to believe that line officials respect staff officials who act in this way, for such behavior simply reinforces the stereotypic view that staff does not carry its own weight. Moreover, some of the obvious techniques of presenting a good impression—language, dress, and the like—may have the effect of making it difficult to achieve close relations between the lower line and staff. Thus creating a good impression—especially if it means defining a good impression in terms of the style of organizational life of the upper line—can have unfavorable consequences for work. Hence the common practice among lower-line officials of referring to staff in such uninspiring terms: "stuck-up," "college punks," "slide rules," "pretty boys," and "apple polishers."[31] The list could be exhausted, at times beyond the limits of relatively restrained discourse.

[30]Dalton, op. cit., p. 100.
[31]Ibid., pp. 87-88.

Wink While You Work

Nature is harsh to sustaining officials seeking diagonal or horizontal relations. That is, the first two techniques for keeping in the good graces of the upper line are not likely to prove sufficient, whether used singly or in combination. Consequently, staff may have to resort to partnership with the lower program officials in keeping information from their mutual program superiors. The quid pro quo often includes a superficial placidity in line-staff relations, which may be taken by some to indicate satisfactory working relations, and an occasional good word about staff officials by lower-level line officials to their supervisors.

Such "cooperation" covers a wide spectrum. Thus sustaining officials may contrive to stall a program which has been approved by the upper line but whose implementation might embarrass lower-level program officials, or violations of rules might be overlooked by supporting officials, and so on. And it is cooperation in the true sense, for both line and staff may derive benefits from such relations. Dalton provides a striking illustration of the reciprocal benefits which participants may derive. He cites the case of a staff assistant caught in some nasty trouble. The line executive whose unit bore the brunt of the errors did not complain to higher management about staff ineffectiveness thereby hoping to soften criticism directed at him. Rather the line executive took the blame. Christian charity did not provide its own reward, however. The line official used the incident as a protection for various kinds of free-wheeling. He employed shortcuts forbidden by policy, he refused to allow inspection of his production at the appropriate time, and he unjustly laid the blame for defects in materials at staff's door. These adventures often required that staff falsify records. These reports, Dalton informs us, "sometimes dealt with extensive operations that called for reworking of the product and manipulation of funds, time, and personnel."[32] Organization, that is, is pervasively political as well as patently technical.

Commonly, no easy judgment concerning such accommodations can be made. For such line-staff cooperation might serve the purposes of both the organization and its personnel. Mutual greasing of the ways may help avoid uncomfortable and costly friction. One need not be stiff-collared in order to note some unfavorable consequences of such cooperation, however. Most prominently, the upper line must operate on the basis of falsified, or inadequate,

---

[32]*Ibid.*, p. 105.

information. The results can be disastrous. Moreover, if such cooperation is common, it may be difficult for program and sustaining officials to regard each other with the mutual respect on which sound working relations must be based. At best, the relation is tense because the upper line often would love to crack such conspiracies and might respond warmly to a confession of wrongdoing from one of the parties.

There is much pious tongue-clucking about such cooperative arrangements. It neglects the political character of life in organizations. The point here is not so pious or pretentious as the common nods of disapproval directed at such behavior. Rather, the point is that the traditional pattern of line-staff relations encourages much undesirable cooperation. There is no thought of trying to eliminate program-sustaining cooperation of various kinds. This would be a pipedream, and ineffective and dangerous in the bargain. Subsequent analysis will try its hand at designing a pattern of program-sustaining relations which encourages cooperation while it avoids the risks of the NII model.

Working Toward Mutual Respect

Yet another alternative exists to the reasonable desires of sustaining officials to have their contributions recognized and rewarded. It involves striving toward effective work relations based upon mutual respect by program and sustaining officials for each other and for each other's contributions to the task. This seems the idyllic relationship.

Once having counted one's self on the side of the angels, however, problems still remain. No doubt many program and sustaining officials have achieved such a state, and certainly most program and sustaining officials have profited from such work relations at one time or another. Both experience and relevant literature, however, place a low probability on such a state of affairs. And, in any case, the NII concept of staff hardly encourages moderate and mature relations. In addition, the pressures of the principles are such as to thwart even the best intentioned. For the allures and demands of vertical fragmentation can be compelling. Finally, most people are highly receptive to even very subtle cues in their environment about legitimate ways of behaving. Thus the NII concept will tend to be accepted as legitimate by many officials, even by most of those who are forced into various accommodations that conflict with the concept. Since the NII model neither describes existing relations nor prescribes effective relations, it may leave a legacy of guilt, even in those cases in which violations of the model contribute to greater effectiveness.

Directions for Further Analysis

These brief considerations may be summarized quickly in terms of four variations on the theme: The NII model seems to heighten the normal tensions that exist between program and sustaining activities. First, the NII model tends to fragment sustaining units from program units in geographic, social, and psychological senses. Second, the NII concept aids and abets the tendencies of the

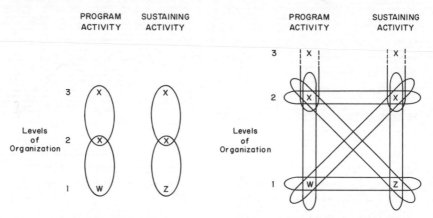

FIGURE 8A. Identifications Encouraged by the NII Concept.   FIGURE 8B. Identifications Encouraged by an Ideal Concept.

FIGURE 8.   Two Contrasting Patterns of Identifications of Program and Sustaining Officials.

principles to compartmentalize an organization into vertically fragmented sub-organizations cohering around one of the several functions or processes. Third, the NII concept decreases the likelihood of "horizontal integration," or (more conservatively) does nothing to encourage it. Fourth, the horizontal and diagonal contacts between program and sustaining officials, encouraged by the pursuit of such prizes of organization success as budgets, promotions, and the like, do not necessarily aid efficiency. On balance, in fact, these contacts seem to have the opposite effect.

The argument also has important implications for the direction of the subsequent analysis. Some cartography points the way. Figure 8B depicts an ideal pattern of identification that might usefully

unite personnel performing program and sustaining activities. Notice that the figure is deliberately simplified by tracing only the relations of organization levels 1 and 2. In Figure 8B, W and Z share an identification that reinforces their efforts on the job by bonds of understanding as well as by formal fiat. At the same time they are identified with their overhead program and sustaining units, respectively. This would temper friendship with due regard for technical standards. The Neutral and Inferior Instrument model, however, encourages the relations depicted in Figure 8A. It increases the tension between units which must integrate their contributions horizontally if operations are to be most effective. Subsequent efforts, indeed, are directed to designing a formal structure which approaches Figure 8B rather than Figure 8A.

Chapter 5

Toward the Colleague Concept of Staff:
The "Team" as an Organizing Device

The Neutral and Inferior Instrument model of staff falls easy prey to the tensions implicit in the character of program and sustaining activities. Consequently, this and the following two chapters strive to provide detailed consideration of one alternative structural pattern. A concluding chapter attempts to place this effort at design and analysis in the context of several dominant themes of the contemporary study of organization.

Organizing for the Colleague Model:
Basic Structure

Specifying the organizational arrangements suitable for the Colleague model is a problem in successive approximations. For it requires extracting a set of relations from research that will become increasingly precise and comprehensive and from practical experience that will become increasingly definitive. But this does not excuse us from attempting the best approximation possible today. Straightaway, then, Figure 9 blocks out the design of a structure for the Colleague model of relations at two levels of organization. Interpretively, a Level II unit (presided over by Heads) monitors several Level I units that are called Sections and whose ranking officers are called Chiefs. Notice particularly the nuclear-like organization chart. It emphasizes the coequal cooperation implied by the Colleague model and portrays visually the intention of organizing so as to facilitate horizontal integration while preserving the traditional vertical controls in a modified way.

As a terminological convention, each set of managerial or su-

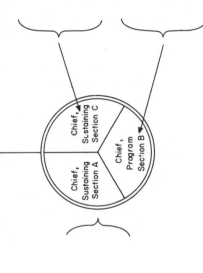

FIGURE 9. The "Team" as an Organizing Concept: The Colleague Model of Program and Sustaining Activities.

Where "substantive" and "technical" matters are distinct, these sets of responsibilities may be given to each of the program and sustaining units cf sections.

policy determination on "technical" matters affecting sustaining units only

supervising technical performance within individual sustaining sections

establishing and monitoring measures of the performance, or the profitability, of individua sustaining sections

training and development of sustaining personnel

policy determination on "technical" matters affecting program units only

supervising technical performance within individual program sections

establishing and monitoring measures of the performance, or the profitability, of individual program sections

training and development of program personnel

responsibility for performance of each individual sustaining section

responsibility for disciplining members of each sustaining section

responsibility for implementing and enforcing "technical" policies applicable to a sustaining unit, and when necessary assuring the necessary compliance of other program and sustaining sections or individuals on their team

responsibility for performance of program section

responsibility for disciplining members of program section

responsibility for implementing and enforcing "technical" policies applicable to a program unit, and when necessary assuring the necessary compliance of other program and sustaining sections or individuals on their team

Where "substantive" and "technical" matters blend, the teams of program and sustaining officials at the two levels have such sets of responsibilities:

policy determination, e.g., concerning the degree and nature of delegation to lower-level teams

hearing appeals on matters not resolved in lower-level teams

granting promotions and pay increases to chiefs of the sections of lower-level teams

establishing and monitoring measures of the performance, or the profitability, of lower-level teams

a major role in determining the nature of the work environment, as in isolating the several major flows of work and in tying wage-and-salary programs to performance within these flows of work

responsibility for performance, or profitability, of each lower-level team

decision-making on matters delegated to lower-level teams, consistent with broad policies

granting promotions and pay increases to employees of each team in both program and sustaining units

pervisory personnel (heads or chiefs) in Figure 9 will be called a "Colleague group." The total organizational unit monitored by each Colleague group will be called a "Colleague team." That is, Figure 9 details one Colleague group at each of two levels of organization. Two kinds of Colleague teams also are depicted. Thus the upper-level Colleague group monitors and is a part of a Colleague team composed of all lower-level Colleague groups plus their operating personnel. And each lower-level Colleague group plus its operating personnel constitutes a second kind of colleague team.

Other features of Figure 9 will be developed at length below, but additionally here note the centrality of the distinction between "substantive" and "technical" issues. The underlying distinction is rudimentary; it is intended to be defined and redefined on a continuous basis as work is grappled with; and the distinction is to be defined in an environment encouraging quick and effective decisions. In the present context, that is, a "substantive" issue is one *defined by organizational participants* in dual terms: as being of significance to more than one of the activities represented on a Colleague team; and as an issue about which representatives of the affected activities have not reached agreement. A "technical" issue, relatedly, is defined as one that affects only a single activity or as one that affects several activities but about which agreement exists. The desired flow is to make "technical" issues out of "substantive" issues, although the exigencies of work may sometimes reverse the flow. If a substantive issue cannot be settled at lower levels before performance is or can be significantly affected, an upper-level Colleague group will intervene while its members indicate their displeasure at being forced into such a role. The patent expectation is that the shared identifications of the individuals performing the several related program and sustaining activities in a flow of work will encourage the kind of collaborative effort that will require few such interventions.

Figure 9, of course, is bare bones. This is intentional, for the purpose is to outline a form of organization applicable at all levels, which dictates an emphasis upon the general character of the proposed relations. The approach has its pluses and its minuses, but the former carry the day. The major liability is that the general structural form must be tailor-made for any specific level of organization in any specific company. This fact makes life more difficult than Figure 9 implies. The general form of Figure 9 is convenient for analytical purposes, however, an overriding plus indeed. Moreover, this chapter will provide detailed illustration of

Toward the Colleague Concept of Staff:

how the Colleague model can guide attempts to organize. If with some caution, then, we may make the best of convenience.

Organizing for the Colleague Concept: Guide Lines

Setting this study's cap for the best of both convenience and realism is not impossibly utopian. Substantial flesh may be added immediately to the skeleton of Figure 9 without complicating the model. Seven major emphases will do the job. The seven serve as guidelines that should be observed in organizing around the Colleague model, or they imply benefits that derive therefrom, or both.

Guide Line I: Freedom From Hair-Splitting

First, the Colleague approach avoids the sticky problem of determining just what is a sustaining function. The purpose here is to organize sustaining functions, not to identify them. This note is not flip, simply because the Colleague model does not distinguish between units "in the line of command" and those which are "purely advisory." Thus no effort need be wasted on hairsplitting, and on hairsplitting which is of grave significance. Let a concern define what are program and sustaining activities *for its purposes* and the Colleague model will apply.

This characteristic is not trivial. For the Neutral and Inferior Instrument concept requires the search for some characteristics that distinguish specific organization units as line and staff, and this procrustean search has not been fruitful. As Sampson concludes:

> Finding a precise definition of the functions of staff people is well-nigh impossible. I found eight different descriptions of what staff work should be in the first ten books on management at which I looked. Most of the descriptions agree in the main, but differ in classifications of techniques, kinds of staff work, functions of staff people, and staff and line relations.[1]

This abort is not surprising, for the search for distinguishing characteristics requires dealing with constructs of the mind as if they are real. This is a dangerous game. As Don Quixote, one should expect to be unhorsed by windmills one sees as dragons. That being line or

---

[1]Robert C. Sampson, *The Staff Role in Management: Its Creative Uses* (New York: Harper, 1955), pp. 4-5.

staff often is important in determining an official's (or unit's) leverage in organizational affairs only aggravates matters. Solemn nonsense is the most dangerous variety.

Guide Line II: Building Upon Experience

Second, the Colleague model is not a total stranger to practice. Such relations do occur, sometimes by planned effort, more often as a spontaneous reaction to the demands of work and smooth functioning. We shall illustrate both spontaneous and conscious approaches to the Colleague model, with the singular intention of suggesting the breadth of the range of the structural content encompassed by the unorthodox approach to line-staff relations. Examples to be given later will provide more specific details.

Spontaneous approaches to the Colleague model exist in ample number, from which we shall select but two from research and manufacturing contexts. For example, Marcson found that research teams succeeded as they approached "colleague authority" and as they avoided authority based on "incumbency in office." The former concept, according to Marcson, "emphasizes ... association, alliance, and working together, while at the same time accepting whatever inequality in status may be present." Status inequalities still exist, but (we are told) they "are subordinated to the assignment of colleagues for work purposes."[2] Marcson emphasizes superior-subordinate relations. The Colleague model of staff would apply somewhat analogous notions to the relations of line and staff officials at the same level.

IBM drew still closer to the Colleague model, but that firm's approach similarly was a spontaneous reaction to specific work demands that were inadequately met by the NII model of line-staff relations. IBM faced the problem of beginning production on some of its equipment before the engineering work was completed. The pressure of events forced a jerry-built collaboration of program and sustaining personnel which was theoretical heresy, but which was also highly effective. The final pattern of relations generally resembles that prescribed by the Colleague model. Thus D. L. Bibby, a high-ranking program official at IBM, summarized his firm's experience with staff teams in favorable terms:

---

[2]Simon Marcson, "Organization and Authority in Industrial Research," *Social Forces*, XL (October, 1961), 75.

Our former foremen get together their own staffs of people, from tool engineering, methods, production engineering, education and the like, and work with them to perform their assignments.... This approach has produced satisfactory — in fact, superior results. Of necessity, the manager has had to go beyond the confines of his daily routine work and to become acquainted with phases of the business with which he would not normally have become familiar. He has had to make decisions, solve problems, and coordinate the efforts of people from many different sections of the business when fulfilling his assignment.[3]

Complementarily, the Colleague model also has been applied in a wide variety of situations by perceptive design. The "product-consumer centers" of Texas Instruments fall in this category. Lambersteen, in addition, describes a Colleague-like application in a nursing team which is called the primary formal operating unit in the organization of the ward of the modern hospital. A team is assigned to care completely for the needs of a set of patients and performs a wide range of activities to this end. Some of these activities can be characterized as staff, some as line. Each unorthodox team meets once during each eight-hour tour of duty. These meetings range from four to twenty-five minutes in one set of observations and provide an opportunity to "think, plan and evaluate together."[4] The traditional pattern of organization, in contrast, prescribes that each nursing employee perform but one restricted set of operations for many patients. And if these employees report to different organization units, as often happens, integrative difficulties assume great importance.

Perhaps the most conscious efforts to depart from the traditional pattern of line-staff relations, however, are reflected in structural patterns designated as "project management," or "program management," or "matrix overlays."[5] Basically, project management as

---

[3]D. L. Bibby, "Building Satisfaction into the Supervisor's Job," *Personnel*, XXXI (March, 1954), 408.

[4]E. Lambersteen, *Educating for Nursing Leadership* (Philadelphia: Lippincott, 1958).

[5]A large literature on "program management" exists, and applications cover a tremendous range anchored by seminal uses in aircraft, defense, and space technologies. More detailed accounts of this unorthodox structural variation may be found in: Paul O. Gaddis, "The Project Manager," *Harvard Business Review*, XXXVII (May-June, 1959), 89-97; A. K. Wickesberg and T. C. Cronin, "Management by Task Force," *Harvard Business Review*, XL (November-December, 1962), 111-118; Auren Uris, "Balanced Talents Bring Team Success," *Nation's Business*, L (December, 1962), 66-68, 70; Joseph A. Litterer, "Program Management: Organizing for Stability and Flexibility," *Personnel*, XL (September-October, 1963), 25-34;

far as possible assigns to basic units of organization all of the activities required for some particular task or project. However, project management is an organizational half-way house to the Colleague model. Generally, a second structure also exists in firms using project management, and that structure is patterned after the traditional theory of organization. Thus Martin Marietta had a "Subroc Project" to which were assigned all of the required specialties, but all members of Subroc also had permanent homes in some functionally-oriented department such as a Department of Engineering. Project teams exist only until their goal is accomplished. That is to say, project teams temporarily serve to cut across traditional organizational boundaries that develop between departments organized around processes or functions. When the task or project is completed, however, team members return to their separate and original organization units which are set up around functions or processes. Harvey Sherman illustrates the nature, advantages, and challenges of project management from the experience of the Port of New York Authority. He explains that:

> Such a plan was recently adopted in the engineering design work of the Port Authority. Prior to the change, engineering design work was performed by fixed organization units in the mechanical, electrical, structural and architectual fields. Under the new plan, these units were abolished, and project teams made up of an appropriate number of each type of specialist were set up to handle active projects in process. Small staff units of senior men in each specialty were set up to advise and assist the project teams.
> The task force approach permits substantial flexibility since members with appropriate skills can be added or subtracted from the team as needed, new teams can be set up rapidly to handle new projects, and team members tend to be "purpose" or "objective" oriented rather than "process" oriented. The major problem is to schedule staff so as to keep them in full use.[6]

Approaches toward the Colleague model at higher levels of organization are common, as in the top management committees—

Allen R. Janger, "Anatomy of the Project Organization," *Business Management Record* (November, 1963), 12-18; David I. Cleland, "Why Project Management?," *Business Horizons*, VII (Winter, 1964), 81-88; John M. Stewart, "Making Project Management Work," *Business Horizons*, VIII (Fall, 1965), 54-70; and National Industrial Conference Board, *The Product Manager System* (New York: National Industrial Conference Board, 1965).
[6]Harvey Sherman, *It All Depends: A Pragmatic Approach to Organization* (University: Univ. of Alabama Press, 1966), p. 140.

composed of both line and staff officials — that so often play a major role in administering today's larger enterprises. Thus one study of the role of top-level general management committees found that the making and enforcing of decisions was relatively common. Some 25 per cent of these management committees were "authoritative," that is, they had the power to make their decisions effective. Some 25 per cent of the committees were "nonauthoritative." The remaining committees had authority to act only in limited areas.[7]

The role of management committees permits sharp contrast of two approaches to organizing complexity. The development of group decision by management committees that have the authority to effectuate their decisions is one response to the growing complexity of business. The NII model of staff is also an adaptation to complexity. It admits the need for diverse and expert knowledge, but it often pays a price for attempting to preserve the notion that some line official is the supreme decision-making center. Although the principles of organization and the NII model do not sanction authoritative group decision, then, this often seems unfortunate. Perhaps the most well-known example of an opposed approach at top levels is Du Pont's executive committee.[8]

Curiously, even successful approaches to the Colleague model often either are offered apologetically or are explained in terms of the NII model (if only with great labor). Thus particular circumstances might be cited as forcing a "departure from orthodox practice." Or, like Bibby on p. 123, commentators may fall back upon the NII concept of the supremacy of program officials. Such is the strength of the traditional staff concept and of the principles.

This much having been said, organizing for the Colleague model is not thereby the inevitable winner. For example, technical factors may restrict the applicability of the model. If Krugman's analysis is accurate, for example, types of operations might be distinguished to which the Colleague model applies ill or well. Krugman concludes that "very complex or intricately coordinated operations" — like those in manufacturing, the military, and government — "need the discipline that is best maintained by tall structure" patterned after the principles. Flat structures, he notes, are more appropriate for "loosely supervised and technically simple, though individually more challenging, operations, such as those of sales, service, politi-

---

[7]M. R. Lohmann, *Top Management Committees* (New York: American Management Association, 1961), p. 10.
[8]William H. Mylander, "Management by Executive Committee," *Harvard Business Review*, XXXIII (May-June, 1955), 51-58.

cal, and religious organizations."[9] This would seem to rule out the Colleague model in many cases for, as later analysis will show, that model is congenial to "flat" organizations. As noted, the NII model decidedly leans toward a "tall" structure. Krugman's analysis, however, may be too straightforward. That is, "very complex or intricately coordinated operations" often are an artifact of man rather than a law of organizational nature. But more of this later.

Guide Line III: Toward "Functional Leadership"

Third, the Colleague concept implies what may be called "functional leadership." In contrast, the NII model implies "fungible leadership." That is, the Colleague model implies a fluidity which allows leadership to pass from individual to individual at the same level of organization (whether program or sustaining official) as the problem demands different information or talents. The NII model oppositely presumes that the program official always possesses the necessary talent to exercise leadership and/or that there is virtue in preserving the fiction of fixed leadership even when the program superior does not have the talent.

This posturing may be very unsatisfying to the program official, and it is very likely to be unnerving to the sustaining official. Thompson reflects the common discontent of the staff expert with the all-seeing, all-knowing program head when he complains that: "At the upper reaches of large bureaucracies the executive job and the hierarchical role become almost synonymous, and as specialization advances they undoubtedly will become completely so...." These are strong words, but Thompson does not shrink from his position. "In short, the most symptomatic characteristic of modern bureaucracy is the growing imbalance between ability and authority."[10]

Briefly, the myth of "fungible leadership" may have been acceptable, perhaps necessary, at less-advanced technological levels. Today it is far less likely to exist, however skilled the role-play.

"Functional leadership" is not adamantly set against the tide of organization history. The Colleague model attempts to create that environment within which the various specialists can feel free to make their contributions to effective performance. This is a more

---

[9] Herbert E. Krugman, "Organization Structure and the Organization Man," *Personnel*, XXXVIII (March-April, 1961), 22.
[10] Victor A. Thompson, *Modern Organization* (New York: Knopf, 1961), p. 6. Emphases in original.

difficult matter than it seems, especially when employees have experienced the "boss who is always correct, right or wrong."[11] Consider the experience of Lou, a line foreman.[12] At first, he prominently wore the badge of the Neutral and Inferior Instrument model. He proclaimed that getting the new product into production rested on his efforts. "I am the production foreman," he noted, "the job of the industrial engineers is to help me get set up for production." The engineers were not impressed by Lou's concept. They denied his authority. In addition, he complained that ". . .they make it clear that I do not exist for them personally. They do not care that I am on the spot. Now I have to prove that my ideas are as good as theirs." Lou, in sum, expressed the quintescence of fungible leadership and experienced some of its consequences. Some months later, although no formal changes had been made in the relations of program and sustaining officials, Lou reflected the lessons of experience in his relations with other sustaining personnel on a similar job. He articulated his new-found approach toward functional leadership in these terms. "I am not alone," he expressed this new emphasis. "We are a group of people working together on this. We each have a place. . . ."

Lou's experience may seem to hoist this analysis on its own petard, since functional leadership was attained without specific structural alterations. This observation scores a point in logic, but it neglects a very practical consideration. Tersely, there is no convenient and continuing way to enforce functional leadership within a structure based upon the "principles" and the NII model. Indeed, strong forces discourage functional leadership under such conditions. In any case, massive reinforcement of "useful" learning (as Lou's) is perhaps the basic psychological requirement in organizations. Of course, training can provide yeoman service, but only the Colleague model does a real job in reinforcing such training over time. The concept at once reinforces and legitimates the flexible interplay of program and sustaining activities. This will reduce much of the defensiveness implicit in program-sustaining relations that, for example, characterized Lou's early experience. Moreover, the team responsibility for performance implied by the Colleague model will place a premium upon functional leadership. Its primary focus is upon contributions, as opposed to an insistence about hierarchy. Finally, the Colleague model will free individuals

[11] Robert H. Guest, *Organizational Change:The Effect of Successful Leadership* (Homewood, Ill.: Dorsey Press and Irwin, 1962), p. 62. This author's emphases.
[12] Harriet O. Ronken and Paul R. Lawrence, *Administering Changes* (Cambridge: Harvard Univ. Press, 1952), pp. 123, 129. This author's emphases.

from their role as apologists for their specialty, a role induced by the principles and the NII model and reinforced by concern over promotions and pay increases.

Guide Line IV: Activities Represented on a Team

The question of assignments to teams, fourth, can be settled only at specific work sites. Nothing more than general injunctions may be given here. In general, the Colleague group will be small. But individual colleagues may or may not have direct responsibility for large operations and large numbers of employees. The size of the Colleague team, that is, can cover a wide range. The handful of officials without operating responsibilities on the Executive Committee at DuPont constitute a Colleague group which monitors a smallish Colleague team of immediate supporting units. Or a Colleague team may include officials directly managing assembly operations that require thousands of operators.

Other assignment details are similarly specific to the case. Thus the size of Colleague groups and teams may differ at various levels of organization. Moreover, the skills required may change over time in any concern and certainly will vary from concern to concern. Thus the skill composition of Colleague groups or teams also is a variable. In addition, depending upon the work load, a sustaining official may be assigned to more than one team. High in the hierarchy such assignments are more likely to be to a single team.

These contingencies making assignments a case-by-case matter may be illustrated by the installation of a new work process. The set-up might require certain sustaining functions such as industrial engineering. Once the process is off the ground, however, these sustaining contributions no longer may be necessary. Upper-level teams then will exercise general oversight to assure that out of sight is not out of mind as far as such sustaining activities are concerned.

Not much greater specificity is possible when one considers the activities that cannot be represented on a Colleague team. At least two classes of such activities seem obvious enough. First, decision-making about major managerial objectives patently cannot be left to lower-level teams. Such objectives include interrelated decisions concerning the "market niche" an enterprise hopes to fill, the "market standing" that it would like to attain, and the "institutional style" in which the enterprise will seek its niche and standing. These objectives constitute the "images" in terms of which organi-

Toward the Colleague Concept of Staff:

zations are defined by their relevant publics, and whose development and sustenance is the peculiarly executive responsibility.[13] Second, decision-making about hardware also is an activity that seems generally inappropriate for lower-level teams. Thus it might not do to have several competing teams decide independently on the technology to be employed when the items include, for example, a multimillion dollar drop hammer.

Even such "cannots" must be offered tentatively, however, for lower-level teams should participate in some aspects of these two areas of decision-making. Thus modifications of an existing productive set-up might provide one occasion for teams to exercise their power in shaping an environment that is congenial to their particular needs. Indeed, perhaps it is safest here to note only that each activity represented on a lower-level team must have a counterpart representing it on the team at the level immediately above. However, an activity may be represented at one level of organization without having a counterpart unit at the next lower level. For example, "finance" seldom need to be represented very far down the organizational ladder, although it can seldom go unrepresented at (or near) the top of an organization.

Relatedly, also, the following question defies a generalized answer: Which specific activities can be lowered (for example) to a team at the first level of supervision? Many activities could be. In the job enlargement program at IBM, for example, foremen got into such activities as hiring, training, promoting, and organizing the work of their subordinates. To encourage the first-level supervisor to act "as though he were the sole owner of a small business," the job title was changed to "manager." More broadly, numerous elements of many of the activities below could be delegated to Colleague teams at the first level of supervision:

1. program activities, e.g., production
2. sustaining activities
   a. material control
   b. development of work standards, as by time and motion study
   c. inspection
   d. maintenance
   e. accounting.

These activities are common to many organizations, of course.

---

[13]Philip Selznick, *Leadership in Administration* (Evanston, Ill.: Row, Peterson, 1957).

The Colleague model's basic intention in all this may be summarized usefully. Although the assignment of specific activities to a team will depend upon the job to be done, the Colleague model aims at permitting the fullest integration of activities at the action level by the personnel who perform or directly supervise the activities, rather than at higher levels of organization by personnel who often are located far above the activities they are to integrate. The sense of identification with a team is encouraged by the mutual responsibility for performance of all program and sustaining officials on a team. The NII model, in contrast, does not meet the challenge of horizontal integration of a complete flow of work near the action level. Indeed, the traditional emphasis upon functions and processes assumes that no such problem exists that cannot be resolved from the "top, down."

The Colleague model's goal of facilitating integration is not pursuit of the unattainable. Under the goading of necessity or convenience, and often apologetically, organizers have approached the Colleague model rather closely. Following sections and Chapter VII will provide substantial detail concerning the specific ways in which this can be done under a wide variety of conditions. Consistent with the Colleague model, for example, the Sun Oil Co. assigns to each team in its new refineries the full range of activities necessary for an entire flow of work. As one official explained:

> In this refinery all the men except the accountants and laboratory technicians are part of a single operating team. There is only one department—the Operating Department. The men have been trained somewhat as the crew of a submarine, in that every man can fill almost every breach. They are not concerned whether someone is doing their work, or whether they are doing someone else's work. Their interest lies, as a team, in keeping the operation going. All of the operating work is their work.[14]

These generalities imply an important agenda item for subsequent analysis. Although the bias of the Colleague model is decidedly integrative, not all organization activities can be or should be represented on each team. Sometimes the boundaries for exclusion are clear enough. Long-range planning, for example, is an activity that will have representation only on high-level Colleague teams. But the boundaries for inclusion are still vague.

---

[14]Clarence H. Thayer, "Automation and the Problems of Management," Address to the Wilmington, Del., Chapter of the Society for the Advancement of Management, October 14, 1958.

Toward the Colleague Concept of Staff:

Generally, the crucial practical problem involves determining the several products or "discrete sub-assemblies" that constitute the major and relatively autonomous flows of work in an enterprise. Chapter VII provides substantial detail on the project.

Guide Line V: Unity of Command on "Technical" Matters

Figure 9 on p. 119, fifth, raises a significant challenge to the principle of the unity of command, a central emphasis in the traditional theory of organization. For unity of command has a wide acceptance, plus a plausibility that is difficult to fault. As Luther Gulick explained the rationale underlying this principle in 1937 in the influential set of *Papers on the Science of Administration:* "a workman subject to orders from but one superior *may be* methodical, efficient, and responsible."[15]

Gulick's counsel is reasonable, of course, albeit given two assumptions: that the adequacy of a decision is based upon its issuance by a superior rather than upon its demonstrable correctness; and that the issuance of an order is *the* significant act, which inevitably sets in motion a chain of events leading to consensus among peers and subordinates concerning the order. These are not always viable assumptions and particularly so on substantive questions. "Substantive" questions, recall, are defined *by the participants* as problems of some significance to more than one organizational unit within a Colleague team and as problems about whose solutions little consensus exists. The two assumptions just given would be more likely to hold on "technical" questions, here defined simply as questions that affect but a single activity on a Colleague team, or as questions that affect several activities but about whose disposition agreement exists. More specifically, the two assumptions would apply rather strictly to command-obey sequences covering only a brief period of time. This is to say that the two assumptions in fact do apply awkwardly to the kind of decision-making that is coming to be increasingly characteristic in organizations. These issues are of great complexity, they persist over very long periods of time, and they may never be "solved" in the narrow sense.[16]

---

[15] Luther Gulick, "Notes on the Theory of Organization," in *Papers on the Science of Administration,* ed. Luther Gulick and Lyndall Urwick (New York: Institute of Public Administration, Columbia Univ., 1937), p. 7. This author's emphasis.
[16] Robert Dubin, "Business Behavior *Behaviorally* Viewed," in *Social Science Approaches to Business Behavior,* ed. George B. Strother (Homewood, Ill.: Dorsey Press and Irwin, 1962), pp. 30-34.

Simple command-obey sequences cannot encompass such properties.

A sharp contrast may be made. The Colleague model preserves unity of command as commonly understood in technical matters; but communal decision-making is prescribed in substantive matters. The NII model and the principles neglect the distinction. This is a significant datum for at least two reasons. Thus it is dangerous to think (and worse to act) as though substantive matters are as congenial to the two assumptions mentioned as are technical matters. Moreover, the view that these two assumptions are correct, or should be, gives slavish devotion to unity of command as opposed to unity of purpose. This seems unfortunate. For unity of command and unity of purpose need not appear together, and the latter is the goal in any case. Indeed — as Chapter VII demonstrates — the techniques commonly used to attain unity of command often have the unintended consequence of reducing the unity of purpose.

The present heresy has ample support. Thus many organizations at the upper levels of necessity modify the principle of the unity of command, as in general management committees with authority to make decisions. At the lower levels, in addition, the pressures of work often encourage similar deviations. The attempt here is merely to extend the practice and to legitimate it. That is, unity of command will be preserved by a careful delineation of spheres within which program and sustaining officials act as superiors or as colleagues.

If evolutionary, the Colleague model in this respect does not therefore avoid all difficulties. For example, technical and substantive spheres will not come ready-made. Considerable early attention in applications of the Colleague model must be devoted to defining the two areas; and new issues will require further or novel delineation over time.

The problems of making the required distinctions, fortunately, probably will not be as sticky as they seem. Potent factors encourage consensus within a team about the distinctions, among them being the elemental datum that the failure to achieve consensus will affect team performance, for which both program and sustaining officials are responsible. Consequently, practice should result in increasingly clear and prompt distinctions between technical and substantive areas. To illustrate, the nature of quality-control techniques and associated factors initially may have substantive implications, that is, they may affect the performance of several of a team's constituent units. Therefore, the team faces a policy question, in whose resolution the chiefs of program and sustaining units participate as colleagues. As matters are progressively settled—by the choice of techniques, scheduling, and the like—elements may be spun off to program or sustaining units for implementation. An upper-level team will monitor these activities, of course, albeit largely in terms of results achieved rather than of details. Beyond that and an adherence to broad policies, the teams will largely operate in the psychologically healthy climate of the implementing of decisions by those who make them and hence accept them.

The matter of desirable relations on technical and substantive questions, then, may be suggested graphically. The analogy of nuclear fission—an example of the power of integration altogether fitting the study of productive organization—helps convey the sense of the relations envisioned. Fission begins when the critical mass is achieved by bringing together previously separate chunks of fissionable material. Similarly, the critical mass is reached in the Colleague concept on substantive matters but not technical ones. Technical questions will be characterized by autonomous operation of the program and sustaining units whose chiefs comprise a Colleague group, then, as in steady-state operations. On many occasions, however, matters will "go critical" under the stress of a substantive issue, as in setting up a new work process.

The situational sensitivity of the Colleague model contrasts sharply with the assumption implied by the NII model that once work is well-designed it merely goes on and on. The assumption is an important crutch for the principle of unity of command, which wobbles on the shaky foundation of such questionable notions as (1) organization is a matter of mechanical integration, (2) technology is relatively simple, and (3) technology changes but slowly, if it is not stagnant. The common actual state of affairs—a complex inter-mixture of technical, social, and psychological factors, operating in a technology increasingly characterized by change—provides far more opportunity for matters to go critical. Hence the growing discontent with the NII concept.

Guide Line VI: Encouraging Effective Team Performance: Utilizing the Power of the Group

Sixth, great effort must be devoted to making each colleague team an important reference group for its members. The pattern of formal organization will encourage such identification, but other reinforc-ing features must be developed. Some of these reinforcing features, at least, seem clear. Thus the team should be held responsible for performance. Program and sustaining officials will do their best to perform integratively and effectively, therefore, or they will both come off losers.

The NII model does not immediately put both types of activities on the same spot. The line official alone is held responsible or, commonly, no operating official has immediate and clear-cut responsibility for a "total contribution." In addition, team performance under the Colleague model should receive great weight in awarding pay increases and promotions. This is necessary to release the potential for cooperation which most individuals have in untapped abundance. Heightened team performance should result. Illustratively, a sustaining official who cannot or will not make his way with his team is in difficult straits. The Neutral and Inferior Instrument model, in contrast, permits such a man to exploit the common sympathies within his own staff hierarchy against those "stubborn program people."

These reinforcing factors present a mixture of promise and difficulty. Great social pressures can be generated by the Colleague model, but that potential does not come scot-free. For example, the measurement of the performance of the teams will remain a more or less pious hope in the absence of some substantial rethinking of the traditional bias toward organizing around functions or processes. Relatedly, interteam competition may develop under the Colleague model. This need not affect output adversely, of course. Indeed, given reasonable management, output may be stimulated. Particular attention must be devoted to organizing the teams so as to make them as autonomous as possible, however, thereby increasing the probability of the latter consequence while facilitating performance measurement.

Management sensitivity can do far more to encourage identification with the team. For example, upper-level management should hold each team accountable for settling its sometimes conflicting interests. This might be done by making it clear that the immediately superior Colleague group will sit as a board of appeal in cases in which colleagues are in disagreement, but that it does not enjoy being put in such a position.[17] Adequate measures of performance, or profitability, would assure that merely cozy agreements would not be reached at the expense of operating effectiveness. Contrast this with the tendency under the Neutral and Inferior Instrument model. Disagreements between program and sustaining units may

---

[17]The Executive Committee of DuPont, for example, takes just this position. See Mylander, *op. cit.*

Toward the Colleague Concept of Staff:

rattle up and down the several hierarchies, in part, because sustaining officials (as program officials are quick to point out) have no responsibility for performance but often have power enough to wage enervating resistance. In addition (and program officials will not often raise the point), program officials may act inflexibly because they face no formal necessity of making peace with their "advisors." The Colleague model of relations does not provide such convenient rationalizations.

The effects of the atmosphere associated with the Colleague model also could encourage identification with the team and integration of the efforts of program and sustaining officials. The effects of atmosphere upon behavior are both subtle and profound, as a wealth of research demonstrates.[18] "Atmosphere" is generated by a host of factors, and the formal structure is important among them. That is, if an organization structure is based—as are the NII model and the traditional theory of organization—upon a distrust of the individual, most individuals will behave accordingly; if a structure organizationally separates activities required for a flow of work, organizational units often will go their separate ways. The Colleague model, then, should do much to encourage the attitudes and behavior necessary for the horizontal integration of program and sustaining activities.[19]

The intention of the Colleague model in this respect may be put straightforwardly, although the full meaning and required techniques will put the following three chapters to a difficult test. The Colleague concept attempts to organize around "discrete sub-assemblies," or products, thereby inducing "natural pressure" in the very organization of work. In contrast, the principles of organization and the NII model often require "artificial pressure," or pressure originating outside of the flow of work, in order to bring off the integration impeded by the traditional structure. In the former case, pressure comes from the demands of work; in the latter case, pressure must be supplied (as by a supervisor or a staff unit) in order to goad the performance of work and to overcome the vertical fragmentation encouraged by the principles and the NII model. That model, therefore, both induces integrative difficulties and at one stroke attempts to apply the pressure to remedy them. This seems ill-conceived.

Even at this stage, there are obvious pitfalls in the Colleague approach against which safeguards must be developed. Some of

---

[18]Illustratively, see Howard Baumgartel, "Leadership Style as a Variable in Research Administration," *Administrative Science Quarterly,* II (December, 1957), 344-60.
[19]Guest, *op. cit.,* p. 165.

these difficulties may be described briefly. Upper-level Colleague groups and their constituent program and sustaining officials must be alert for "sweetheart arrangements" between program and sustaining personnel on lower-level teams, for example. Thus the neglect of maintenance might show up in the short run as a more favorable operating ratio. Cooperation should not extend this far.

Setting and enforcing boundaries for cooperation within Colleague groups or teams is crucial. Hence the Colleague model attempts to free upper-level Colleague groups for the development and monitoring of standards suitable for the general supervision of the performance of underlying teams. Consequently, the task should not prove overwhelming. Relatedly, no team member should be at the mercy of his team. His technical performance will be monitored by the upper-level unit of the activity he represents to prevent injustice, although the individual is generally responsible for achieving the acceptance of his team.

Assignments to Colleague group or teams also must preoccupy upper-level units, for mistakes will be costly to the individual and to the organization. Fortunately, much has been learned concerning the kinds of individuals who may be expected to "get along" with one another. One line of experimentation, for example, attempted with some success to measure deeply rooted personality predispositions and to make assignments to teams on the basis of these measures. The personality predispositions tapped in this research have an obvious relevance for behavior at work. The three major predispositions considered make this point with much to spare:

1. a power orientation, which attempted to determine the predisposition of an individual to become a person with high formal authority or to be subject to such a person;
2. a personalness-counterpersonalness orientation, which attempted to determine an individual's predisposition to seek warm, close interpersonal relations; and
3. an assertiveness orientation, which attempted to determine the individual's predisposition to make his views known in group situations.[20]

Such work has great promise. Compatible groups differed from incompatible collectivities in very significant ways. Thus liking, satisfaction, and output on several tasks were higher in compatible groups, and conflict was greater in incompatible groups.

---

[20]William C. Schutz, "What Makes Groups Productive?," *Human Relations*, VIII (November, 1955), 430-31.

This line of research has a way to go. But it suggests the future delicacy with which assignments to teams may be made so as to safeguard both the individual and the organization. Notice particularly that high compatibility does not require selection of individuals that "run to a common type." High compatibility groups can be formed around individuals high on "personalness" or around individuals high on "counterpersonalness," for example. More will be made of this point later. Here note only that the possibility of using personality testing for diverse compatibility assignments should please those who agree with William H. Whyte's criticism of the run-of-the-mill use of personality testing.[21]

Preliminary details must not obscure the basic rationale underlying the design of a structure for the Colleague concept, however. That rationale, bluntly, is to take advantage of the enormous potential for social control implicit in man's group relations. In contrast, the principles deny the existence of the group or prescribe ways of restricting group development. The limited span of control reflects this individualistic bias, for example.[22] The traditional theory pays heavily for its denial of the existence of the group. The point has been demonstrated at great length elsewhere,[23] so we may rely on Seashore's straightforward conclusion: "... it is becoming clear that the individual employee's behavior cannot be understood except in the context of the team or group of which he is a part."[24]

The research literature amply supports building a recognition of group phenomena into the very organization of work. A brief reference to structural integration suggests the magnitude of the costs of neglect. "Structural integration" is a measure of the degree to which the group ranking of individuals corresponds to their formal status in an organization. There is considerable evidence, both experimental[25] and from on-going organizations,[26] that high structural integration commonly is associated with such favorable consequences as high productivity and high employee satisfaction, ceteris paribus. Even when important factors are not held constant,

[21]Robert T. Golembiewski, *Men, Management, and Morality* (New York: McGraw-Hill, 1965), Ch. 4.
[22]Waino Suojanen, "The Span of Control: Fact or Fable?," *Advanced Management*, XX (November, 1955), 5-13; Waino Suojanen, "Leadership, Authority and Span of Control," *Advanced Management*, XXIII (September, 1957), 17-22.
[23]Robert T. Golembiewski, *Behavior and Organization* (Chicago: Rand McNally, 1962).
[24]Stanley Seashore, "Basic Elements of Planning Constructive Supervision" (Ann Arbor: Institute of Social Research, Univ. of Michigan, mimeographed, n.d.), p. 11.
[25]Christoph Heinicke and Robert F. Bales, "Developmental Trends in the Structure of Small Groups," *Sociometry*, XVI (February, 1952), 7-38.
[26]Stuart Adams, "Status Congruency as a Variable in Small Group Performance," *Social Forces*, XXXII (October, 1953), 16-22.

high structural integration commonly is associated with a favorable profile on productivity and satisfaction two, three, or more times as often as is low structural integration.[27] The generalization is arresting, since increments to productivity of even a percentage point or two would be very well received indeed by the management of any enterprise.

The question then becomes this obvious one: Do the traditional theory of organization and the NII model contribute to structural integration? The direct experimental test of this proposition has not yet been brought off, but compelling indirect evidence suggests a firm "No." That organizing for the Colleague model does violence to group properties can be illustrated in two ways. First, all other things being equal, the degree to which supervisors control their work environment seems directly associated with structural integration.[28] But the principles and the NII model tend to reduce supervisory "power," that is, control over their environment. The limited span of control has this effect, for example.

Second, the list of favorable consequences that Worthy ascribes to organizing around products or "discrete sub-assemblies" may be reworked usefully in terms of structural integration. Worthy notes that, in contrast to departmentation based on functions or processes, the unorthodox structure

> Employees have a much better opportunity to know each other, so that cooperation between individuals and departments can develop on a more personal, informal basis and not be so largely dependent on impersonal systems and administrative controls. Employees can see much more readily where they themselves "fit" into the organization and the significance of their jobs in the whole scheme of things.[29]

Several implications of Worthy's description are relevant here. Thus groups will develop norms regulating behavior.[30] The only question in organizations is whether these norms will favor high or low output. Organizing around autonomous flows of work decreases the probability that workers will so perceive their environment that

[27]Robert L. Kahn and Daniel Katz, "Leadership Practices in Relation to Productivity and Morale," in *Group Dynamics: Research and Theory*, ed. Dorwin Cartwright and Alvin Zander (rev. ed.; Evanston, Ill.: Row, Peterson, 1960), p. 558.
[28]Rensis Likert, *New Patterns of Management* (New York: McGraw-Hill, 1961), p. 56.
[29]James C. Worthy, "Factors Influencing Employee Morale," *Harvard Business Review*, XXXVIII (January-February, 1950), 68.
[30]For an interesting study of the complexities of dealing with norm phenomena, see Martin Patchen, "Supervisory Methods and Group Performance Norms," *Administrative Science Quarterly*, VII (December, 1962), 275-94.

they feel constrained to protect themselves, e.g., by restricting output. This can hardly be called a trivial happenstance. For if a group's norms sanction low output, the supervisor faces two noxious alternatives. He may strive to achieve high structural integration, which will usually imply that he must become a defender of the group's norms and therefore a party to restricting output. Or the supervisor may elect to eschew high structural integration and apply pressure to increase output with consequences that are likely to be self-defeating *except* under particularly stressful conditions that the employee cannot avoid or under socioeconomic conditions (e.g., a depression) that are relatively uncommon.

It might be argued in oppositon that, since the traditional theory of organization stresses "specialization," the advantages of the Colleague model are available to the traditional theory where the specialization is by product rather than function. Several factors discourage such an outcome and discourage it quite flatly. First, although traditional usage of specialization is quite broad enough to include both products or discrete sub-assemblies, other properties of the traditional theory are not so hospitable. Thus traditional usage prescribes a limited span of control. Organizing around products permits a very broad span of control, however. Second, practice clearly establishes that the "other properties" commonly have prevailed. Defining "specialization" as product-oriented has been rare in organization practice, and where it exists it does so, as it were, over the dead body of "specialization" defined in terms of functions or processes.[31]

From another angle, organizing for the Colleague model encourages the development of output norms that have an upward orientation. That is, the Colleague ideal is to have several competing teams performing the same or similar relatively autonomous sets of activities. In contrast, the principles emphasize organizing around processes or functions. Norms of output would tend to have a downward orientation in this case. The logic of the situation is compelling. Bluntly put, it would require enormous social forces to lift productivity beyond some minimal acceptable level when functions or processes are the bases of departmentation. Consider only that a *single* organization unit can reduce the output of a total flow of work, but only *all* such units in a traditional structure can raise output. The key factor, of course, is that each organization unit controls but a single activity required for some total flow of work.

---

[31] Alfred D. Chandler, Jr., *Strategy and Structure* (Cambridge: Massachusetts Institute of Technology Press, 1962).

These restraints are absent under the Colleague concept, or at least exist in substantially reduced strength.

By way of summary, then, the Colleague model relies on microstructures that follow the grain of work; the NII model and the principles develop around macrostructures whose component units fragment the flow of work. The social demands differ significantly. In the former case, a single team can raise productivity because it controls all of the necessary activities and is more insulated from retaliation by other units than is true in a structure patterned after the principles and the NII model in which any one organizational unit controls only a single activity of the several required for some total flow of work. Although upward-oriented productivity in Colleague teams seems most likely over the run of a considerable number of cases,[32] more precise prediction will require the specification of a number of variables. For example, some work units may pay for a high level of performance by a relatively low level of satisfaction. The questions, then, are whether this LoSat-HiPro condition will decay over the long run into a LoSat-LoPro condition, and under what mixes of personalities, structure, and the like it will most tend to do so. From another angle, it certainly is sometimes the case that high satisfaction of employees exists along with low levels of aspiration or with low productivity.[33] These interesting cases seem in the definite minority, but they do require close investigation.

In any case, organizing for the Colleague model has a number of features that minimize the dangers of our present lack of knowledge. For instance, providing for self-choice of teammates and for mobility between teams allows the individual to seek a congenial level of aspiration. And the difficulties of limiting output under the Colleague model will encourage a level of aspiration that, in general, will be higher than that probable under the traditional concepts of organizing. Indeed, given reasonable administration of the Colleague model, there is every reason to expect an upward-oriented

---

[32]This is a major hypothesis. The argument here rests basically on the logic of the situation. A great deal of evidence also supports the hypothesis, as in the cases of the "Autonomous Group" and other descriptive studies that will be reviewed shortly. The supporting studies include: P. G. Herbst, *Autonomous Group Functioning* (London: Tavistock Publications, 1962); Seymour Melman, *Decision-Making and Productivity* (New York: Wiley, 1958); and Leonard R. Sayles, *The Behavior of Industrial Work Groups* (New York: Wiley, 1958), particularly in his comparison of "strategic" and "apathetic" groups. The hypothesis also is supported on the small-group level by much evidence reviewed in Robert T. Golembiewski, "Small Groups and Large Organizations," in *Handbook of Organizations*, ed. James G. March (Chicago: Rand McNally, 1965), pp. 87-141.

[33]Adams, *op. cit.*, pp. 16-22.

level of aspiration that may feed on changed employee attitudes and on labor-saving innovations that the team develops and utilizes. Something of the sort seems to explain the extraordinary cost reductions and lower direct labor cost per unit achieved in the Lincoln Electric Company.[34]

These few comments must suffice to suggest the social forces that encourage this effort at structural design. Fortunately, there will be numerous occasions on succeeding pages to amplify and supplement these considerations. These future efforts should be referred back to this introduction of the attempt to rectify an enormous historical accident that has colored so much thinking about and acting within organizations, the disregard of man as a social creature.

Guide Line VII: Pity the Poor Program Chief?

It may seem, seventh, that the program head comes off poorly in any application of the Colleague model, for one can envision the case in which sustaining heads will ally themselves against the program head. Which head will see that production does not suffer?

There seem ample safeguards against the worst in this particular. Thus each supervisor on a team will share responsibility for performance, which should encourage any "political combinations" within a team to aid performance. There is a danger that things will work out differently, but the danger seems less than that implied by the fiction of the NII model in holding one individual responsible for output. This person cannot control many of the factors affecting performance, but he must integrate the efforts of others who are not responsible for output but who can affect it significantly. There seem reasonable grounds for optimism about achieving an effective balance between team members, in addition. For example, should the sustaining officers become overly concerned with short-run output under the Colleague model, there will be upper-level sustaining officials to whom such neglect must be explained. Should the sustaining heads become overly enamored with the technical elegance of their own specialties, on the other hand, their collective responsibility for performance should bring them up short. The first-level program head, compared to the "man in the middle" who is today's foreman, seems in a favorable position.

---

[34]James F. Lincoln, *Incentive Management* (Cleveland: The Lincoln Electric Company, 1951).

Organizing for the Colleague Concept:
Approaching the Model Despite the Formal Structure

These guidelines depart from the conventional model. But the departure has its advantages, as is demonstrated by the integration of program and sustaining activities without structural change in a study by Guest. The traditional staff concept, that is, was accepted both before and after a change in the manager of Plant Y. The new manager made changes that had the effect of softening many of the harsher consequences of the NII model. This record gives some heart to supporters of the traditional model. As will be shown, however, only very qualified optimism seems in order.

A plain recitation of facts sets the stage for the demonstration of the favorable effects of an approach toward the Colleague model. Before the change in managers, tersely, Plant Y was a loser. Consider this unfortunate record:

1. plant efficiency was the worst of the six plants in the division, and this by a wide margin;
2. plant safety left much to be desired, Plant Y being consistently in the lowest quarter of the 126 plants in the corporation; and
3. average monthly quits and discharges were twice the level of the five other plants in the division.[35]

The richness of detailed factors which contributed to this poor record is far beyond the present analysis. The difficulties, however, seem a classic example of the vertical fragmentation aggravated by the NII concept of line-staff relations, which was the official guide in Plant Y. As one program superintendent phrased this familiar refrain:

> The line and service departments never get together to decide on a policy. If the material department wants to do something, they run to the front office, get backing from the top, and then they cram it down your throat. We do the best we can, but the next thing we know someone higher up comes down and threatens: "If you can't do it that way, we'll get somebody in here who can."[36]

NII sustaining officials obviously had found ways to supplement

[35]Guest, *op. cit.*, pp. 38-39. Similarly, the same kind of structure has been associated with sharply-different behavioral outcomes. See J. M. Dutton and Richard E. Walton, "Interpersonal Conflict and Cooperation: Two Contrasting Studies." Paper No. 92, November 1964, Krannert School of Industrial Administration, Purdue University. In sum, structure does not determine behavior. But structure does influence behavior mightily.
[36]*Ibid.*, p. 33.

their organizational inferiority, although not with happy results all the way around. The consequences of such vertical fragmentation were marked and severe.

In a few years under the guidance of a new plant manager, Plant Y reversed directions. Plant efficiency improved by 14 per cent; its safety record improved so markedly that it stood fourth among the 126 plants in the corporation, many of whom had less accident potential in their work; and the monthly turnover rate dropped from 6.1 per cent in 1953 to 4.9 per cent in 1956. Most striking was the general change in attitude: Doing what was the "right thing for the plant" replaced the former dominant attitude of "doing the right thing for the individual departments."[37]

The human improvements may be illustrated by the changes from 1953-1956 in relations of program units with a sustaining official, the plant comptroller. Although he reported to the plant manager, the comptroller was the direct link between the corporation and Plant Y. Originally, the relations of the comptroller's unit with other sustaining and program units left much to be desired. The efficiency reports coming from the comptroller's office were misunderstood, disliked, and considered "downright harmful." The figures had come from a remote comptroller's office, whose officials were seldom well informed about operating problems, and the figures had been used as a bludgeon by the old manager whose guiding principle was: "If you can't do it, get out." With it all, these figures were not particularly useful for program officials bent on improving their performance. Indeed, the figures often had the effect of placing responsibility on program officials for factors influencing production which they could not control. Consequently, secrecy and perhaps duplicity characterized the relations between program and sustaining officials. As one official put matters in the language of the bridge player: "Everyone played the cost figures close to their chests."

With the inspiration and support of the new plant manager, a new comptroller sought to improve these relations. In effect, the Colleague model of program-sustaining relations was approached. First, specifically, attempts were made to reduce vertical fragmentation, as by getting the comptroller's people at the problem-site together with the other program and sustaining officials involved. As the comptroller explained:

> I got into another kind of activity which is different from the kind usually thought of for a comptroller. Cooley

[37]*Ibid.*, pp. 77, 99-103.

would often bring me in when they were going to make
some kind of rearrangement in the shop. Take like in the
trim department *when we made* those big changes. I and
my people would often go down *as a group* with Cooley
and the heads of other operating and service departments.[38]

The very act was symbolic of horizontal integration. And the comptroller's use of the term "we" suggests that more than symbolic
behavior was involved. Such trips made the comptroller less remote and thereby reduced the fragmenting tendencies implicit in
the Neutral and Inferior Instrument concept of program and sustaining relations.

Second, such visitations, complemented by regular meetings of
program and sustaining officials, served to expand what Guest
calls the "span of cognition." This concept refers to the awareness
of the problems of others and of the impact of one's actions upon
others. The NII concept serves to restrict the span of cognition.
That is, vertical fragmentation encourages the philosophy of "doing
what's right for the department" as opposed to "what's right for the
plant." Moving toward the Colleague model encourages a wide
span of cognition by making both program and sustaining officials
responsible for performance. One of the new comptroller's visits to
the shop, for example, helped him formulate requests to headquarters for capital outlays. "We could observe the operations themselves to see why the changes needed to be made," the comptroller
explained. This made his job easier, that of preparing the information required for requests for money outlays. "It meant a lot more to
us," he noted, "when we had the actual experience of seeing the
problem itself and in having a part in making suggestions."[39]

Third, relatedly, changes also were made in the direction of
functional leadership. The effort proved advantageous. Thus the
comptroller of Plant Y reacted favorably to "being cut in on the
deal" on proposed changes.[40] Not unrelatedly, the comptroller's
office instituted a new set of reporting practices to aid program
officials in supervising their work. The traditional set of figures was
still forwarded to headquarters. As the comptroller recounted his
experience, however:

The [traditional] figures in themselves were not wrong,
but they certainly weren't useful to [the program units],
which amounts to about the same thing. For example, if
you simply come out with a figure and tell a foreman that
he is 10 per cent over standard costs, that doesn't mean

[38]*Ibid.*, p. 81. This author's emphases.
[39]*Ibid.*, p. 81.
[40]*Ibid.*, p. 81.

too much to him unless he understands why. As we found out in our talks with the foremen, there could be six or seven different factors which would account for a foreman's being over standard, and some of these factors could be beyond his control. We worked a long time figuring up a formula which the foremen and general foremen and superintendents could use to analyze efficiency figures quickly. Also, we broke down the efficiencies, after we got the over-all figures, into individual elements and laid a program out on that basis. Next, we got all of supervision in and presented the idea to them, showing that the idea had basically come from our talks with them.[41]

This story of Plant Y and the comptroller's office could be expanded, but the main point should be clear. The improvement in performance derived from increases in horizontal integration which resulted, in turn, from overcoming many of the difficulties implicit in the traditional theory of organization. The approach reflected the spirit of the Colleague model, but without corresponding structural changes.[42] This poses a challenge to the present analysis: The search for a new structure for organizing program-sustaining relations may seem a waste of effort. All that is necessary is to have other managers do what the new manager of Plant Y accomplished.

There is one hitch in this antirevisionist argument: The probability that the generality of managers will act appropriately does not seem great.[43] The high conflict between line and staff, indeed,

---

[41]*Ibid.*, p. 79.

[42]*Ibid.*, p. 81.

[43]The importance of structural change is implied, for example, in the distinction between "hygiene factors" and "job factors" made by Frederick Herzberg, *et al.*, *The Motivation to Work* (New York: Wiley, 1959). Briefly, hygiene factors act only as satisfiers, that is, they operate so as to prevent employee satisfaction from falling to dangerously low levels. Hygiene factors include such items as pension programs, physical working conditions, and the like. Only job factors have proved positive motivators of individuals at work, and job factors include such elements as the organization of tasks and their structuring into broader organizational relations. For evidence supporting Herzberg's findings, see Milton M. Schwartz, Edmund Jenusaitis, and Harry Stark, "Motivational Factors Among Supervisors in the Utility Industry," *Personnel Psychology*, XVI (Spring, 1963), 45-53; Frank Friedlander and Eugene Walton, "Positive and Negative Motivations Toward Work," *Administrative Science Quarterly*, IX (September, 1964), 194-207. Herzberg's duality does not isolate orthogonal dimensions, however, as is demonstrated by Ronald J. Burke, "Are Herzberg's Motivators and Hygienes Unidimensional?," *Journal of Applied Psychology*, L (1966), 317-21.

More directly, the relevance of structural redesign is implied by considerable experience with the "laboratory approach" to organization change, without question the most used and useful contemporary technology for inducing and reinforcing change. Consult, particularly, Edgar H. Schein and Warren G. Bennis, *Personal and Organizational Change Through Group Methods* (New York: Wiley, 1965). Early critics attempted to force some users of laboratory methods into posing the basic issue as individual change *or* structural change. Chris Argyris was thus interpreted,

suggests that the long-run forces toward vertical fragmentation implicit in the NII concept are all but irresistible. And vertical fragmentation induced by the NII concept, in turn, does not encourage charitable attitudes in either program or sustaining officials. For the sustaining official must seek to know, and the program official must reveal. Little discouragement is needed to convince both parties the effort is not worth the prize.

The moral seems clear. Heroes may succeed despite the formal structure by modifying their behavior (and the behavior of others) appropriately, although probably only under exceptional circumstances. The rest of us require the support of the formal structure, for good or ill, and few of us have the innovative zest to fly in the face of the principles and the NII model as did the new manager in Guest's study.

The point seems to apply even to Plant Y. "Some of the older supervisors were smart enough to see the handwriting on the wall and changed when they got the new regime," we are informed. But other supervisors were just barely willing to go along as long as necessary. Thus one manager warned that: ". . . if there should be a change in top management, they could slide right back into their old ways. That old horsewhip attitude is still underneath with some people. . . ."[44] This puts a crucial matter straightforwardly. What would happen, for example, if top-level corporate management became aware of the new comptroller's style and dual set of reports? Corporate management probably would react unfavorably, and their direct order certainly could wipe out the relations so newly won. There seems a definite advantage, then, in having the Colleague model (or some formal structure) support the new pattern of relations induced by the personal skills of the manager in Plant Y.

Organizing for the Colleague Concept: Approaching the Model via Structural Change

The Colleague model has been approached via specific structural changes at high levels and low. The present section provides specific detail supporting this summary conclusion, albeit with a strong bias on lower and middle levels of organization. Higher levels of organization receive only passing notice here. *Kollegialleitung* (Colleague Management), as widely practiced in Germany, ex-

---

particularly. But he has unequivocally noted the complementarities of individual/ structural change. See his *Integrating the Individual and the Organization* (New York: Wiley, 1964).

[44]Guest, *op. cit.*, p. 62. Emphases in original.

emplifies the approach to the model at high levels of organization. Several executives share in the collegial management of a firm under this model. Many types of executive leadership are possible under Kollegialleitung, varying from a permanent primus inter pares to a subtle sharing of command as the particular interests and abilities of the several colleagues become more or less relevant.[45]

Automation often forces a similar approach at low levels of organization. An engine plant of the Ford Motor Co. illustrates the point. It was a mass-production plant in the "old style" which produced uniform products rather than uniform parts. The plant was reequipped with automatic transfer machinery, and this minor change required major organizational innovation. The older technology tolerated—perhaps required—the traditional chain of command of organizationally separate units handling a single process or function. But the new technology required a "task force" pattern of basic organization. The new pattern emphasized many small centers of communication and decision-making close to the work level, manned by specialists representing the several activities required for the flow of work. In contrast, the traditional pattern was characterized by separate units organized around individual specialties. Its emphasis was upon one centralized center of communication and decision-making far removed from the work level and capable of integrating the several monoprocessual units beneath it.[46]

Approaches to the Colleague model also may be illustrated usefully in greater detail by two cases from lower-middle levels of management at Sears, Roebuck and the Glacier Metal Co. Sears rejected the tyranny of thinking in terms of "function" basically, as in Figure 10B. In sum, the buyers' organization at Sears rests upon forty separate "flows of work," with each Buying Department handling all of the operations necessary to purchase a specific line of products.[47] Each Buying Department has a profit-and-loss responsibility, it being relatively easy to determine whether (for example) too many snowshoes were purchased at the wrong price. In briefer summary, each department is equipped to handle the complete buying process for certain products.

Figure 10A, in contrast, eschews an emphasis upon the horizontal integration of work. It is a conventional structuring of organiza-

---

[45]Heinz Hartmann, *Authority and Organization in German Management* (Princeton, N.J.: Princeton Univ. Press, 1959), pp. 18-19. More generally, see D. Ronald Daniel, "Team at the Top," *Harvard Business Review*, XLIII (March-April, 1965), 74-82.

[46]Peter F. Drucker, *The Practice of Management* (New York: Harper, 1954), pp. 219-20.

[47]James C. Worthy, *Big Business and Free Men* (New York: Harper, 1959), pp. 94-98.

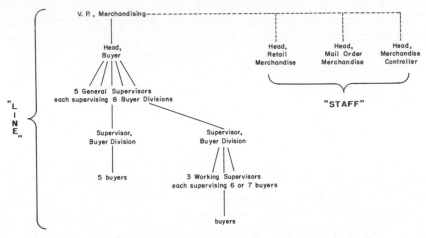

FIGURE 10A. Organizing the Buyers in Terms of the Principles of Organization.

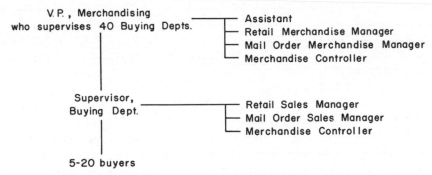

FIGURE 10B. Organizing the Buying Process in Sears, Roebuck (1959).

FIGURE 10. Two Ways of Organizing the Buyers at Sears, Roebuck.

tion relations. Notice also that the full formal organization of only the buyers is sketched.

Line and staff roles in the two structures, similarly, reflect consistent differences. Figure 10A provides no challenge: The NII model prescribes the relations. The Sears structure is more elusive, however. The officials on the figure's right are designated as staff, but, in point of fact, a Colleague-like relation seems to dominate. Theodore Houser, once the chief executive at Sears, put it simply. Any staff executive can challenge any feature of local operations that falls within his speciality. This is the price, Houser tells us, that local management must pay for the wide autonomy granted them in the Sears organization.[48] Illustratively, the vice-president's office seems to act as an overhead team monitoring the forty departments.

[48]Theodore V. Houser, *Big Business and Human Values* (New York: McGraw-Hill, 1957), p. 24.

Toward the Colleague Concept of Staff:

That is, one-line authority is not the prescriptive order of the day. Overhead staff officials can act authoritatively with respect to both the supervisors and their counterpart staff officials at the department level. Indeed, something like the substantive *vs.* technical distinction introduced early in this chapter (see p. 120) seems to guide relations. Finally, the several heads of the units of each of the departments seem a Colleague group in the present sense. Each Colleague group—composed of the head of the buyers and of the several sustaining activities—monitors a relatively small Colleague team of one hundred members or so. At the very least, the departments reflect little of that extreme difference between line and staff that is implicit in the NII model.

The renowned effectiveness of Sears suggests that approaches to the Colleague model must be taken seriously, and the experience of the Glacier Metal Co. in industrial operations reinforces that suggestion. Glacier had followed the NII model and suffered the usual difficulties. As the firm's president observes: "... we found that these so-called advices or services that [NII] specialists gave were not only felt to be instructions by those who received them, but that they had in fact to be instructions if the Company was to get its work done efficiently."[49]

Glacier decided to legitimate what was actually happening in many cases and what should happen if the work were to be done expeditiously. Beginning from the bottom of the organization upwards, "sections" of from ten to seventy men were set up. Several sections performing operations required for some flow of work, in turn, were grouped into "units" of no more than 350 employees. Each unit had its own complement of sustaining personnel, e.g., specialists in production engineering and production scheduling and control. In contrast, the earlier organization had a "top, down" bias, and staff officials performing different activities were members· of separate organizational units.

In similar marked contrast with their earlier role prescribed by the NII model, the new Glacier policy provided that within their own unit sustaining officials were "... to carry recognized staff authority within their own fields, in relation to their manager's subordinates."[50] More fully, the "Policy on Specialist Organization" provided that staff was to have:

1. *advisory responsibility* for giving technical advice to a manager;
2. *service-providing responsibility;*

---

[49]Wilfred Brown, *Exploration in Management* (New York: Wiley, 1960), p. 152.
[50]*Ibid.*, p. 155.

3. *staff responsibility,* that is, of assisting a manager in coordinating the work of his immediate subordinates in particular fields by exercising authority and by issuing orders; and
4. *technical coordination responsibility,* as by providing technical guidance or by reviewing the effectiveness of specialist work in a staff man's field but not under his executive control.[51]

A brief summary may be useful. In Glacier's manufacturing operations, the group of "near-Colleagues" often had three members at the lowest levels. That Colleague group included the program head of a section, a Production Controller, and a Production Engineer. This group monitored the performance of a Colleague team of some 300 to 350 personnel, at a maximum.

The specific relations developed at Glacier within this policy framework also suggest an approach to the Colleague model. The picture is not a monochrome, to be sure. Thus the chief sustaining official at the unit level was considered to be of subordinate formal rank to the program head of that unit, and the chief sustaining official at the unit level was considered the equal-in-rank of the program head of a section, or the next lowest level of organization. Moreover, much of the terminology of Glacier's policy implies an Alter Ego role for the sustaining official. But there are substantial hints of further departures from the NII model. Consider the reaction of a program official to one of his sustaining officials after the latter complained that program officials at the section level were slow in implementing a new policy:

> Well, make them, give instructions, use your authority. You are trying to get me to do your job for you. You are a Staff Officer responsible for seeing that my policy goes, get cracking, your authority is clear. If they are in real difficulties, find out and let me know, but otherwise see that they get on with it quickly.[52]

Moreover, a sustaining official at the unit level was free to give a wide range of orders to program personnel in the sections. The boundaries were general and generous. Thus all organization members were obliged to question any order they felt unable to carry out within existing policy with the resources available. "In the absence of any such query," reads the relevant company policy, "his manager may take it that the member has accepted the instruction as being reasonable."[53] This ground rule implies a distinction like that drawn between technical and substantive issues. Sustaining officials have command powers over both program and sustaining members at lower levels on the former issues but not on the latter.

---

[51]*Ibid.,* p. 158.
[52]*Ibid.,* p. 162.
[53]*Ibid.,* p. 159.

Two conclusions seem to be relatively clear. The program and sustaining officials at the unit level approach a Colleague group, although sustaining officials are not formally considered the equals of the program manager. Moreover, the satisfaction at Glacier with the new program-sustaining implies the usefulness of developing structural relations alternative to the NII model.

Organizing for the Colleague Concept:
Two In-Process Perspectives

This introduction to the Colleague model of line-staff relations has gone only a small part of the way toward outlining an alternative structure, but at least two major facets should be clear. We give them brief notice here.

First, the structure appropriate for the Colleague model attempts to provide for an appropriate mix of these apparently paradoxical demands made on the manager: to foster stability, to encourage change, and to do both without compromising the one to the other.[54] With only a little overstatement, the single underlying demand acknowledged by most thought about organizing has been that of achieving some kind of equilibrium, some stable and smooth "meshing of gears of a well-oiled organization." The present end-vision is more complex. Sherman has articulated the challenge to which this manuscript responds in forceful terms. "What we need is a new model or concept which regards change as a continuing process," he observed, "which recognizes that change may mean ambiguity and uncertainty but that these results are not necessarily 'bad,' and which sees the organization as constantly changing (whether rapidly or slowly) rather than reaching set stages of equilibrium in between periods of change."[55]

The Colleague model is a concept that regards change as a continuous process, then, and progress as a set of limited approximations to some ideal. The present orientation may be put otherwise. This book does not argue that the Colleague model is applicable everywhere in principle, or that it may be applied successfully anywhere in practice. Rather, the argument is more limited. Where the technology permits that the Colleague model can be approached, and where man's skills are competent to capitalize on the opportunity, there advantages will accrue.

Second, the focus on structural change in approaching the Col-

[54]Leonard R. Sayles, "The Change Process In Organizations: An Applied Anthropology Analysis," *Human Organization*, XXI (Summer, 1962), 62-67.
[55]Sherman, *It All Depends*, op. cit., p. 140.

league concept reflects multiple needs: to change basic attitudes about organizing, to encourage more favorable relations between organization members and units, to overcome unfortunate organization histories, and to reinforce more useful behavior and attitudes. That is to say, although we have rarely stressed the point, moving toward the Colleague model often must be tied to programs of widespread behavioral change that "unfreeze" old patterns. The Colleague model can then help to develop new patterns, as well as to "freeze" them in a reinforcement sense. Specifically, moving toward the Colleague model often will be facilitated by so-called "laboratory programs" of organizational change.[56]

The point cannot be given its due here,[57] but several assertions can at least clarify the present position. Thus lasting behavioral change is more probable if the new behavior is reinforced as, for example, by appropriate structural relations at work. The Colleague model purports to provide reinforcement for behaviors different from those commonly induced and reinforced by the NII model of line-staff relations. Moreover, applications of laboratory approaches to organization change tend to move in the direction of the Colleague model. For example, lab programs emphasize the organic versus the mechanistic nature of work.[58] And lab programs commonly call for "team development" to include the competencies necessary to do the job, the demands of hierarchy notwithstanding.[59] Needless to say, there is little of the principles of management or the NII model in all this.

An example should drive home the significant reinforcing features of structural arrangements that approach the Colleague model and of mass behavioral changes in organizations accomplished through laboratory programs of development. The example is taken from the early experience with Project ACORD—or Action for Organization Development—in the U.S. Department of State. Two interacting elements formed the vitals of this laboratory program of organization change: laboratory, or sensitivity, training; and appropriate restructuring of work relations. The former was de-

[56]Schein and Bennis, *Personal and Organizational Change Through Group Methods, op. cit.*
[57]More expansively, see Robert T. Golembiewski, "Integrating Small Behavioral Units Into Large Formal Organizations," esp. pp. 37-47, from a paper delivered September 30, 1966, at the Symposium "People, Groups and Organizations: An Effective Integration of Knowledge," at Rutgers University.
[58]Herbert A. Shepard, "Changing Interpersonal and Intergroup Relationships in Organizations," in March, *Handbook of Organizations, op. cit.*, pp. 1115-43.
[59]Harold J. Leavitt, "Unhuman Organizations," in *Readings In Managerial Psychology*, ed. Harold J. Leavitt and L. Pondy (Chicago: Univ. of Chicago Press, 1964).

signed to free members from some of the burdens of personal and organizational history, as well as to develop relations that could support more effective performance. As it were, structural reorganization was at once facilitated by this preparatory building of relations; and reorganization also raised the probability that these new relations would persist. Not surprisingly, one of the early emphases in Project ACORD was the creation of autonomous "program managers" who managed "activities that formed a coherent unit" and who reported directly to the Deputy Undersecretary of State for Administration. The early experience seems very favorable. For example, one individual now reports directly to the Deputy Undersecretary. Prior to the reorganization, this towering chain of command loomed above him: Division Head, Office Director, Deputy Director of Personnel, Director of Personnel, Deputy Assistant Secretary for Administration, Assistant Secretary for Administration, and Deputy Undersecretary.[60] A technology facilitating behavioral change, in short, undergirded a basic restructuring of work in this case. Much the same also will often be true in attempts to implement the Colleague concept of line-staff relations.

[60]Alfred J. Marrow, "Managerial Revolution in the State Department," *Personnel*, XLIII (November-December, 1966), 6-7.

Chapter 6
The Colleague Concept:
How It Lives with Program-Sustaining Tensions

The examples of Sears and Glacier discussed in Chapter V imply the value of detailed attention to the Colleague model. Consequently, this chapter begins the heavy work of giving greater definition to the structural relations appropriate for the model, as well as of placing those relations within the context of a congenial broader theory. Immediately, the Colleague model will be put to the same test that was applied to the NII model in Chapter III. That is, the efficacy of the model will be tested against the nine sources of tension common in program-sustaining relations. Subsequent chapters will range farther afield in detailed analyses of aspects of the model.

Testing the Colleague Model

As Table 4 reflects, the Colleague model does rather well in moderating the tensions implicit in program and sustaining activities. Six emphases will do the job of specifically supporting these tabular conclusions. The Colleague model reduces the tension from sources I and II, first, and it does so simply. The concept recognizes that "service" and "control" are often associated and that sustaining units handle scarce resources. And the concept confers the status which is a reasonable correlate of these facts of life. Consequently, program officials need not be scandalized that sustaining officials atttempt to make their contributions more effective. And sustaining officials need not feel that their contributions go unrecognized organizationally and thus that their effectiveness is compromised.

The Colleague model, in short, attempts to reflect reality rather than to prescribe that man dissociate himself from the things that are. Men being men, we cannot expect most of them to operate with a disregard for themselves and for the power potential in their environment. Matters probably ought not be otherwise, for an agency program for which one is not prepared to do battle probably will be short-lived and perhaps should be. This is no argument for obstinacy by specialists. Indeed, the NII model encourages extreme devotion to sub-organization programs by its focus on particularistic functions or processes. In contrast, the Colleague model discourages vertical fragmentation by organizing around discrete flows of work—about which much will be written on succeeding pages—and by assigning common responsibility for a total flow of work. The Colleague model, that is, provides the room to adjust status to the realities of the changing contributions of individuals cooperatively engaged in the same flow of work and communally responsible for performance.

The Colleague model also will discipline power phenomena in organizations. That is, staff units under the NII model can derive great leverage from their plant-wide or corporation-wide jurisdiction, bargaining being implicit in the necessity of allocating services at specific times and at specific costs among the component units of an organization. The Colleague model moderates such byplay by prescribing that sustaining officials have pervasive iden-

TABLE 4. NORMAL SOURCES OF TENSION BETWEEN PROGRAM AND SUSTAINING ACTIVITIES AS AFFECTED BY THE COLLEAGUE MODEL

Normal Sources of Tension	Colleague Concept
I. "Control" is the correlate of "service."	reduces tension
II. Sustaining activities handle scarce resources.	reduces tension
III. Program and sustaining activities have differing time orientations.	reduces tension
IV. Sustaining units or officials: (a) are ordered to play, or (b) face a greater temptation to play, the role of the informant.	reduces tension
V. This may be a potent taunt to sustaining officials: "Can you look the paymaster in the eye?"	reduces tension
VI. Sustaining units and officials are oriented toward change and program units and officials toward stability.	reduces tension
VII. Cultural differences exist between program and sustaining activities and officials.	reduces tension
VIII. Sustaining activities induce high levels of frustration.	reduces tension
IX. The integration of sustaining activities often is a major problem.	reduces tension

tifications with their team as well as with the counterpart upper-level unit of their particular activity. Upper-level officials, that is, must respect the dual identifications of their fellow specialists. The possibilities of playing organizational activity against activity, then, face a rather strict set of limiting conditions. One is usually careful about goring one's own ox. Consequently, Table 4 assigns the designation "reduces tension" to sources I and II.

The differing time orientations of program and sustaining activities, second, also are accommodated by the Colleague model. Thus the concept attempts to mesh both the long-run and the short-run, the lubricant being direct and mutual responsibility for performance and coequal organizational status. It would require very convincing argument that either time orientation can be underrepresented, a condition encouraged by the status differences built into the NII model. In this one specific sense, at least, the traditional line-staff distinction does not facilitate the melding of today and tomorrow. Moreover, the demands of today and tomorrow would tend to be much less extreme under the Colleague model. For neither today nor tomorrow—as represented by program and sustaining units and officials, respectively, to make a rough but useful distinction—would be condemned to an a priori organizational inferiority. And it would not do under the Colleague model to have a team locked in conflict, since its performance would suffer and nonarbitrary measures would establish the exact degree to which performance had been affected.

This desire to permit the coequal scuffling of the long-run and the short-run may seem perverse. Thus it might be argued that both temporal orientations ought to be represented, for few organizations can afford either the punctilious adherence to procedure or the docility common when sustaining services are undervalued. But those agreeing with this proposition also might argue that the coequal status permitted by the Colleague model is out of the question. For, to illustrate what may be a common feeling, one can hardly consider some wage-and-salary clerk as a peer of a supervisor. The point cannot be avoided if the traditional theory is respected. However, job enlargement of sustaining activities will be the order of the day under the Colleague model. Later sections of this chapter illustrate how sustaining jobs might be upgraded to make the assignment of coequal status something more than an extravagant way of achieving a desired end, a kind of burning of houses to roast pigs.

The tension deriving from source III, then, probably will be reduced by the Colleague model of program-sustaining relations. Different temporal orientations will tend to characterize the two types of activities, and they should do so lest the organization perish from living too much in the present or too far in the future. The Colleague model attempts to make the best of differing time orientations, that is, by encouraging some balance and by structurally reinforcing that balance.

The Colleague concept, third, also controls the tension induced from sources IV, V, and VI. As for IV, the sustaining official will be less tempted to employ information to enhance his organization status. No doubt the temptation can never be eliminated. However, the Colleague concept develops a team identification, and officials of both program and sustaining activities are responsible for performance. Any information, then, can be put to direct use. Any "indirect" uses would run the risk of an accounting before one's immediate colleagues. Moreover, the Colleague model provides formally coequal status. The organizational inferiority of NII staff, in contrast, may encourage informal tattling by way of compensation and certainly does place staff in the role of an "outside" informant. Finally, the job enlargement of sustaining activities (to be discussed presently) consistent with the Colleague model should provide the ambitious sustaining official with ample opportunity to display his talents and to improve his position in ways that do not imply great dangers to smooth functioning.

Ample evidence demonstrates the awkwardness of the several accommodations encouraged by the NII model in the use of information. Consider the increasingly common practice of holding lower-level managers responsible for results and of redefining the sustaining role as, e.g., one of raising the question of irregularities with the manager rather than with the manager's superior. Traveling auditors in General Electric, for example, do not report their findings upward. Their role is to inform initially the responsible executive in the field to assure that he is aware of the condition. The local executive decides what to do with the information. The increasing incidence of such arrangements suggest that, whatever the value of the information communicated upwards by sustaining officials under the NII concept, the costs of the traditional staff concept can be extreme in larger organizations.[1] Sustaining activities, in short, can prove ineffective in a punitive climate.

In his role in a formal organization based upon the Colleague

---

[1]Harry D. Kolb, "The Headquarters Staff Man in the Role of a Consultant," in *Organization Theory in Industrial Practice*, ed. Mason Haire (New York: Wiley, 1962), pp. 143-46, for example, outlines such a set of unorthodox structural relations. The attempt is to avoid the many difficulties associated with staff services provided by an "outsider" that are perceived as punitive. For one recitation of such difficulties, see R. Blackwell, "The Impact of Work Study on the Operative," *Time and Motion Study*, V (July, 1956), 12-14.

model, continuing with source of tension IV, the sustaining official often will play a regulative part. But he no longer need go "up and over and down" with information about an irregularity. Technical matters can be enforced by a sustaining official, whether orders are issued to program or sustaining personnel. Or the question of nonenforcement can be raised by a sustaining official sitting as a colleague. In either case, initial communication is within the team. This should serve to reduce tension while required modifications of work processes or procedures can be made with less heat and almost certainly with more dispatch. That other competitive teams might make such modifications first facilitates the process, of course.

Two points deserve particular underscoring in relation to source of tension IV. First, approaches to the Colleague model probably will reduce tension; they do not merely shift its locus downward. Consider the possibility of an operator receiving conflicting instructions from program and sustaining officials. This can happen under the Colleague model as well as under the NII model. The saving grace of the Colleague model is not simply that the level of conflict is lower in the hierarchy. Rather, many factors associated with the Colleague model make the "quantitative" change in levels a "qualitative" one as well.[2] Only two of these factors will be noted here. At the Colleague team level, sustaining and program officials share a direct and mutual organizational identification. Fragmented identifications around separate line and staff units are more likely under the NII model. The immediate interests of program and sustaining officials under the Colleague model, therefore, are not starkly squared off in a kind of organizational cat-and-mousing, as they tend to be under the NII model.

The Colleague model will not eliminate tension, second, if that can or should be accomplished by any structural arrangement. However, the inherent tensions are reduced in contrast to those situations in the NII model in which one's program superior is informed of deviations down the line by an outsider, a sustaining official at a higher level. If nothing else, such "reminders" often prove unnecessarily and perhaps abortively embarrassing to both program officials. The primary emphasis upon intrateam communi-

---

[2] A similar effect was patent in a wide range of "qualitative" variables, for example, as a consequence of a "quantitative" change in the number of hierarchical levels in a large firm. See F. L. W. Richardson, Jr., and Charles R. Walker, *Human Relations in An Expanding Company* (New Haven: Labor and Management Center, Yale Univ., 1948).

The Colleague Concept:

cation alone should remove a major irritant to program-sustaining relations. And, in the bargain, the possibility of direct (and, perhaps, freer) communication will reduce the time lag before corrective action is taken. Such a lag can produce much tension in many ways. In extreme cases, a team may not be able to reconcile differences between its program and sustaining officials. Upward reporting will not be required even in these cases, for measures of comparative performance will bear ample and early testimony to any derivative difficulties, whether they stem from failure to enforce "technical" procedures or failure to agree upon which matters are "substantive." The upper-level team must intervene in such cases, albeit not without indicating great displeasure.

Consequently, the term "reduces tension" is applied to source of tension IV in Table 4.

These changes in the mission and roles of sustaining officials also may take some of the sting out of the taunt, "Can you look the paymaster in the eye?" This is source of tension V. Particular sore spots that must be ameliorated by any staff model derive from the size and growth of sustaining services and the high probability of failure of staff services, as aggravated by the difficulty of measuring their contributions.

The Colleague model in several senses moderates the problems associated with the size and growth of sustaining services. For example, both program and sustaining officials will be involved in the determination of requested force levels. So if anyone is not carrying the weight of his salary, the others have only themselves to blame. And these officials also will consider recommendations for pay increases and promotions for team members. This provides program officials and sustaining officials with authority they probably did not have in one another's affairs. Moreover, sitting through the review will make it difficult to give credence to reports which flourish when the review of, for example, sustaining officials is made in the original instance by other sustaining officials.

An important bridge may be built here. To set the stage, every Colleague group will react to program and sustaining activities primarily in terms of their perceived contributions to team effectiveness. This implies a kind of "shoe-pinching" reaction, valuable because a team monitoring a complete flow of work can tell if the "shoes fit." There are potentially serious difficulties, however. For example, evaluation of technical competency of sustaining officials is implicit in such shoe-pinching reactions, and these evaluations will not necessarily be accepted gracefully. Many sustaining specialists, that is, might prefer to have fellow specialists judge their performance. There are some safeguards against worse coming to worst, however. Thus overhead Colleague groups will monitor lower-level evaluations to safeguard against gross injustice. More significantly for present purposes — and particularly so at lower and middle-management levels — the Colleague model makes shoe-pinching reactions particularly meaningful most directly because that model permits and encourages programs of job enlargement for both sustaining and program officials.

The job enlargement possible under the Colleague model will be emphasized later, but we may sketch here how the possibility of using the technique will moderate source of tension V. Consider only that the Colleague model encourages the assignment of sustaining "generalists" to teams at the first level of supervision. Such a generalist, for example, might tailor all or a wide range of personnel policies for his particular team. Neglecting the details temporarily, some attractive consequences are to be found. Thus such assignments would eliminate many paper-manipulating jobs required by the NII model and the principles. That is, primary communication in the Colleague model is within the team, rather than upward through the sustaining hierarchy and across and down the appropriate program hierarchy. As one result, upper-level sustaining units can prune the many employees whose task it is to see that "papers are shuffled" up and across the organizational gap prescribed by the NII approach. Many so-called staff jobs are of this debilitating kind which goes a long way toward explaining much that is curious in the behavior of many sustaining personnel, such as their sometimes-monumental devotion to form and detail.[3] Certainly, at least, fewer sustaining officials will be needed to police the integration of operations under the Colleague model.

Evidence is in short supply, but one large British manufacturer sharply cut "indirect labor" following a structural reorganization consistent with the Colleague model. After the reorganization, there were but 15.7 administrative, technical, and clerical employees for each 100 production workers in the company. Comparably, a Detroit tractor plant (under much the same technological and demand conditions) had *at a minimum* 36 indirect employees for each 100 directly engaged in production. If other criteria are utilized to allocate staff personnel that serve more than one plant in

---

[3]James C. Worthy, "Democratic Principles in Business Management," *Advanced Management*, XIV (March, 1949), 18.

the American concern, the ratio rises to 58:100. Either difference is significant, even though American firms typically have a higher ratio than European firms.[4] Significantly, the American plant was organized and managed in "accordance with conventional industrial practice," that is, in accordance with the principles and the NII model.[5] Such advantages of the Colleague model should take some of the acid from this taunt to sustaining officials: "Can you look the paymaster in the eye?"

Organizing for the Colleague model, in addition, should reduce tension deriving from the innovative nature of many sustaining activities and from the difficulty of developing useful measures of the performance of sustaining units or officials. That is, tension deriving from source V will not be heightened. The following chapter considers the point in great detail. Here note only the possibilities in the Colleague model of attaching reasonable values to activities that tend to defy measurement. Take communication programs, for example. The difficulties of measuring consequences of such programs on a company-wide level encourage unfortunate extremes: the neglect of communication programs or profligate spending on them. Many firms ricochet from one extreme to the other. The Colleague model permits judgments about such programs that are more firm, a team at any level being in a favorable position to observe a program at close range and to judge whether the costs are justified. Circumstances would dictate how a team might make its opinion felt. Basically, each team would make significant decisions concerning its particular communication program and the share of its resources allocated to it. Upper-level teams can make available such broader communications services as a company-wide newspaper. Even in such cases, however, the other teams need not stand mute. Thus teams might refuse to purchase such a newspaper if they do not think the costs justified, which should contribute to keeping the paper's staff on their reportorial toes. This philosophy of "internal purchasing" ought to be applied as widely as possible in organizing for the Colleague model. In contrast, given the orthodox arrangement, the justification of a plant-wide program of communications is an extraordinarily diffi-

---

[4]The point is a commonplace one. Various aspects of it are developed, for example, in Ernest Dale, *Management: Theory and Practice* (New York: McGraw-Hill, 1965), esp. pp. 613-19.

[5]Seymour Melman, *Decision-Making and Productivity* (New York: Wiley, 1958), pp. 175-76. The significance of the data is supported by other evidence, as from a West German Volkswagen plant which approaches the Colleague in many respects. *Ibid.*, pp. 198-99.

cult matter,[6] a difficulty met only in part by such techniques as polling to measure the change of employee attitudes over time.

All in all, then, the Colleague model implies distinct advantages in managing tension source V. The model makes it more difficult to play the game underlying much line-staff conflict induced by the NII model, gaining credit for the successes and avoiding blame for the failures.

The related tensions deriving from source VI probably also would be moderated by organizing for the Colleague model. Sustaining officials might cry less stringently for change, thereby attempting to prove they really are worth their keep. To consider one case only, the NII model often requires extreme efforts by staff to get the attention and support of the upper-line, the better to prompt the lower-line into some desired action. This is a time-consuming approach, and its dynamics also lend credence to the common complaint of program officials that sustaining officials often are perversely devoted to change for its own sake. The NII model encourages the game of organizational hares-and-hounds in which the interests of sustaining officials and program officials must conflict in the deadly serious contest to establish, maintain, and/or increase power.

The Colleague model should take much of the edge off the common over-eagerness of the sustaining official and the common defensiveness of program officials. Consequently, the use of information in a tattling sense by sustaining officials as a lever of change might be limited in the process. Similarly, program officials probably will be more amenable to worthwhile proposals for change, since change would no longer be something that sustaining officials propose and program officials bear the brunt of. Such moderation of the extremes encouraged by the NII model, then, motivates assigning the designation "reduces tension" to source VI in Table 4.

Cultural differences between program and sustaining units, fourth, probably would decrease under the Colleague model. Some — educational differences between program and sustaining officials — might be beyond any structural change. But the Colleague model seems capable of doing much to moderate the impact of such differences. Others common under the NII model — differing organizational identifications, for example — may be changed by structural variations.

The dual utility of the Colleague model with regard to source of

[6]Robert Newcomb and Marg Sammons, *Employee Communications in Action* (New York: Harper, 1961).

tension VII may be sketched. Note, for example, that tension seems heightened by geographical and psychological separatism fostered by the Neutral and Inferior Instrument model. The very fact of greater face-to-face interaction contributes mightily toward horizontal integration under the Colleague model, as in the case of the new comptroller in Plant Y (see p. 144). Moreover, face-to-face interaction has no equal in destroying the attitudes which reinforce separatism.[7] In addition, the assignment of sustaining officials to specific teams ought to counterbalance the psychological identification of sustaining officials with the "front-office" or headquarters. In many cases, indeed, it may be possible to physically relocate the sustaining officials, thereby further diluting the vertical fragmentations that are so common when the principles and the NII model are the pattern for a formal structure.

Similarly, the several factors encouraging identification with the Colleague team also serve to reduce the cultural chasms between personnel performing program and sustaining activities. Rewards and punishments consistent with the Colleague concept, in short, place a premium on the integration of the two types of activities. The NII concept, especially in placing responsibility for performance in the line alone, is not so straightforward on this matter. Indeed, the NII concept fosters cultural distinctions between program and sustaining activities if only because of its tendencies toward vertical fragmentation.

The Colleague concept, finally, might act more subtly to reduce the common cultural differences between program and sustaining units. Thus the "upward orientation" of staff no doubt accounts for significant cultural differences, if that orientation is not deliberately cultivated by management so as to decrease the probability that sustaining officials will identify closely with the units about which they are providing information to top management. The Colleague concept does not so exaggerate this upward orientation. Here note only that a lower-level bias in assigning sustaining personnel would reduce the degree to which they play the "headquarters role." That is, low-level sustaining personnel working out of a central site (headquarters, "up front," and the like) are precisely those who feel the greatest need of distinguishing themselves from program operatives, even though the work of the latter may demand more skill and command higher pay. Attempts to develop and preserve sharp differences between "the office" and "the floor,"

[7] U. S. War Department, *Opinions about Negro Infantry Platoons in White Companies of Seven Divisions* (Washington, D. C.: Information and Education Division, Army Service Forces, Report No. B-157, 1945).

when office work often is as fully routinized and repetitive as that of production work, suggest the point. Driving much of this sustaining work down to the operating level, wiping out many of the paper-manipulating jobs, and enlarging both sustaining and program jobs over the longer haul would encourage less-pained relations between program and sustaining personnel. Any improvement would be significant, for the tone of relations at such levels is crucial and often unsatisfactory.

These assignment changes require rethinking by management of the staff role, but the effort seems worthwhile. Many sustaining officials would breathe a sigh of relief, for example, since their previous central location encouraged a style of living beyond their incomes. Some psychic loses would be felt by employees who revel in their "superior" identification. But scattered evidence supports the present point, on balance. Consider the case of a public agency which controls a number of bridges connecting several states. Much conflict had existed between program personnel and low-level sustaining officials who checked toll receipts against a tape indicating the number and type of vehicles that had passed through the toll stations monitored by program personnel. Originally, the sustaining officials were located at headquarters. This location, plus the fact that the sustaining officials were minor political appointees, encouraged much "phony pulling of rank," as a toll booth attendant put it, "by a guy whose job is no tougher than mine." A considerable time lag also existed between the receipt of monies and their check against the tape. Apparently, the lag reflected the efforts of the sustaining personnel to emphasize the importance of their work by dragging things out. "Inspection trips" by these headquarters officials usually would follow the discovery of some discrepancy, invariably long after the fact. These trips were looked upon by the toll-takers as punitive and as a phony pulling of rank. At the very least, the trips did little to improve operations. The time lag tended to make these sessions "hell-raising about ancient history," since the underlying difficulties often had been ironed out long before.

Subsequently, the sustaining officials were relocated at the several toll-collecting sites. Conflict between them and the attendants virtually disappeared. Tapes and monies were correlated twice daily, and deviations reported directly and promptly to attendants who could make the required adjustments before matters got out of hand. The sustaining officials tended to derive "real status" from providing such timely aid, and this without painful by-play. Moreover, the sustaining officials were relieved not to have to

The Colleague Concept:

keep up with practices common at headquarters, for example, eating at a good restaurant. Almost all of these officials brown-bag it and can do so without arousing the social criticism that would have greeted such practices at headquarters. Periodic inspections by a small headquarters unit, incidentally, assure that friendly relations between toll collectors and sustaining officials do not go too far.

The several probable advantages of the Colleague model in reducing "cultural conflict" derive support from the existing experimental research literature. Consider "feedback," which may be defined as the mutual transmission of authentic information between two sources. The Colleague model attempts to induce high feedback between line and staff officials in a common flow of work; the NII model encourages low feedback. Experimentally, such differences in feedback have proved significant. Thus low feedback has been associated with low confidence in, and high hostility toward, specific others with whom one interacts[8] and with high resistance to change.[9] Other related evidence also supports the Colleague model, according a high probability to increased effectiveness under it. Thus research indicates that the performance of work units is likely to be high when the problems of those in a common flow of work are mutually understood and when the work unit has a high degree of autonomy in work-related matters.[10] The Colleague model attempts to induce the first condition, of course, and it is organized around the second condition. The NII model compares unfavorably in these two regards. In sum, many factors support the notation "reduces tension" opposite source VII in Table 4.

The Colleague model, fifth, in all probability would reduce the frustration of performing sustaining activities. The multifaceted argument of this chapter suggests a general decrease in frustration. Specific attention here will be concentrated on one factor having such a consequence, the release of "tension systems" associated with work. As has been well established,[11] tension systems develop in the individual when the completion of a task is prevented.

[8]Harold J. Leavitt and R. A. H. Mueller, "Some Effects of Feedback on Communications," *Human Relations*, IV (November, 1957), 401-10.
[9]Bernard M. Bass, *Leadership, Psychology, and Organizational Behavior* (New York: Harper, 1960), p. 16.
[10]Bernard P. Indik, Basil S. Georgopoulos, and Stanley E. Seashore, "Superior-Subordinate Relationships and Performance," *Personnel Psychology*, XIV (Winter, 1961), 357.
[11]Bluma Zeigarnik, "Über das Behalten von Erledigten und Unerledigten Handlungen," *Psychologische Forschung*, IX (1927), 1-85.

Witness the marked tendency to recall tasks whose performance is prevented experimentally and to forget tasks that are completed. It is not an extravagant hypothesis that frustration will soon set in if tension systems are not released. The NII concept encourages the unrelieved intensification of such tension systems in two major senses. Thus the NII model's separation of "thinking" and "doing"prevents sustaining officials from reducing tension systems. Moreover, by fragmenting sustaining units and program units the model inhibits the release of such tension systems by individuals who provide the several required functions or processes and who identify strongly. These simple psychological data may explain many of the attempts by NII sustaining officials to "take command" or to take actions "for the good of the organization" on matters "beyond the knowledge of the line chief." Literally, there may be no other psychologically acceptable alternative.

The Colleague concept, in contrast, permits release of such tension systems. The point is not that sustaining officials will do everything under the Colleague concept; it is more subtle. That is, the individual himself need not complete the task in order to accomplish release. The performance of the task by a group with which the individual identifies will do the job equally well.[12] The thrust of the Colleague model tends toward just such group identification with a team performing a discrete flow of work. The "frustration head," in short, can be reduced by organizing for the Colleague model. In both general and specific senses, then, the tension implicit in source VIII probably will be reduced by the Colleague concept of organizing relations between program and sustaining units and officials.

The Colleague model, sixth and last, reduces the tension implicit in the integration of sustaining activities. There is nothing mystical about this effect. The concept does not eliminate the problem, but organizing around the Colleague model permits certain liberties that reduce the pressure to integrate the increasingly large number of sustaining specialties in most organizations.

The cushioning effect of the Colleague model in this regard may take many forms. Thus the very organization by teams, on which are represented all or many of the activities required for some discrete sub-assembly, encourages the integration of program and sustaining activities. In practice, such integration has markedly characterized approaches to the Colleague model. IBM's experi-

---

[12]Mark Mulder, "The Power Variable in Communication Experiments," *Human Relations*, XIII (August, 1960), 241-57.

ence is relevant. That firm established Colleague-like teams at low levels of organization when production changes were necessary. A foreman became a manager of a project, and he worked closely with whatever sustaining personnel were necessary to handle problems of design, production layout, job set-ups, and the like. Descriptions of the dynamics of such teams strongly imply a Colleague-like arrangement. The innovation has paid off in many ways: superior design, better production engineering, and more satisfactory production records.[13]

Relatedly, program officials under the Colleague model may be less resistant to taking directions from sustaining officials. Like it or not, such mutual directive cues from multiple sources are part-and-parcel of administration. The only question concerns the techniques used to do the job. The NII model encourages techniques, e.g., getting top-level support to force the hand of lower-level program operatives, which imply a great potential for conflict. The Colleague model does less poorly on this score even if we consider but two factors associated with the Colleague model. The program official will run the gauntlet of the team in seeking promotions and pay increases. This is powerful medicine. And there will be less occasion for members of upper-level teams to encourage diagonal contacts, given the basic organization around discrete flows of work which permits ready measurement of performance.

Finally, the Colleague model encourages job enlargement, a powerful technique for easing the integration of the several sustaining activities in any organization. Indeed, the Colleague model aims directly at facilitating the integration of the several vertically fragmented hierarchical chains that rise above the point at which action is necessary. Thus the several activities of a Personnel Department may be integrated through a single representative of that department assigned to a lower-level team. This is a crucial point and explains particularly the designation "reduces tension" opposite source IX in Table 4. The consequences of the NII model seem less favorable. Thus the line official is not likely to bring off the integration of the several sustaining activities, as he is commonly enjoined to do. In practice, rather, the NII model encourages line officials to give formal or informal powers of command to sustaining officials to attempt the integration, which implies an interesting conflict with the NII model. Or sustaining officials may begin making decisions "for the good of the company" on their own.

---

[13]D. L. Bibby, "Building Satisfaction into the Supervisor's Job," *Personnel*, XXXI (March, 1954), 407.

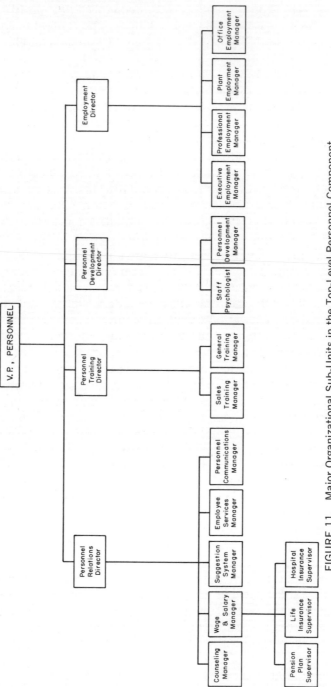

FIGURE 11. Major Organizational Sub-Units in the Top-Level Personnel Component.

"Staff" Job Enlargement: An Integrative Emphasis

The integration of sustaining specialties through job enlargement merits extended analysis. Consider two levels of organization of the sustaining activity personnel under the Colleague model. The personnel component of the top-level team is headed by a vice-president, and the team at the work level is represented by a single personnel man.

The personnel component headed by the vice-president might be a relatively large and complex organization. There is no end of variety possible in the administrative units that might be represented on this upper-level team. For illustrative purposes, the structure proposed for the personnel function at Johnson and Johnson headquarters may be employed. Figure 11 describes this top-level structure in some detail. Its use is motivated particularly by the facts that Johnson and Johnson is a relatively decentralized firm and that the spirit of decentralization encourages substantial delegation to lower-level teams implied by the Colleague model.

If the principles of the traditional theory of organization are respected, two major problems are encountered. First, such respect compounds one of the chief problems of modern administration, the overspecialization of sustaining services.[14] In Figure 11, for example, there are fifteen major functional subdivisions. Thus any lower-level supervisor faces the prospect of making a multitude of contacts upward, and this to get directly the several bits and pieces of the policies of the personnel department. This implies problems aplenty. For example, sustaining units incline toward change. But if sustaining sub-specialties are narrow, any change may involve a program official with a large number of component units. Efforts by a sustaining unit to induce change, then, may threaten a massive headache for the program official. Hence his common resistance. More specifically, if the principles are respected, the offices of both the General Training Manager and the Wage and Salary Manager have their own little hierarchies, and upward identification is very probable. Not uncommonly, the interests of these minihierarchies are not entirely consistent. The common interests-in-opposition between training and job evaluation programs illustrate the point. The latter tend to place rank in the job. For many training purposes, oppositely, rank is conveniently in the person. The opposition is greatest under a strict job evaluation system whose integrity wage-

---

[14]Robert C. Sampson, *The Staff Role in Management* (New York: Harper, 1955).

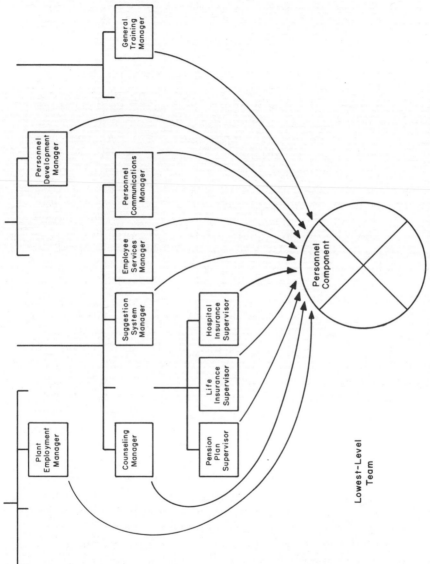

FIGURE 12.   Schema for Integrating Personnel Activities within a Lower-Level Colleague Team.

and-salary people have reason to feel will be compromised by exceptions.[15] Whatever its intensity, the difficulty is commonplace.

Following the principles, second, makes little use of "staff job enlargement." The advantages sacrificed thereby can be significant. Thus the person with a very narrow specialty probably has less security than job enlargement permits. Certainly some individuals relish limited work confines, but the person with a very narrow specialty often faces (and deserves) the taunt that he cannot really help the program official. This is unfortunate enough, but the effects need not end here. The sustaining official, in turn, may be motivated to reinforce his miniscule contribution to work by various supplementary techniques (such as informing) that do not necessarily aid job performance but are intended to get program officials to accept "help." Moreover, the possibility of buck-passing under conditions of very narrow specialization will increase the pressure for integration and consequently will induce close supervision and multitudinous checks on performance. Hence the common complaint that a little staff service costs a great deal of staff control. These features do not often contribute to effective performance. In addition, wider specialties are likely to attract more capable and more motivated personnel, if only because the training opportunities in such jobs are greater. The enlarged job, Sampson explains, not only would integrate overspecialized sustaining services, but it also would help develop acceptance for other phases of sustaining work. That is, becoming a more general source of help would benefit both the sustaining official and the organization.[16]

The Colleague model attempts both to avoid overspecialization and to profit from job enlargement. Thus the personnel representative on a lower-level team would integrate the several personnel specialities as they apply to a particular team. He might perform the following activities for each of the overhead personnel specialties: administering procedures, applying policies, acting as direct liaison with the overhead specialties, and gathering data. Figure 12 sketches one possible integrative staff arrangement. At higher levels *considerable specialization would be possible and necessary.*

The development of the advantages of approaching the Colleague model via staff job enlargement has been pitched at a generalized level, but it is possible to complement this approach by outlining a specific practical case. Raytheon's Wayland Lab, for

[15]Paul P. Van Riper, "The Senior Civil Service and the Career System," *Public Administration Review*, XVIII (Summer, 1958), 189-200.
[16]Sampson, *op. cit.*, p. 194.

example, has experimented successfully with a "personnel general-ist." His role as intregrator of the full range of personnel activities at low levels of organization approaches the Colleague model. There were significant differences, however. Thus the personnel general-ist worked for a particular line manager and apparently had no formal responsibilities to overhead personnel units. In sum, then, the Raytheon approach attempted to establish effective horizontal relations between the staff generalist and the line manager. The Colleague model attempts to influence both horizontal relations and vertical ties of the staff man and overhead counterpart units.

Despite the acknowledged differences in formal relations be-tween the Colleague model and Raytheon's approach, there seems a significant commonality in intention. And if the results at Raytheon are any criteria, the two should also be similar in the advantages they permit. The advantages accruing to Raytheon may be sug-gested in terms of the liabilities that were said to inhere in the NII model of line-staff relations that had been respected in the firm. Knudson emphasizes five such liabilities of the traditional model:

1. line managers faced the problem of dealing with several specialized representatives of the personnel department;
2. personnel specialists operated throughout the organization and consequently tended to lose contact with specific line managers whose problems they knew in detail;
3. the abilities and experiences of specialized personnel repre-sentatives — being "theoretical" and generalized in nature — often were insufficient to gain the confidence and respect of line managers who were enmeshed in "practical" and specific situations;
4. specialization by personnel representatives left even the best of them operating within narrow, and sometimes artificial, areas; and
5. specialization increased the probability that personnel repre-sentatives would perform their services from their offices, which added another barrier to communications and under-standing.[17]

Relying on the general case and the specific, then, a rather bold statement of the advantages of approaching the Colleague model in this particular seems appropriate. First, approaching the Colleague model patently provides for the integration of the several sustaining

---

[17]Harry R. Knudson, Jr., "Enter the Personnel Generalist," *Personnel*, XXXVII (March-April, 1960), 33-41.

specialties, and this at the level of application. Second, the approach facilitates training and reduces the probability of the parochialism of the narrow specialist. Third, the Colleague model permits the tailoring of the program of the overhead sub-units to the particular needs of a team, with the goal being an integrated package. Fourth, the approach provides for continuous and direct overhead contact by the team representative with the several sub-specialties he is attempting to integrate at the work site. This reduces the likelihood that the several sub-specialties will apply pressure from inconsistent directions on the program official. Fifth, savings of time might result. Sixth, the personnel representative can specialize in the outside contacts which a program head might not be able to sustain because of the pressure of work and/or because of cultural differences between himself and overhead sustaining officials.

The Colleague Model and Horizontal Integration: The Special Case of the Foreman

As does the NII model, the Colleague concept faces the problem of sub-organization development. However, the latter does so more successfully: It avoids many of the cross-pressures associated with the development of sub-organizations in formal structures based upon the principles and the NII model. The key is the emphasis upon discrete sub-assemblies and the assignment of all necessary activities to each team. That is, of course, the ideal. Technological conditions will not always permit attaining it.

Ample reason to fully exploit any technical conditions that do permit organizing for the Colleague model is provided by the NII model's tendency to heighten three forces fragmenting organizations. Thus the NII approach reinforces the inherent tendency for the very act of organizing to induce divisive forces that can disrupt the flow of work. Moreover, the NII model supports the tendency for informal groups to develop as vertically integrated sub-organizations with members drawn from the same organizational activity. Finally, the NII approach complements the impetus of the traditional theory of organization toward encouraging vertical fragmentation.

The Colleague model moderates these three forces toward divisiveness. Illustratively, each team contains all (or many) of the activities necessary to do the job, and each team is responsible for seeing that the job is done. Any competition between these autonomous sub-organizations prescribed by the Colleague model, then, probably will raise the productivity of the competing teams. In contrast, traditional organization theory, reinforced by the NII approach to program-sustaining relations, tends to develop sub-organizations which include one (or a few) of the activities necessary for a complete job. Competition between these sub-organizations is likely to hinder integrative performance. In short, cliques also will develop under the Colleague concept. But these cliques will serve to horizontally integrate the several program and sustaining activities in task performance. The NII model encourages vertical fragmentation, in contrast. It tends to separate the activities involved in task performance, and this in geographical, social, and psychological senses.

Some Assignment Effects: The General Case

The present point can be enriched by more detailed analysis of the probable consequences of assigning an individual to a specific team, with rewards and punishments reinforcing the implicit structural instructions to cooperate. In sum, such assignment encourages the identification of program and sustaining units and officials and thus enhances the horizontal integration of their activities. The literature on small groups is a mine of supporting evidence that such "instructions" can have profound effects upon member production and satisfaction. Consider a simple case. In one experiment some groups of individuals were instructed to behave "cooperatively" and others to behave "competitively." Table 5 demonstrates impressively that such instructions have a profound impact upon behavior. Significantly, these instructions were reinforced by suitable rewards. In the competitive situation, the rewards for performance were made to individuals, as might be expected. In the cooperative situation, rewards were made to the best performing groups.[18]

The reported results are from a laboratory experiment, but they have obvious analogs in organizations. The NII model and the traditional theory of organization both imply competitive instructions between the several program and sustaining activities, no matter what nice things are said about cooperation. The Colleague model implies cooperative instructions in its emphasis upon the

---

[18]Morton Deutsch, "The Effects of Cooperation and Competition upon Group Processes," in *Group Dynamics: Research and Theory*, ed. Dorwin Cartwright and Alvin Zander (rev. ed.; Evanston, Ill.: Row, Peterson, 1960), esp. pp. 348-52.

performance of Colleague teams and upon individual contributions to team effort. A profound change in attitudes—and, if existing experiments can be given any credence, favorable changes in productivity and satisfaction—may be expected if changes are made in the direction of the Colleague model.

TABLE 5. EFFECTS OF DIFFERENT INSTRUCTIONS ON THE BEHAVIOR OF INDIVIDUALS

Variable	Differences between Cooperative (Coop) and Competitive (Comp) Conditions
1. Difficulties in communicating	1. Coop groups expressed significantly fewer difficulties than Comp collectivities.
2. Working together	2. Observers rated Coop groups as more highly coordinated than Comp collectivities.
3. Self-pressure for achievement	3. On several tasks, Coop groups exerted more self-pressure for high achievement.
4. Productivity	4. In general, Coop groups performed significantly better on two tasks than did collectivities in the Comp condition.
5. Behaviors, such as "blocking" and "self-defending," which do not maintain the group as a behavioral system	5. Collectivities in the Comp condition were significantly higher on such behavior.

Supervisory Relations: A Specific Case

Even further narrowing of scope helps demonstrate the forces toward horizontal integration latent in the Colleague model. Recall the increasingly narrow specialization of the first-line supervisor in socioemotional affairs and the growing participation of staff officials or units in line activities. The prime consequence is an institutionalized schizophrenia that has to be reconciled at work, a task complicated by the fact that the foreman is "responsible." In addition, the NII concept causes or complicates several particularly important problems bedeviling the job of the first-line supervisor.

The Colleague model promises to minimize vertical fragmentation deriving from such sources. Thus the Colleague concept, first, tends to ameliorate vertical fragmentation of the people vs. policy variety. Some such tension no doubt will exist under all circumstances. However, the Colleague model does not reinforce the tension by setting up separate organizational units. The team membership of a sustaining official requires that he give considerable thought to, and be answerable for the workability of, policies and procedures not only in some technical sense but as they apply to the people in *his* team at *their* work. That the sustaining official sits as an organizational colleague of other program and sustaining officials raises the probability that this wedding of technical and human approaches will occur early in the game. The organizational separateness implicit in the NII concept, in contrast, encourages that policies percolate upwards slowly within one of the vertically fragmented hierarchies of the various functional or processual units, gathering such internal support that massive interdepartmental political conflicts often may be necessary to preserve power status.

The Colleague concept, second, will tend to reduce the severity of problems facing the first-line supervisor, particularly in "intermittent manufacturing." Five of these problems were discussed earlier (see p. 109); (1) poor downward communication to foremen: (2) inadequate upward representation of foremen in policy decisions; (3) disagreement regarding supervisory job responsibilities; (4) salary inadequate to make the foreman feel "a part of management"; and (5) limits of foremanship as a training ground.

Much is yet to be written in this volume about the specific ways in which the Colleague approach may develop. Note here merely one of the most patent senses in which organizing consistent with the Colleague model will help ameliorate such problems. Consider problem (3) just mentioned. Each Colleague group must determine the intrateam responsibilities of its members. Any major unresolved disagreement soon will become apparent in a request for intervention by the overhead team and/or in the poor performance of the lower-level team for which all members are responsible. The overhead team should react unfavorably to both circumstances, a feature encouraging early and amicable decisions in the lower-level team. Under the NII model, oppositely, any disagreements between program and sustaining officials tend to fester into issues complicating the inevitable jockeying for power and to reinforce the organizational separateness prescribed by the traditional concept.

The reader can apply the subsequent analysis to develop the ways in which other features of the Colleague approach serve to mitigate the five problems. For example, problems (1) and (2) will be reduced in significant part by the wide limits of team autonomy. And the upgrading of the foreman's job in the several particulars to be outlined should have favorable consequences for problems (4) and (5). But enough of this here. The weight of subsequent analysis will add much to this fragile demonstration.

The Working Supervisor: Decline and Rise?

Approaching the Colleague model also suggests an avenue of solution to a critical and common problem: the role of the working supervisor. There are two types of working supervisors, those who do much the same work as the employees over whom they exercise some quasi-supervisory authority, and those whose technical position or skill on a work team is such as to encourage the deference of fellow members. The role of the working supervisor always has been ambiguous and, indeed, the second type of supervisor often receives no formal grant of authority. Ambiguous or not, however, working supervisors can play a significant part in inducing smooth operations. As Strauss notes:

> The old-time working supervisor [was] the "non-com" who partially bridged the gap between management and the rank-and-file worker. The secret of his success was his lifelong knowledge both of the processes with which he worked and of the "face-to-face" work group. In addition, working supervisors were the first rung in the promotional ladder which in many companies might lead through foreman and general foreman, right up into top management. Thus the working supervisor's job served the dual function of providing management with a reservoir of possible promotable material and of symbolizing to the average worker the continuance of the American Horatio Alger ideal that every man can rise to the top.[19]

The arrival of the "new supervisor" on the industrial scene forced some clarification of the role of the working supervisor. These new supervisors, largely college-trained, became management's vehicle for meeting the following host of pressures that beset work:

1. the increasingly complex production processes which require that shop skills be complemented more and more by engineering theory;
2. the increasing interrelationship of processes which reduces the usefulness of experience with a single work process or a single department;
3. the increasing attention to the skills of human relations which college training was thought to facilitate; and
4. the greater complexity and tact of the supervisory job because of the union contract.[20]

---

[19]George Strauss, "The Changing Role of the Working Supervisor," *The Journal of Business*, XXX (July, 1957), 206. Copyright © 1957 by the University of Chicago and reprinted by permission of the University of Chicago Press, publisher.
[20]*Ibid.*, pp. 204-6.

The new foremen are commonly rotated through several departments of a plant, then become assistant foremen with the expectation that they are the personnel pool from which managerial talent will be selected.

The clarification of the role of the working supervisor required by the emergence of the new supervisors seems in general to have caused as many difficulties as it resolved. Consider this partial list of unintended consequences. First, the working supervisor generally has no opportunity for promotion, and this has the unfavorable consequences on morale that one might expect. Second, the new supervisor tends to regard the working supervisor as a rival and to lack appreciation for his role. Consequently, by-passing the working supervisor is common. This reduces the latter's power over employees while the new supervisor cannot take up the slack, not only because of a lack of time and ability to be everywhere at once, but also often because of a lack of that specific knowledge about work processes possessed by the working supervisor. Third, communication suffers. Thus the new supervisor has a high "social distance" from his employees. His status sharply differentiates him as a "management man," while the working supervisor's ambiguous status permits him, for example, to be a member of the employee's union. Moreover, the college and technical training of the new supervisors often makes communication difficult with both employees and the working supervisor. Finally, the new supervisor is "upward-oriented," being sharply differentiated from those below him in the possibility of promotion and no doubt often in attitudes toward his work and personal relationships. Such forces discourage the development of sound communication links downward, while they also discourage both the working supervisors and operators from taking initiative and assuming responsibility.[21]

These conditions are not inevitable or irreversible. Thus the natural division of responsibilities between the two jobs also permits an approach to the Colleague model. On the technical level, the college-trained supervisor knows what should be done in theory while the working supervisor knows how it can be accomplished. These differing orientations can complement one another. Similarly, a natural division of contributions exists in that the two jobs can serve to link upper-level management with the operators. As Strauss puts it: "The college-trained man can handle relations upward and outward (with higher management, staff agencies, and the union), while the supervisor deals with purely

[21]*Ibid.*, pp. 206-8.

internal problems."[22] The working foreman and foreman, then, can be two members of a Colleague group.

Successful adaptation to the problems posed by the new supervisors is possible without structural change, but the arrangements seem unstable. That is, arrangements between supervisor and straw boss in terms of the principles of organization theory are susceptible to breakdown because they depend upon restraint by the supervisor that is not reinforced by appropriate structural arrangements. Strauss describes one workable arrangement in these terms: "The chief requirement is that the foreman channels his orders through the working supervisor and gives him sufficient discretion to carry them out. Of course, on serious matters like formal discipline the foreman must have primary responsibility. However, before making his decisions, he should consult with the working supervisor."[23] Such arrangements are perhaps acceptable, given a devotion to traditional organization theory. In essence, however, they suffer from their attempt to preserve the fiction of the principle of unity of command on some issues while encouraging greater leeway on more trivial matters. The integration of the different skills and orientations hangs by the proverbial thread of supervisory restraint that is uncommon under any circumstances and seems heroic when the inferiority of the working supervisor is prescribed by the organization structure.

---

[22]*Ibid.*, p. 209.
[23]*Ibid.*, p. 210.

Chapter 7
Organizing for the Colleague Concept:
Details of Design and Major Side Effects

The Colleague model itself cannot do the entire job of reducing the pressures toward vertical fragmentation of the several activities required for the performance of a common task. For greater effectiveness, the tail of the Colleague concept must wag the dog of organization theory. The traditional theory of organization, in short, must be violated in significant ways so as to exploit the full potential of the Colleague model.

This chapter attempts to build the Colleague model into a congenial theory of organization. The design of this structure and commentary about its consequences will be of immediate interest. If anything, this analysis will sin boldly on the side of full development, the cost being a degree of restatement. Particular attention will be given four major "side effects" of organizing for the Colleague concept. For these side effects have the felicitous consequence of reducing both the incidence and the severity of a number of problems that bedevil attempts to organize, and particularly in enterprises of some scale.

Detailed Design of a Colleague Structure:
Organizing Around a Product or Discrete Sub-Assembly

The present strategy is straightforward. Developing the detailed design of a structure suitable for the Colleague model of program-sustaining activities requires that the analysis be pitched to several levels of organization. Consequently this and the following chapter will contrast two approaches to organizing the several top and bottom levels of an hypothetical organization. One approach will be patterned after the principles and the NII model, while the other will be patterned after the Colleague model.

A Bird's-Eye View: Two Top Levels of Organization

Developing a formal structure at the top levels consistent with the principles of organization is a straightforward matter. Figure 13A details such a hypothetical structure for the program function C and two sustaining functions A and B. The structure sets up separate chains of command for each of the three functions, with lower-level representatives of any function reporting upward. The NII model, then, may be characterized as "particularistic": It generates a structure of several separate chains of authority which are tied together only toward, or at, the top of the hierarchy.

Illustrating the top-level organization consistent with the Colleague model is quite another matter. Experience is lacking at high levels, and even cartographic conventions are not available for the illustrative effort. But these conditions are not crippling for two major reasons. First, the Colleague model should be most useful at lower- and middle-management levels. There, also, we need not be so tentative. Second, some high-level analogs consistent with the Colleague model do exist. The "collegial rule" in some German firms (to be sketched later) fits the mold, for example. Without arguing for anything but its illustrative qualities, moreover, one possible formal arrangement is that actually followed by the Forest Service of the Department of Agriculture. The Service's limited line of services and sharp sense of organizational mission, however, urge caution in making extrapolations. Directly, in any case, Figure 13B suggests two major goals of the Service: to present a balanced organizational effort and to stress the sense of *the* Forest Service, that is, of an entity as opposed to an aggregation of conflicting specialties. Various policies and procedures reinforce these goals implied in the top-level formal chart of organization. Illustratively, the several Assistant Chief Foresters on a rotating regular basis have considerable responsibility over internal administration of the total agency, in addition to having full operating command of their own specialized unit. The Chief Forester is heavily occupied with external contacts and with broad policy matters. Kaufman sketches the arrangement in these terms:

> The Chief and his six assistant chiefs are commonly treated as a single administrative unit, referred to as "staff." Each month, a different assistant chief assumes the responsibility for serving as acting chief. Theoretically, the assistant chiefs are merely arms of the Chief, extensions of his official will and personality, and everything that emanates from staff is to be regarded as coming

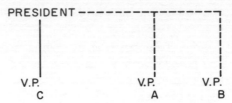

FIGURE 13A. Organizing by Function, Top
Two Levels of an Organization, Consistent
with the Principles and the NII Model.

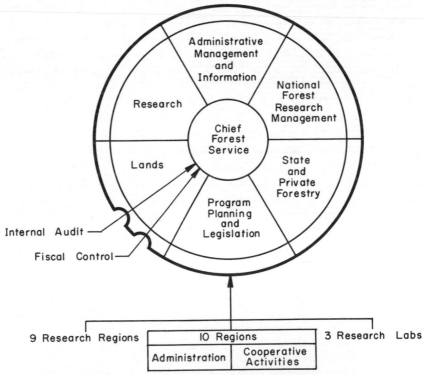

FIGURE 13B. Organizing by Product or Total Organizational Mission, Top Two
Levels of an Organization, Consistent with the Colleague Model. Based upon
Herbert Kaufman, **The Forest Ranger** (Baltimore: Johns Hopkins Press and Re-
sources for the Future, Inc., 1960), p. 43.

FIGURE 13. Two Ways of Organizing Top Levels.

Organizing for the Colleague Concept:

from the Chief. (In practice ... things are not quite so simple and clear-cut.)[1]

The integrative bias of the formal structure has firm foundations. Thus all the various levels of foresters throughout the agency have been through a planned and concerted program of training and rotation (both geographical and functional) as a precondition of moving up the hierarchy. These and other factors tend toward reinforcing the sense of *a* Forest Service.

The consequences of the Forest Service model may be sketched. Given the top-level structure and the training undergirding it, for example, no head of a top-level specialized unit is likely to act upon the particularistic identification endemic to the NII model and to the traditional theory of organization. Practically, also, any representative of any headquarters staff unit can question operations at any level in any unit throughout the organization. Particularism is not likely at lower levels either, that is.

The illustration from the Forest Service thus reflects a dominant property of the Colleague model. In general terms, a structure consistent with that model has a strong bias that may be characterized as "total" in its stress on organizing around the full range of the several top-level activities required for some product or service.

A Worm's Eye View: Two Lower Levels of Organization

The gross characterizations of the structures generated by the Colleague and the NII models as total *vs.* particularistic apply as well at lower levels of organization. And here we need be less tentative than at the top levels. Thus the principles and the derivative NII model prescribe organizing around line and staff units distinguished also in terms of processes performed at lower levels. Figure 14A presents the traditional organization of supervisors and operators, required for four processes — stamping, chamfering, polishing, and finishing — that yield "discrete sub-assemblies" 1 and 2. The figure has a patent particularistic bias. Interpretively, S_s supervises the stamping operations for all three sub-assemblies, which is one particularistic contribution to performance. The integration of the four operations s, c, p, and f therefore is crucial, since the efforts of all supervisors and all operatives must be brought into proper

---

[1]Herbert Kaufman, *The Forest Ranger* (Baltimore: Johns Hopkins Press and Resources for the Future, Inc., 1960), p. 43.

phase. In addition, necessary staff services must be integrated successfully at appropriate points. In Figure 14A, these staff services are provided by individuals designated as a-a_3 and b-b_3. Later examples will deal with a larger and more realistic number of sustaining activities.

The Colleague model prescribes assigning all operations necessary for some flow of work to a team, as far as possible. Figure

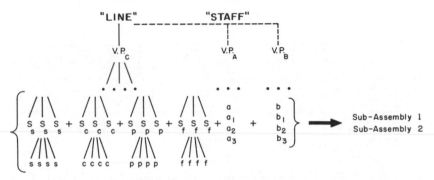

FIGURE 14A. Organizing by Process, Bottom Two Levels of an Organization, Consistent with the NII Model and the Principles.

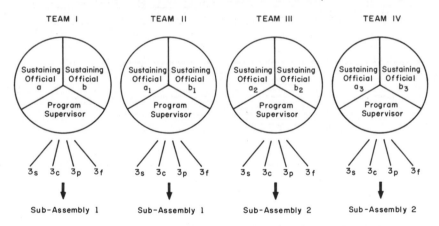

FIGURE 14B. Organizing by Discrete Sub-Assemblies, Bottom Two Levels of an Organization, Consistent with the Colleague Model.

FIGURE 14. Two Ways of Organizing Lower Levels.

14B is an ideal case: Its structure is organized around discrete sub-assemblies 1 and 2. Figure 14B contains approximately the same number of operating personnel as Figure 14A, but fewer supervisors.

The particular nature of work will determine the specific discrete sub-assemblies around which teams might be organized. In

Organizing for the Colleague Concept:

general, these bases of organizing should have the following char-acteristics, whether in administrative or manufacturing work: (1) The work must be either an identifiable and significant component of some larger assembly or a complete product; (2) a substantial number of processes should be involved; and (3) the completed sub-assembly or product must be testable as an entity.

These guidelines are admittedly rough. The assembly of the audio system of a radio or the repair of a telephone, however, clearly fit them and illustrate the nature of the low-level discrete sub-assemblies in an industrial context. In an administrative situation, processing all of the categories of incoming mail would consti-tute a discrete sub-assembly. Several Colleague teams might be formed, each of which would handle all of the classes of mail received from, for example, senders with surnames beginning with specified letters of the alphabet. Therefore, each supervisor could "get all the way around" the job and make meaningful decisions for a complete flow of work. The traditional pattern, in contrast, would assign individual supervisors and operators to one class of mail, volume permitting.

Notice that a discrete sub-assembly cannot be defined in terms of the size of the work force or of the total organization. Since defini-tion is tied to specific work contexts, size cannot be specified in general. Depending upon the technology, the number of contribu-tors to a discrete flow of work might vary from several dozen to several hundred. The assembly of an auto might require large teams; the factory repair of a telephone permits much smaller teams. The significant point here is that the Colleague model seems amenable to guiding the structural relations of large as well as small discrete sub-assemblies.

If a discrete sub-assembly must be grounded in a specific techno-logical context, its importance has not gone unnoticed in enlight-ened managerial practice, and particularly at higher levels of organization. The reorganization of the DuPont complex in the second decade of this century, for example, was guided in signifi-cant ways by this rule-of-thumb: "The most efficient results are obtained at least expense when we coordinate related effort and segregate unrelated effort." That is, the DuPont committee study-ing proposals for reorganization felt they could isolate relatively discrete flows of work at various levels. It might seldom be the case that an activity Z contributes nothing to a flow FW, but its contribu-tions might be so attenuated as to make it reasonable to exclude activity Z from the activities given organizational representation for the flow of work FW.

DuPont's rationale for reorganization is no bare-faced restatement of the traditional emphasis upon functions and processes. The reorganization committee, oppositely, forcefully noted that its guiding proposition did *not* imply, as "it is so often said, that good organization results from putting like things together." Just the opposite commonly was the case, the committee stressed: ". . . it is related effort which should be coordinated and not 'like things.' In fact it is often more necessary to combine related efforts which are unlike." The point was underscored by this example:

> For instance, it is natural to think that all engineers and engineering work should be grouped in one engineering department. Now, surveying a farm, designing and building a bridge, running a locomotive, or operating a power house, are all "engineering," but it is quite obvious that they are so unrelated that to group them under one head would be uneconomical. On the other hand, the operation of a boiler house at Carney's Point is similar in name and reality to the operation of a boiler house at Haskell, yet one would not think of grouping them under one head in exchange for the authority exercised over each of them by the plant superintendent.[2]

All this was not so much impractical speculation: Product rather than function became the basis for organizing at DuPont.

Organizing around products or discrete sub-assemblies, in sum, has two major general motivations. It is biased toward decentralization rather than centralization, that is toward forcing downward the locus of effective decision-making. The present approach to organizing also is biased toward increasing the power of lower-level participants in organizations, a related but distinct matter.

Neither motivation of organizing around products or discrete sub-assemblies wants for support in the literature. Decentralization, for example, is a complex phenomenon. In general, it yields positive consequences.[3] Boundary conditions restricting applications of the

---

[2]The quotations in this paragraph are from the *Report of the Subcommittee an Organization to the Executive Committee*, E. I. DuPont de Nemours & Company, March 31, 1919. The quotations are reproduced in Alfred D. Chandler, Jr., *Strategy and Structure: Chapters in the History of the Industrial Enterprise* (Cambridge: Massachusetts Institute of Technology Press, 1962), pp. 69-70. Copyright © 1962 by The M.I.T. Press.

[3]William F. Whyte, *Man and Organization* (Homewood, Ill.: Dorsey Press and Irwin, 1959), pp. 11-16; Ernest Dale, "Centralization vs. Decentralization," *Advanced Management*, XX (June, 1955), esp. 15-16, illustrate the evidence supporting the efficacy of decentralization. One of the major problems in interpreting such findings is the variety of meanings of "centralization-decentralization." For an interesting attempt to grapple with these designatory difficulties, see Thomas L. Whisler, "Measuring Centralization of Control In Business Organizations," in *New*

technique do exist, of course, as they exist for all techniques. Illustrative boundary conditions include this variety of factors: Some types of work are not easily amenable to decentralization beyond very large units,[4] some individuals have personality characteristics that are inappropriate for the demands of this structural form,[5] and decentralization implies significant training burdens that may be unrealistic under some circumstances.[6] With it all, decentralization has much to recommend it as a general strategy for organizing, and it has at least been a crucial element in the histories of many firms that have grown to large size as well as a useful technique in smaller concerns.[7]

Increasing the control of lower-level participants over their work also has much to support it. Again, boundary conditions for successful applications of appropriate techniques exist. Fortunately, we can rely on extensive treatments of both usefulness and boundary conditions from a number of points of view.[8] Thus some supporting arguments have emphasized improved performance and reduction of immediate dollars-and-cents costs;[9] other treatments have centered upon longer-run savings and the development of self-actualizing man in organizations;[10] still other cases have been made from the point of view of the contributions of increased control over work to achieving and maintaining emotional health;[11] finally, arguments have stressed that moral commitments of Western society can be served in organizations by techniques that increase man's control over his work.[12]

Perspectives In Organization Research, ed. William W. Cooper, Harold J. Leavitt, and Maynard W. Shelly, II (New York: Wiley, 1964), pp. 314-33.

[4]Robert T. Golembiewski, *Men, Management, and Morality* (New York: McGraw-Hill, 1965), Ch. 8.

[5]William D. Fitzinger, "Entrepreneurial Prototype in Bank Management," *Journal of the Academy of Management*, VI (March, 1963), 36-45; Whyte, *op. cit.*

[6]Herbert E. Krugman, " 'Just Like Running Our Own Little Store'," *Personnel*, XXXIV (July-August, 1957), esp. 46-47.

[7]Chandler, *op. cit.*, well documents the point for the large organization. Counterpoint for smaller units is provided by Paul R. Lawrence, *The Changing of Organizational Behavior Patterns* (Boston: Graduate School of Business Administration, Harvard Univ., 1958).

[8]The most useful and extensive effort of this kind is Chris Argyris, *Integrating the Individual and the Organization* (New York: Wiley, 1964), pp. 37-42.

[9]George F. Faris, "Congruency of Scientists' Motives With Their Organizations' Provisions for Satisfying Them: Its Relationship to Motivation, Affective Job Experiences, Styles of Work, and Performance." (Ann Arbor: Department of Psychology, Univ. of Michigan, November, 1962, mimeographed).

[10]Chris Argyris, *Personality and Organization* (New York: Harper, 1957), esp. pp. 175-208.

[11]Arthur Kornhauser, "Mental Health of Factory Workers: A Detroit Study," *Human Organization*, XXI (Spring, 1962), 43-46.

[12]Golembiewski, *Men, Management, and Morality*.

Four Major Side Effects:
Consequences of a Colleague Structure

The uncomplicated graphics used in the preceding discussion tend to underplay the magnitude of the differences that derive from organizing around the Colleague model, and this misperception must be laboriously prevented. Four major side effects of the basic design of an organization structure compatible with the Colleague concept will accomplish the necessary job. The basic structures in Figures 13B and 14B generate these consequences, although from time to time it will be necessary to develop the design of an even more detailed structure consistent with the Colleague concept.

The major consequences of the Colleague model derive from these several sources: reducing the pressure for the integration of activities by organizing around discrete sub-assemblies or products, measuring and motivating performance, handling errors in organizations, and training and developing personnel. The discussion of them parallels the similar analysis of the NII model in Chapter IV.

Reduces the Pressure of Integration:
A Side Effect of Organizing for the Colleague Concept

First, the pressure for the integration of activities will be eased by organizing in ways consistent with the Colleague model. The point has been made earlier in several ways. Note here, therefore, only that the very existence of the other teams provides an incentive for integration within a team of all of the activities necessary to perform the complete task. This reduces the need for supervisory pressure. Moreover, a friendly competition may result in that the success of one team need not be achieved at the expense of the others. Success comes from putting out work more economically than others performing the same or similar operations rather than from bargaining ability. Virtue is likely to be rewarded, in short.

The traditional theory offers less sanguine probabilities. For competition in an organization patterned after the principles is between units organized around a partial contribution to some discrete sub-assembly or product. This puts human nature to a difficult test. The awkward consequences of this temptation, for example, were reflected in the case discussed on p. 103 of the $3,000 order which had been improperly filled. Several organizational units did compete, but in attempting to avoid the charge rather than in terms of their partial and largely noncomparable

Organizing for the Colleague Concept:

contributions. Consequently, the success of any unit in avoiding a charge for the cost of rectifying the error implied the failure of one or more of the other units. The competition was hardly friendly under these "zero-sum" conditions. Nor was the "solution" particularly happy. For the difficulty of assigning responsibility, given the several overlapping partial contributions, did not permit a just and nonnegotiated assignment of the change.

The pressure for integration induced by the Colleague model also eases in the sense that a breakdown in one of the teams will not affect others at the same level. This is due to the representation of all necessary functions or operations on a team. Under the principles and the NII model, in contrast, organizational subunits perform only one function or operation. Figures 15A and B—

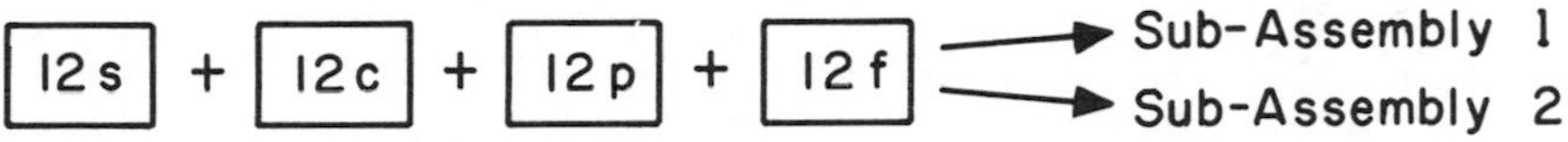

FIGURE 15A. Traditional Organization Theory: Organization by Process.

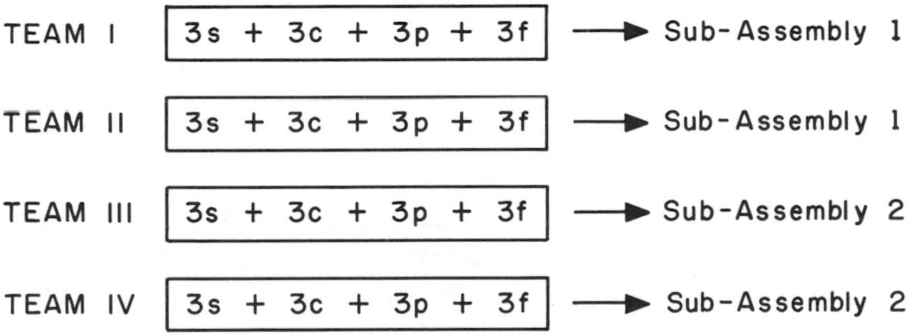

FIGURE 15B.   The Colleague Model: Organization by Discrete Sub-Assemblies.

FIGURE 15.   Two Ways of Organizing Lower-Level Operations.

simplifications of Figures 14A and B—present some straightforward graphics which demonstrate that the integration of activities required by the traditional theory of organization can be a source of great difficulty. Thus output could be reduced to zero as a minimum in the structure in Figure 15B, given a single obstreperous unit of organization. In Figure 15B under the same condition, output would fall by only $1/N$, where N is the number of similar autonomous teams.

The point need not rely on simplified graphics alone. Thus a group leader on the "graveyard shift" had trouble getting his work unit to meet his expectations for output, although plant management was satisfied with production. One of the major contributing factors was the example provided by an inspector/tester unit whose members made use of their work hours to catch up on their sleep. The group leader had no authority over the inspector/tester unit, since the principles guided the organization of effort. In addition, the group leader's foreman (who *could* communicate across to the head of the inspector/tester unit) was hesitant to take action, apparently because he was satisfied with production and/or because he feared retaliation via a sudden increase in the number of "rejects" counted against the record of his group leaders. The "purely advisory" formal status of the inspector/tester unit, that is, apparently did not lull the foreman into underestimating the unit's power. Moreover, although the group leader felt he was losing output, others were feeling no pain. And there was no compelling practical reason why they should. The inspector/tester personnel were not responsible for output, in short; yet they could affect output, and they had the power to inhibit counterremedial action. Of such stuff is organizational conflict made.[13] The Colleague model does not encourage similar disregard by sustaining personnel of program responsibilities.

The point may be generalized. Perhaps the major practical consequence of organizing for the Colleague model is the facilitation of the supervisory job for all levels of supervision. This conclusion can stand on the development of a single feature suggested by Figure 14. If we neglect operating employees, Figure 14A requires at least two levels of management above the level of the first-line supervisor consistent with the limited span of control. Figure 14B probably would require but a single additional supervisory level. For the primary integration may take place at the first level of supervision in the latter structure.

The greater stresses generated in A-type structures by additional supervisory levels may be suggested briefly. Thus M_{scpf}, being three levels away from the action level, must exert considerable pressure to "keep on top of things." His anxiety will be increased because he faces great difficulties in measuring performance and in motivating effort. On the motivational side, for example, organization-by-process makes it easier to restrict output informally, if only because of the physical proximity of employees performing similar and narrow operations. The preventative of close supervision, in turn, often will complicate matters. Time pressure also will tend to

[13]"Corelli Case," in *The Administrator: Cases on Human Relations in Business,* ed. John D. Glover and Ralph M. Hower (3rd ed.; Homewood, Ill.: Dorsey Press and Irwin, 1957), pp. 681-85.

be high, for only M_{scpf} can make reasonable decisions for the full range of operations. Thus problems will tend to be passed upward to the manager's level, and decisions will tend to percolate down. The communication bill in time and paper-processing costs may be high. Derivatively, this will reduce the control of all supervisors over their subordinates, the subordinates not missing the obvious fact of nature as to who calls even the relatively trivial shots.

The traditional theory increases the difficulty of integrating work, that is, and this increase tends to be self-defeating. To illustrate, one student directly observed some fifty-six assembly-line foremen. Over 32,000 separate incidents were cataloged. Significantly, foremen who had to cope with fewer "emergencies," such as those implied by the close and constant integration of work, were found to be: (1) more successful in their work as judged by others, and (2) more free to devote time to planning.[14] Relatedly, a kind of multiplier effect seems associated with the recourse to pressure: Pressure not only begets pressure but often amplifies it. Thus the apparently reasonable use of close supervision to assure that operations are integrated often only complicates matters. The result in organizations can be disastrous. As existing research demonstrates,[15] the pressure applied by a high-level official is very likely to encourage officials at the several lower levels to behave similarly. The consequences hardly are favorable in most cases, with, for example, low productivity being far more likely to exist along with such manifestations of pressure as "close supervision" than is high productivity.[16]

---

[14]Robert H. Guest, "Of Time and the Foreman," *Personnel*, XXXII (May, 1956), 478-96.

[15]Robert L. Kahn and Daniel Katz, "Leadership Practices in Relation to Productivity and Morale," in *Group Dynamics: Research and Theory*, ed. Dorwin Cartwright and Alvin Zander (rev. ed.; Evanston, Ill.: Row, Peterson, 1960), pp. 559, 561.

[16]Thus "directive supervision" has been associated with low output, high absenteeism, and high grievance rates. For examples of supporting studies see, respectively, Rensis Likert, *New Patterns of Management* (New York: McGraw-Hill, 1961), esp. pp. 20, 45; Michael Argyle, Godfrey Gardner, and Frank Cioffi, "Supervisory Methods Related to Productivity, Absenteeism and Labor Turnover," *Human Relations*, XI, No. 1 (1958), 23-40; and Edwin A. Fleishman, "Patterns of Leadership Behavior Related to Group Grievances and Turnover," *Personnel Psychology*, XV (Spring, 1962), esp. 50. The present generalization does have exceptions, of course. Martin Patchen, "Supervisory Methods and Group Performance Norms," *Administrative Science Quarterly*, VII (December, 1962), esp. 286-87, 290, for example, presents evidence that goes against the grain of most research.

The issues are devilishly complicated, but both "rule" and "exception" seem reconcilable in terms of other variables. Thus individuals who are highly "authoritarian" will respond less enthusiastically to "supportive supervision," if they do not rebel against it. On this point, see John R. P. French, Jr., *et al.*, "A Study of Threat and Participation In An Industrial Performance Appraisal Program," *Behavioral*

Aids Measuring and Motivating Performance:
A Side Effect of Organizing for the Colleague Concept

Simplified measurement and motivation of contributions to performance, second, will prove a particularly attractive side effect of organizing for the Colleague model. This is no mean claim. For if there are problems in the measurement and motivation of behavior in the macroscopic organization, these problems are even more acute in constituent sub-units. Figures 13-15 may be exploited to illustrate the present point.

This puzzling question frames our inquiry: How does one determine how much activity S did contribute and should contribute to total performance in a Figure 14A structure? Approaching this question will prove a complex business. By way of introduction, the form of organization in Figure 15B avoids many of the problems of measuring and motivating contributions to performance. Not that the form of organization isolates the imponderable and solves the unanswerable. Rather, the form of organization reduces the importance of the imponderable and the unanswerable, thereby making measurement easier and facilitating motivation.[17]

Research Service Report (New York: General Electric, 1962), pp. 109-119; Victor H. Vroom, *Some Personality Determinants of the Effects of Participation* (Englewood Cliffs, N. J.: Prentice-Hall, 1960). Relatedly, the larger the basic unit of organization, the greater the reliance upon, and the greater the toleration of, "directive supervision." Supporting evidence on this point is provided by M. G. Ross and C. Hendry, *New Understandings of Leadership* (New York: Association Press, 1957), pp. 47-81.

Similarly, many other studies permit more precise prediction than this summary generalization. For example, see the distinction between "rewarders" and "punishers" in David Kipnis, "The Effects of Leadership Style and Leadership Power Upon the Inducement of an Attitude Change," *Journal of Abnormal and Social Psychology,* LVII (September, 1958), 173-80; Lynn R. Anderson and Fred E. Fiedler, "The Effect of Participatory and Supervisory Leadership On Group Creativity," *Journal of Applied Psychology,* XLVIII (August, 1964), 227-36.

Macroscopic variables also might account for still more variance in studies of the consequences of various styles of supervision. For example, some have argued that different technologies may be differentially sensitive to different styles. The point is developed forcefully, for example, by Robert Dubin, *Leadership and Productivity* (San Francisco: Chandler, 1965), pp. 11-19. Dubin relies on the general distinctions between "small batch," "large batch," and "continuous process" technologies. It is also possible that different leadership styles will have different consequences in different types of organizations. For some early taxonomic work, see Raymond V. Bowers, *Studies on Behavior in Organizations* (Athens, Ga.: Univ. of Georgia Press, 1966), pp. 157-80.

[17]Peter F. Drucker, *The Practice of Management* (New York: Harper, 1954), pp. 62-87, details some of the measurement problems in orthodox organizations. For insight into some of the mensural problems that persist in decentralized organizations, see the discussion of "transfer prices" in Andrew Whinston, "Price Guides In Decentralized Organizations," *New Perspective in Organization Research, op. cit.*, pp. 405-48.

The abortive search for "absolute standards" illustrates the specific problems for measuring sub-organization performance created by the traditional theory of organization. The bare assumption that an "absolute time" could be determined for particular motions,[18] for example, buoyed a revolution in viewing work. Early students like the Gilbreths saw that measuring performance was tied closely to motivating effort. Many grave problems thus would disappear if "absolute times" were determined. Consider only that workers on piece-rates or standard-plus-bonus arrangements tended to "soldier" on the job to protect themselves from such management action as raising standards. Soldiering would be impossible and unnecessary if "absolute times" were determined. For rates would be set once and for all and set at precisely the correct level. Workers therefore would have no grounds for apprehension concerning changes in standards and, consequently, restrictive arrangements would cease.

Approaching the measurement and motivation of individual contributions in terms of absolute standards has proved an elusive task, however. Standard times are used but infrequently, as a consequence. March and Simon describe the more common practice in this way:

> At present, time standards for industrial jobs are still usually estimated directly, and only in a minority of cases are they synthesized from standard data on component units. The human organism, even when it is regarded as a neuro-physiological "machine," has proved far more complex than pioneers like Gilbreth hoped and expected when they undertook to analyze human work into its component therbligs.[19]

The problems of measuring and motivating the contributions to performance of sub-organizations are even more formidable than those associated with individual performance. These problems will be particularly acute when — as the traditional theory prescribes — an organization is built around major functions and, at lower levels, around processes. Here the allocation of some crucial costs tends to become arbitrary and therefore a complex and essentially political matter. The complexity can be illustrated by analyzing disputes over the allocation of costs.

Costing as an Illustration. Let the comparative focus be upon the relative difficulties of costing in two structures. Under the

---

[18]James G. March and Herbert A. Simon, *Organizations* (New York: Wiley, 1958), p. 16.
[19]*Ibid.*, p. 16.

traditional theory of organization reflected in Figure 15A two problems must be faced in costing. That is, the total cost of the discrete sub-assembly 1 must be determined. In general, this is not a formidable problem. In addition, costs must be apportioned among the work units S_s, S_c, S_p, and S_f. This is a much more difficult problem. Illustratively, since the activities s, c, p, and f must be integrated, S_c may pay for the inventiveness (or worse) of S_s. Thus S_s might convert some scrap into a component which meets standards but still makes the task of S_c somewhat more difficult. S_c might demand consideration in such a case, a matter all the more sensitive because there are often no hard-and-fast rules for apportioning costs and because a supervisor's record may depend upon even small costs.

Political battles may rage over costing issues with two major consequences. First, staff growth is encouraged. For example, five inspections are necessary to eliminate most arguments about responsibility for costs in Figure 15A, one before and after operation s and one after c, p, and f. Second, staff units derive influence from riding herd over such disputes, thereby being privy to many agreements made by the lower line to avoid conflict. These agreements, such as the following novel technique, need be neither nonarbitrary nor related to effectiveness. The participants (unknown to higher levels) have an abacus-like toy, and the representatives of the several units each are awarded beads in number corresponding to the power status of their organizational unit. Where costing disputes cannot be settled by negotiation, participants may surrender one or more of their beads to remove their organizational unit from consideration in the allocation of charges in that particular case. This alternative might be chosen by a department with an already unfavorable cost record for the month. Since the object is never to get caught short of beads, interestingly enough, settlements-by-negotiation are encouraged by what seems a trivial technique.

More conventional approaches also may increase the power of sustaining officials. Larson—a lower-level "internal costing and pricing consultant"—typifies how such influence may come to even the relatively lowly in organizations. Larson's very title reflects the guiding hand of the NII model, but that title did not restrict his behavior. Dealing with program officials several levels in the organization above him in an emergency matter while his superiors were out of town, Larson explains his actions in this way:

> The two divisions couldn't agree on a policy, I had their
> representatives in my office for two afternoons in a row.

Organizing for the Colleague Concept:

Where they couldn't agree on what to do, I made the decision. I checked a number of things in advance with the vice-president. It was taking too much time for the divisions to settle the differences themselves. We needed to get a decision.[20]

The vice-president of control and planning was the final authority in such questions, formal decisions being issued over his signature. However, Larson and his superiors had much room for action in other than emergency situations. In one case, for example, top management apparently spent less than two hours reviewing recommendations evolved after six months of preparation. Moreover, as Larson reports, the vice-president "always signs letters exactly as we write them."

These costing pressures are much reduced by organizing for the Colleague concept. Thus only the cost of producing, for example, sub-assembly 1 in Figure 15B is crucial for evaluating a team's performance, and that calculation is not particularly troublesome. This would be the case even for individual performance under a job enlargement program at all levels, a program which is consistent with the Colleague model. In such a case, responsibility can be determined more quickly and accurately on the basis of one inspection before operations begin and one terminal inspection. Of course, any Colleague group might request cost accountants to estimate the costs of each of the four operations, information which might be very useful. This implies a significant advantage. For under the NII model, costing reports will often be perceived as arbitrary and punitive efforts by an outsider to goad greater effort. Under the Colleague model, these reports can be perceived as objective and helpful efforts contributed by a fellow team member. The difference is enormous, psychologically viewed.

Organizing for the Colleague concept, then, permits avoiding the tough problems of apportioning costs. And the tough problems are the ones which a theory of organization should help one to avoid. Or, from another vantage point, the Colleague model makes the crucial calculation a relatively simple one, and the complex and arbitrary calculations become relatively unimportant. Of course, some intrateam squabbles may result from particular internal allocations of costs. But the Colleague model implies significant penalties for dallying and, in any case, the disagreement is localized. The principles and the NII model have neither of these saving graces.

---

[20]William R. Dill, Thomas L. Hilton, and Walter R. Reitman, *The New Managers: Patterns of Behavior and Development* (Englewood Cliffs, N. J.: Prentice-Hall, 1962), p. 57.

Costing disputes can rage within and between the several program and sustaining hierarchies, each with but "partial" responsibilities for performance, and costing disputes often involve heads of the several units, each with resources to wage political warfare and sometimes with reason for doing so.

These considerations suggest that the reliance on statistical controls under the principles and the NII model is likely to face one or both of two awkward consequences. First, overreliance on such controls is likely. Matters come to an especially unfortunate pass when the items measured do not encompass all significant aspects of work, or when the items measured cannot be allocated among an organization's several units. At least the latter feature commonly plagues the principles and the NII model. Second, overreliance upon statistical controls may reduce control by the line in a subtle way. As Yasinski puts the practical effect of such overreliance: "... rather, the accountant with his rows of figures, becomes the dominant voice in the company. He becomes a manager by default, as it were, because knowledge is power, and the knowledge on which action is based is what the accountant puts into his reports."[21]

The matter may be put bluntly. The difficulties and risks are great in measuring performance in a structure patterned after the principles and the NII model. Moreover, there is no reasonable guarantee that facing the difficulties and running the risks in most cases will yield more effective control.

Efficacy of Organizing Around "Discrete Sub-Assemblies." The measurement and motivation of work also may profit from the focus upon discrete sub-assemblies required by the Colleague model. Thus one gets a useful and valid comparison between teams with relatively little overhead cost, for each team performs all of the activities necessary for completing the total job. In terminology having some currency today, discrete sub-assemblies have many of the characteristics of "independent profit-centers." Of course, the present approach does not promise the measure and motivation of performance in terms of absolute standards. However, a relative measure of performance does imply some motivational pay-offs. For it will have the effect of keeping Colleague teams on their collective toes, since innovations by other teams may make yesterday's relative rankings an inaccurate criterion of acceptable performance. That is, again, the opportunity for facile measurement can motivate

---

[21]Frank Jasinski, "Use and Misuse of Efficiency Controls," *Harvard Business Review*, XXXIV (July, 1956), 111.

effective performance. Standards under the traditional theory, in contrast, are often arbitrary and difficult to change in the bargain.

The present argument may seem so much verbal sleight-of-hand. Except in cases where each operator performs all of the required activities, it may seem that the Colleague model only relocates vertical fragmentation at a lower level. This is an empty alternative to vertical fragmentation at the supervisory level.

The objection dissolves upon inspection, however. Consider this set of structural concomitants that make the relocation of the level of vertical fragmentation significant indeed. Under the Colleague model, the advantage definitely resides with the team that can resolve its internal conflicts quickly and with a high degree of consensus as well. The failure to do so will be all too evident in team performance, for which the heads of all team activities are collectively responsible and concerning which they cannot easily raise charges of arbitrariness. Finally, conflict will tend to be localized within teams under the Colleague model even when members disregard these structural limitations on the efficacy of conflict. For the teams are organized around autonomous flows of work, or as nearly so as possible. Consequently, disturbances in one or a few teams need not affect others at the same level. A disgruntled team may be by-passed, directly, rather than be able to clog the flow of work as under the principles and the NII model.

The difficulties of measurement inhering in the principles and the NII model imply significant motivational problems, in contrast. The traditional theory heightens the inevitable controversies over the relative contributions to performance of the several activities organized by function or process that contribute partially and simultaneously to a flow of work. Thus individuals with a cause would be identified organizationally with their functional or processual brothers, and ample room exists for disagreement between honest men about the relative contributions to total performance of the several partial contributors. Overhead support of such causes will be common, in addition, if only because it is politically inexpedient to have one's functional or processual subordinates emasculated by other program or sustaining officials. An organization unit that does not at least take care of its own, in general, will find it difficult to control (let alone motivate) its personnel and to bargain with other units. Conflicts between S_A and S_B and S_C, that is, imply the mobilization of very considerable political forces by substantial units of organization that can paralyze the macroscopic flow of work.

The Colleague model also provides some "vertical" support, but counterbalancing forces exist. Thus every official in a Colleague group will be responsible on technical issues to a counterpart official from a team at the next higher level. But all officials also are responsible to their teams. This horizontal allegiance can have a high salience. Vertical allegiance, ideally, would become most salient in cases of severe violation of policies and procedures within a team.

All this is not to neglect that one is organizing mortal man. Of course, the aggressive individual bent on developing friends and influencing people in high places might neglect his horizontal identifications in his pursuit of vertical and diagonal support. And no doubt many executives will continue to cultivate such sources of information. Under the Colleague model, however, substantial forces operate to reduce both the need for such behavior and the likelihood that it will be rewarded. For example, it is one thing for a personnel man Z to bring an irregularity in a program unit to the attention of his upper-level program contacts when the NII model prescribes structural relations. For the upper-level officials might need such information desperately, and their gratitude might serve to protect and reward Z. Moreover, Z's associates might give him credit for demonstrating that "personnel is on its toes." Under the Colleague model, in contrast, our hypothetical personnel man often would face the wrath of a team done wrong and the less-than-enthusiastic support of upper-level officials who should be less stymied in their attempts to assign responsibility.

This might seem like giving too much the best of it to the Colleague model in problems of mensuration and motivation. For example, one might argue that the Colleague concept does nothing to decrease the problems inherent in schemes of wage-and-salary administration. However, organizing for the Colleague model may ease these problems considerably. Thus a Colleague team might be entrusted with much of the responsibility for developing and administering direct wage programs. This has been tried with success, albeit only under circumstances that may be unusual.[22] For Colleague teams will be judged in terms of their performance on a discrete sub-assembly, and there seems no insurmountable objection to granting teams a very considerable say in their own internal workings. Unions, perhaps, would constitute the most serious roadblocks.

This is no blue-sky speculation. Melman's explanation of the reasons for radically different approaches to providing maintenance

[22]P. G. Herbst, *Antonomous Group Functioning* (London: Tavistock Publications, 1962), pp. 3-20.

services in two similar plants in the automotive industry illustrates the point. In Plant A, maintenance was an unhurried affair. Although the advanced technology of the plant provided for continuous operation, in practice each of the interlocked machines was regarded as if it were itself a production plant. An awkward wage-and-salary system helps account for this bad fit of practice to technique. High output required a high degree of integration of the contributions of line manning sequential operations and of staff providing maintenance. The technology provides for a horizontal, integrated flow. But the traditional theory prescribes separate organization units for the several activities, and the derivative wage program provides individual incentive rates for the operators and straight rates for maintenance. The reward-and-punishment system, that is, encourages "sharp dealing" by operators while the technology requires cooperation and integration. Moreover, the wage program encourages this attitude among maintenance employees: "Why should I work harder so Operator A can make more?" Meanwhile, the technology places a heavy premium on the close and prompt integration of maintenance in the flow of work.

Although there is nothing inevitable about the adaptation made to these cross-pressures in Plant A, one could hardly expect anything better in the normal course of events. Maintenance performed its services at a leisurely pace, and management provided large "banks" of partially finished goods at the several machine sites so that operators could earn incentive rates while breakdowns "up the line" were being leisurely repaired. That is, each machine was treated as if it were a separate plant, a costly adaptation indeed.

In Plant B, the maintenance picture was a polar extreme. As Melman puts it: "The unhurried pace of this emergency maintenance work [in Plant A] was in spectacular contrast with the style we found at [Plant B]. There, a breakdown which obstructs a line sets off alarm signals and a maintenance crew operates on a fire brigade system."[23] The reason for the difference is not obscure. In Plant B, output is measured not for individuals but for rather large groups whose several activities contribute to what has been called here a "flow of work" or a "discrete sub-assembly." Consistently, production bonuses are paid to maintenance as well as to production employees as mutual members of an organizational team that monitors a specific flow of work.

The approaches in the two plants may be contrasted sharply. Plant B supported the integrative technology by organizational

[23]Seymour Melman, *Decision-Making and Productivity* (New York: Wiley, 1958), pp. 8-9, 12.

identifications and by a reward-and-punishment system that encouraged integrative effort. In contrast, Plant A followed the self-defeating course of obstructing an integrative flow of work with structural arrangements and a reward-and-punishment system strongly biased toward fragmenting individual production stations from each other and toward fragmenting maintenance from production.

The results certainly support the former approach. Plant B was among the more efficient in its industry, despite the fact that its hourly wage rates were a formidable 65 per cent above those of competing firms. Again, we find what seems a paradox. The individual profits most when the system of remuneration permits him to profit as others in a related flow of work also profit. Stressing the benefits that will accrue to the isolated individual encourages disruptive behavior that has the consequence of, on the average, sharply reducing everyone's share. The paradox exists, however, only so long as we implicitly accept the theory underlying the principles and the NII model. Given the two theoretical systems underlying this effort, the differences between Plant A and Plant B are reasonable.

The Team and Self-Control: Consensus as a Motivator. The several features aiding the measurement and motivation of performance have a solid foundation in the social and psychological forces that inhere in the group. Organizing for the Colleague model attempts to utilize group forces and to orient them toward superior performance and heightened employee satisfaction, particularly via emphasis upon discrete sub-assemblies.

Ample reasons support the usefulness of mobilizing group forces to motivate effort. Groups may develop within the functional or processual units prescribed by the principles and the NII model, to make the point by contrast, but such groups can use their power more effectively to impede than to facilitate a flow of work. Moreover, all of the favorable consequences of identifying with a discrete sub-assembly or a total flow of work are forfeited by the principles and the NII model. There is an alternative, of course. Groups may develop between such units and informally serve to integrate the activities required for a complete flow of work. Given the pressures generated by the traditional structure, however, this adaptation is not likely.[24] And even if such liaison groups do develop, the traditional theory hardly deserves the credit.

[24]Observers generally agree that "vertical" identifications — that is, those within departmental boundaries defined in terms of functional or processual specialties — are the most prevalent and enduring. Particularly see Melville Dalton, *Men Who Manage* (New York: Wiley, 1959), esp. pp. 57-65.

Organizing for the Colleague Concept:

An illustration drives home the point that the neglect of group forces by the NII model is an unrewarding policy. The illustration is a famous one, which explains the brevity here. In one factory operation, coincident with a minor change in low-level operations, employees were exposed to three degrees of participation in decision-making. All employees were informed that competition required an increase in output. Beyond that, one work unit was simply told what to do and appropriate directions and explanations were provided by management after a no-nonsense declaration that the change would be made. This may be called the No Participation condition. A second work unit was allowed to elect representatives who participated in the actual decision-making about the specifics of the change. This may be called the Partial Participation condition. A final work unit was allowed to come to its own decision about the design of the change and about the new rates, albeit within the general guides that had been laid down by management. This may be called the Total Participation condition. Table 6

TABLE 6. EFFECTS ON PRODUCTIVITY OF VARIOUS DEGREES OF PARTICIPATION IN A MINOR WORK CHANGE

Condition	Productivity at Five-Day Periods After Change					
	5	10	15	20	25	30
Total Participation	64	63	75	71	71	72
Partial Participation	50	53	60	68	64	66
No Participation	45	53	55	51	49	55

From Lester Coch and John R. P. French, Jr., "Overcoming Resistance to Change," in Group Dynamics, ed. Dorwin Cartwright and Alvin Zander (rev. ed.: Evanston, Ill.: Row, Peterson, 1960), p. 300.

dramatically testifies to the importance of participation in, and consensus about, decisions. Organizing for the Colleague concept, of course, requires a pattern approximating the Total Participation condition.

Note also that these same group forces might be turned against the purposes of the organization. The mensural and motivational advantages of the Colleague model, however, will reduce the probability of such a happenstance. Generally speaking, the implied "high cohesiveness" of groups is associated with high productivity and high satisfaction in available studies. But high cohesiveness/low productivity has been observed in a minority of cases.[25] Directly, the Colleague model should reduce the probability of such high/low cases. The supporting rationale can only be

[25]Robert T. Golembiewski, The Small Group (Chicago: Univ. of Chicago Press, 1962), pp. 149-70.

sketched. Any *one* Colleague team can utilize its high cohesiveness to raise output; *all* similar Colleague teams must conspire to reduce output. In contrast, any *one* functional or processual department in the traditional model can lower output, but only *all* such units acting cooperatively can raise output. The implied dynamics strongly suggest an upward bias in productivity in the Colleague model and a downward bias under the traditional model. Some research supports this rationale.[26]

Handling Errors in Organizations:
A Side Effect of Organizing for the Colleague Concept

Organizations exist to increase man's mastery over his environment. Of necessity, then, the handling of errors in organizations must be of some consequence. Errors involve costs and thereby claim importance. In addition, the ways in which errors are handled can mean costs at least as great as the errors themselves.

Structural arrangements have much to do with whether errors are handled ill or well. The NII model encourages a costly handling of errors in both narrow and broad senses. These summary conclusions demand support.

Five Sources of Trouble. Five common sources of resistance to review in organizations help demonstrate the ways in which the NII model adversely affects the handling of errors. Jerome's list of the several sources of resistance will be relied upon:

  1. instinctive resistance to "outsiders," particularly punitive outsiders;
  2. the use of the review to inflate the reviewer's ego and/or to develop power for the reviewer;
  3. narrow conceptions of authority and responsibility by the official being reviewed;
  4. emotional response by the boss to error; and
  5. the use of review as a punitive post-mortem rather than as a guide for future planning and action.[27]

Of course, staff officials—auditors, personnel specialists, cost accountants, and the like—often participate in the review of program units and officials. Consequently, the prevailing model of formal relations between line and staff officials will be significant in

[26]Leonard R. Sayles, *The Behavior of Industrial Work Groups* (New York: Wiley, 1958).
[27]William Travers Jerome, III, *Executive Control: The Catalyst* (New York: Wiley, 1961), pp. 181-86.

determining the outcome of review. Of course, many other variables might wash out the effects of structural arrangements from case to case. That is, this analysis is a statement of general tendencies rather than inevitabilities.

The traditional staff concept, first, heightens the tendency to resist review by an organizational "outsider." Patently, the NII model makes just such outsiders of sustaining personnel via, for example, the separate hierarchies commonly provided for program and sustaining services. Other factors tending to pull program and sustaining officials apart—age, education, cultural characteristics, and so on—have been discussed (see pp. 69-73). In addition, the NII model heightens the intensity of vertical fragmentation, thereby providing the program official with a rationale for resistance to review by a staff official who may have formal status inferior to his own. Moreover, the actions of a sustaining official may not seem neutral and, in any case, his advice or service often will influence the program official's attempts to meet his responsiblity for performance.

The Colleague model reduces the resistance to review in this regard. For the staff man doing the initial reviewing will be a member of the team and just as responsible for production as the program people. Since there would be no formal distinction between sustaining and program officials at the same level or on the same team, constructive mutual cooperation on a common task might be encouraged between officials who need not worry about the stigma of organization inferiority in their dealings with one another. Moreover, the results of the review would be reported where they do the most good, at the work level. In most cases, this would probably result in less subterfuge in the review process, and in easier working relations all the way around. An organization, that is, is not likely to benefit from cat-and-mousing.

Relatedly, the Colleague model helps remove a basic complaint against sustaining activities and officials, that they are essentially punitive. That is, sustaining units and officials under the NII model inform superiors, who discipline offenders. The Colleague model, in contrast, provides that sustaining officials play a rewarding role. They spot and help remedy problem situations at the level at which they occur. Psychologically, one is well-advised as a general rule to reward rather than to punish. The latter orientation encourages resistance; the former may induce and reinforce the behavior desired. Practice in organizations supports what may seem an impractical platitude. As Jerome summarizes his survey of industrial experience:

> The relevant point...amounts to this: irritation with review and appraisal by outside agencies seems to be caused *when the findings are reported at a management level higher than is required for effective corrective action.* In other words, the purpose of review is to help, not to castigate operating management, or to inflate the prestige of the reviewing agency.[28]

The Neutral and Inferior Instrument model, second, also encourages resistance due to the (real or imagined) use of review to inflate the reviewer's ego or to increase his power in the organization. Indeed, the traditional concept of staff encourages this unfortunate standoff: It implies that staff can succeed only where the line fails. This is psychologically awkward and infuses line-staff relations with punitiveness. The NII model encourages inflating staff's ego at the line's expense, for that model assigns to him an organizational inferiority that the staff man may find difficult to bear with equanimity. The record bears ample evidence that line-staff relations commonly take on such a win/lose character, and particularly in the review process. The Colleague model reduces the temptation since it removes much of the rationale for divisive behavior.

The deliverance of sustaining officials from the temptations of the NII model has much to recommend it. Consider two brief contrasting cases cited by Drucker. One company acquired a Gestapo-like reputation because of the conduct of review. In general, members of the control section of the company acted as the Neutral and Inferior Instrument concept prescribed. Its findings were reported directly to the president with only peremptory clearance with the officials of the administrative unit being reviewed. The home office then would take firm action. The review process was a trial for all, and there was no compelling evidence that top management was better off for it. Drucker also cites the case of General Electric's internal auditors, who were representatives of headquarters but who functioned much as the Colleague concept requires. That is, the auditors discussed their findings with the management of the unit being analyzed. Drucker tells us that the findings went no farther up the hierarchy.[29] Review was not bounded by fear and secrecy in this case.

These two cases suggest the problems of review permitted (if not encouraged) by the traditional staff concept. The Neutral and Inferior Instrument concept, by requiring that staff officials report up

---

[28]*Ibid.*, p. 184. Emphases in original.
[29]Drucker, *op. cit.*, pp. 131-32.

and over and down, has several serious disadvantages. Thus it may create the impression that the review process is designed more to build up the staff official than to aid performance. The time lag in such reporting, for example, often results in strong demands for corrective action long after the fact. And demanding that the farmer close the barn door after the horse has been stolen, if it does nothing to return the horse, may well arouse the ire of the farmer. This is especially the case if some control unit is established to make certain the door remains closed forevermore.

The traditional model of staff, third, is likely to cause resistance to review because that model is based upon a narrow concept of authority. If the line is really *the* acting part of the organization, a program official might complain: "Where do staff people derive their power to influence operations?" Calling their services "advisory" is not likely to moderate the intensity of the complaint. For one being advised to death will draw little consolation from a verbal separation of "service" and "command." In a similar vein, injunctions that staff accept line definitions of "help" must be unrealistic, for the professional training common among sustaining operatives encourages their active involvement in a definition of what help is required. And to the degrees that organizational identifications of program and sustaining officials differ, or that sustaining officials feel insecure in their jobs and consequently feel compelled to prove their value, staff restraint is unlikely.

The problem is not that program officials are stubborn or that sustaining officials have an exaggerated notion of their own importance. Rather, the traditional theory is unrealistic about authority. Thus reasonable behavior by sustaining officials will violate the traditional theory. But so much the worse for the theory. Staff officials will participate in command, whatever theoretical fictions deprive them of this role, and they ought to do so in what were described as "substantive problem areas" in Chapter V. The Colleague model permits meeting such organizational realities without guilt. It gives to sustaining activities the voice in command denied them by the traditional model.

The emotional response of a boss to error probably will be reduced by organizing for the Colleague concept, fourth, although no pattern of organization will deprive the boss of all opportunities to display his anger. This response of a boss often stems from such sources as feelings of guilt because he did not know about the error long ago, fear that error reflects unfavorably on his ability, knowledge (or fear) that higher levels will learn of the error through staff officials before he does, unconscious or conscious desires to use the error as further proof of his superiority, and learning of the error when it is too late to take constructive action.

The use of review as a postmortem, fifth, and finally, also is a common source of resistance to review. If a review is largely past history and involves more justification of actions taken than learning from experience, the process is likely to prove ineffective. Review that is a learning experience as well as a rehashing of actions taken can have substantial payoffs. As Jerome explains:

> The proper exercise of review and appraisal contributes to greater present and future effectiveness in these respects: (1) past shortcomings are the stuff of experience — the sort of experience that leads to improved operations; and (2) realization that one's plans, programs, and budgets will be scrutinized against the actual achievements lends necessary rigor and realism to the entire control process. Omit the promise of an eventual review and the pressures of the moment will erode any planning and budgeting structure no matter how sound it may be.[30]

The NII model and its narrow concept of authority heighten the impact of some of these sources of resistance to review, especially three and five. The Colleague model, by changing the rules of the game, tends to change the executive's reaction to error. Again, life in organizations is unkind to the NII model, which encourages an "ancient history" cast to the review process. To make the point positively, review under the Colleague model is more likely to be an ongoing concern within the teams, its own sustaining officials being on the alert for difficulties whose discovery might contribute directly to increased performance. Both program and sustaining officials also would have an interest in displaying alertness in their internal review should their failure encourage an upper-level team to intervene. That is, much of the work of administering programs would be left to each team. The relation of an overhead counterpart unit with any activity within a team, in turn, would be one of general oversight within the boundaries of accepted policies.

Unity: Via Uniformity or Diversity? Perhaps the overriding motivation of the traditional theory of organization has been the quest for unity. Hence the quest for the "one best way" so common in the early writings on scientific management. Thompson summarizes some of the evidence for the position in these terms:

> The entire structure is characterized by a *pre-occupation with the monistic ideal*. The hierarchical institution is

[30]Jerome, *op. cit.*, p. 185.

monocratic. It is a system of superior and subordinate role-relationships in which the superior is the *only* source of legitimate influence upon the subordinate.... Since this was the original organizational relationship, it has dominated organizational theory and practices and still does so.[31]

One cannot disparage such efforts although they often appear extraordinarily prissy. For unity of behavior is at the very heart of any system of organization. But questions can be raised concerning the way in which unity has been commonly sought. That is, the quest for unity has often been perverted into a stress upon uniformity, and pressures toward uniformity often have the effect of encouraging disunity.

Organization theory must learn this fundamental lesson: Unity can spring from diversity as well as from uniformity.[32] The lesson is a necessity rather than a luxury for many of the assumptions of the approach to unity through uniformity limp badly.[33]

That the emphasis on uniformity can abort in disunifying effects may be illustrated by considering supervisory style. How should supervisors treat their subordinates? The traditional theory of organization, of course, implies what may be called a directive style of supervision. The supervisor is an order-giver, he closely scrutinizes work, he is sharply differentiated from his men, and he has considerable and arbitrary power over them. In contrast, research has established that a supportive style often pays handsome dividends. The permissive supervisor is more a motivator of men than one who orders and coerces effort, he seeks their views and gives consideration to them, and he provides general rather than close supervision.

---

[31]Victor A. Thompson, *Modern Organization* (New York: Knopf, 1961), pp. 19-20. Emphases in original.

[32]Mary Parker Follett put the matter with characteristic directness and insight: "What people often mean by getting rid of conflict is getting rid of diversity, and it is of the utmost significance that these should not be considered the same. We may wish to abolish conflict, but we cannot get rid of diversity. We must face life as it is and understand that diversity is its most essential feature.... Fear of difference is dread of life itself. It is possible to conceive conflict [and organize for it as in the Colleague model] as not necessarily a wasteful outbreak of incompatibilities but a *normal* process by which socially valuable differences register themselves the enrichment of all concerned." *Creative Experiences* (New York: Longmans, Green, 1924), pp. 300, 301. Emphases in original.

[33]With particular reference to job descriptions see, at the managerial levels, Dill, Hilton, and Reitman, *op. cit.*, p. 14. The differing technical and social demands at low levels of organization, for example, are reflected in the "American Radiatronics Corporation (B) Case," in Paul R. Lawrence, *et al.*, *Organizational Behavior and Administration: Cases, Concept, and Research Findings* (Homewood, Ill.: Dorsey Press and Irwin, 1961), pp. 344-59.

Which style of supervision should be chosen? Which *one* is best? Many managements have pondered such questions, thereby reflecting the common tendency to think of organization problems in terms of uniformity. Why should *one* style be best? As might be expected, the research literature indicates that the "best" style of supervision will vary with conditions. For example, a favorable mixture of personality characteristics and supervisory style will tie together employees and supervisors, thus unifying the organization. A style of supervision inconsistent with employee personality characteristics may induce lower satisfaction and productivity.

The nuances of choosing a style of supervision are beyond this analysis.[34] However, Table 7 illustrates the gross point being made here. The table reports data from an experiment using the Twenty Questions game. Subjects with different intelligence levels were subjected to different styles of supervision. Notice that the kinds of pairing of styles of supervision with intelligence levels make a very considerable difference in performance.

In sum, a uniform approach to supervisory style will lead to mixed success in unifying an organization. A diversity of leadership styles, sensitive (among other factors) to differences in the intelligence of operators at the same level of the organization, will contribute more toward a unity of employees and their supervisors.

A second illustration will take us more concretely into the innards of organization life. The emphasis upon unity-through-uniformity in organizations is often manifested through such techniques as detailed inspection by a staff unit from headquarters or the "front office." Judging from published work and personal experience, uniformity is what such techniques often get in place of real unity. In discussing the auditing staff of a large plant, for example, Dalton notes that its component units "prepare reports of what *should* occur, and what *is* occurring and what has *occurred* in terms of operating costs and volume of production." This is of course important information, but its gathering from upper levels by outsiders (as the NII model requires) implies substantial costs. Thus Dalton concludes that: "Agencies of this kind precipitate much unofficial activity among those subject to higher interpretations of the reports. . . . Great stress on minute control increases evasion. . . ."[35] This suggests a vicious cycle. Top-level executives may be forced to interpret reports that may be as much fancy as fact, which encourages minute control, which in turn stimulates evasion.

---

[34]Robert T. Golembiewski, "Three Styles of Leadership and Their Uses," *Personnel*, XXXVIII (July-August, 1961), 34-45.
[35]Dalton, *Men Who Manage, op. cit.*, p. 11.

TABLE 7. INTELLIGENCE, ATMOSPHERE, AND PERFORMANCE

	Questions Per Problem	Per Cent Problems Solved
Permissive-Bright	15.5	100.0
Permissive-Dull	31.0	37.5
Directive-Bright	18.5	87.5
Directive-Dull	24.5	75.0

From Allen D. Calvin, Frederick K. Hoffman, and Edgar L. Harden, "The Effect of Intelligence and Social Atmosphere on Group Problem-Solving Behavior," **Journal of Social Psychology**, XLV (February, 1957), 72.

Enough, then, of the negative aspects of the stress upon uniformity. What is there in organizing for the Colleague concept that promises some alternative to attempting to achieve unity via uniformity? Specifically, the emphasis will be upon three approaches to the problem of achieving unity in organizations through diversity. Their common outcomes include increased output and heightened employee satisfaction.

Diversity in Choice of Tasks and Employees. Diversity need not imply an organization at sixes and sevens. A minimal degree of opportunity for diversity is provided by several simple techniques consistent with the spirit of the Colleague model — among them job enlargement or job rotation and the self-choice of workmates by employees — that encourage high output and satisfaction.

There are many varieties of job enlargement,[36] but all share the property of permitting a supervisor or operator to control more (or all) of a total flow of work.[37] Figures 14B and 15B (see pp. 184, 189), for example, illustrate the enlargement of a supervisor's job. Figure 16B (see p. 219) also illustrates one specific approach to job enlargement. Ideally, job enlargement should be carried through to the job of each operative. The bias in traditional thought about organizing on functions and processes as bases for departmentation does not encourage job enlargement for either supervisors or operatives.[38]

More than charity dictates this advocacy of job enlargement. The Colleague model implies a need for knowledgeable managerial personnel at all levels, and there is nothing like a job of some scope for training purposes.[39] These and other good effects of job enlarge-

[36]Argyris, *Personality and Organization, op. cit.,* esp. pp. 177-87.
[37]Golembiewski, *Men, Management, and Morality, op. cit.,* pp. 128-50.
[38]For a case in point, see J. Douglas Elliott, "Increasing Office Productivity Through Job Enlargement," *Office Management Series* (New York: American Management Association, 1953), No. 134.
[39]Whyte, *op. cit.,* pp. 11-16. To be sure, rigorous work with job enlargement has barely begun. For example, see the seminal work in Arthur N. Turner and Paul R. Lawrence, *Industrial Jobs and the Worker* (Boston: Harvard Univ. Graduate School

ment act on both supervisors and supervised, and they need not be accepted on faith. One inadvertant use of job rotation plus a sampling of the available literature provide appropriate support for present purposes:

> While the boss was away, some factory workers in Endicott, New York, switched jobs, just to break up the boredom. Result: it turned out to be just what the doctor ordered. By the time the switch was discovered, the men were all doing so much better that the boss decided to rotate jobs in his department—an International Business Machines plant—as a matter of policy. That was a year ago. Since then manufacturing costs in the department have dropped about 19 per cent.[40]

Despite generally positive consequences, however, job enlargement is no all-purpose cure. Successful applications must be sensitive to both task and personality characteristics, for example.[41] Although job enlargement is a more useful guiding principle than extreme specialization, it does not apply under all conditions.

The positive consequences of job enlargement have complex causes, but tension reduction seems important in any explanation. That is, appropriate applications increase the worker's control over the job environment, decrease monotony, and so on. These factors serve to reduce tension and, in turn, the individual is free to release more of his energies in work as opposed to expending them in self-protection.

---

of Business Administration, 1965). Despite the state of research, much descriptive evidence supports the summary conclusion above and also extends the effects of job enlargement to higher productivity, better quality, greater participant satisfaction, and so on. Some relatively-controlled research provides complex and sometimes-qualified support for the gross position here. For one example of such research, see Louis E. Davis, "Job Design and Productivity: A New Approach," *Personnel*, XXXIII (March, 1957), esp. 419-25.

[40]*Newsweek*, XLIII (March 22, 1954), 79. Useful reviews of the vast supporting literature are provided by Argyris, *Personality and Organization, op. cit.*, pp. 177-87; Georges Friedmann, *The Anatomy of Work* (Glencoe, Ill.: Free Press, 1961), pp. 40-67; and Maurice D. Kilbridge, "Reduced Costs Through Job Enlargement," *Journal of Business*, XXXIII (October, 1960), 357-362.

[41]Golembiewski, *Men, Management, and Morality, op. cit.*, Ch. 5, discusses some of the technique's boundary conditions. Specifically, highly involved individuals are most likely to derive satisfaction from opportunities for self-expression. See Victor H. Vroom, "Ego-Involvement, Job Satisfaction, and Job Performance," *Personnel Psychology*, XV (Summer, 1962), 159-78. Job enlargement therefore may not make work more palatable to those not involved in their work. However, techniques like job enlargement often seem to have the longer-run consequence of increasing the employee's involvement in his work. Moreover, various approaches to job enlargement are likely to have markedly different effects, as sketched by Argyris, *Integrating the Individual and the Organization, op. cit.*, pp. 228-40.

Organizing for the Colleague Concept:

Choice of workmates has similar effects and for many of the same reasons. Of course, self-choice is consistent with the horizontal integration of units monitoring a discrete sub-assembly prescribed by the Colleague model. Consider the comparison of work units on a construction project. One batch of work units was given the opportunity by management to meet its diverse socioemotional needs through selection of team members; the other was formed by having management assign its members. The former type of organization paid enormous dividends. The self-choice crews were markedly superior on four criteria: job satisfaction, turnover rate, an index of labor cost, and an index of materials cost. More concretely, the self-choice crews constructed 104 houses for the same labor and materials costs that it took the management-choice crews to construct 100.[42]

Allowing individuals to meet their diverse needs at work can pay off handsomely for both employer and employee, then, but only given appropriate structural constraints. Self-choice also can prove a dangerous technique under an organization structure such as that based upon the principles and the NII model that does not permit the facile measurement of performance. The heightened group feeling that derives from self-choice may be turned against the formal organization in such a case, as by more effective restriction of output.[43]

Diversity Through Participation in Decision-Making. Unity through diversity need not (perhaps cannot) be approached entirely through techniques which trespass but tentatively on traditional "managerial prerogatives." More substantial opportunities must be provided, although one may be pessimistic about their early and general adoption. Enlarging rank-and-file participation in decision-making illustrates the techniques that permit more substantial possibilities for diversity.

Much research suggests that ambitious opportunities for diversity can be well worth the cost, although matters are far too complex for unqualified statement. Thus four parallel divisions doing routine clerical work were treated in such ways that two of the divisions experienced substantial increases in rank-and-file participation in

[42]Raymond M. Van Zelst, "Validation of a Sociometric Regrouping Procedure," *Journal of Abnormal and Social Psychology*, XLVII (April, 1952), 299-301.
[43]For example, research studies commonly show that high group cohesiveness is associated curvilinearly with output. That is, high cohesiveness implies a high degree of behavioral control over its members. And both high and low output require a high degree of control of member behavior. Stanley Seashore, *Group Cohesiveness in the Industrial Work Group* (Ann Arbor, Mich.: Survey Research Center, Univ. of Michigan, 1954), pp. 61-70, 88-91.

decision-making.[44] The experiment lasted two years so the experimental manipulations had time to "take." For example, the two Autonomous Divisions participated in a wide range of decisions, even concerning methods and procedures and such personnel matters as recess periods and the handling of tardiness. The Hierarchically Controlled Divisions experienced a tightening of supervisory controls, in contrast.

The results generally support the proposition that increased opportunity for diversity encourages organization unity. For example, personnel in the Autonomous Divisions reported significantly higher self-actualization and growth on the job and greater satisfaction with their supervisors. The Autonomous Divisions also reported greater liking for their work after the experiment, while personnel in the Hierarchically Controlled Divisions reported a substantial decrease. Productivity under the two conditions cannot be compared meaningfully. Clerical costs decreased in both pairs of divisions, although more so in the Hierarchically Controlled Divisions. But the turnover in the latter divisions was higher, and their supervisory costs also seem to have been higher. In addition, complaints about the work pressure in the Hierarchically Controlled Divisions reasonably could develop into a major source of long-run irritation. Finally, the experimental period was too brief to allow the benefits of the autonomous condition to become fully manifest. Thus members of the Autonomous Divisions decided that they would reduce the work force (and thus costs in significant measure) only by failing to fill normal vacancies as they occurred. Since the satisfaction of employees in the autonomous condition was higher, however, voluntary turnover was low. Consequently, reductions in clerical costs could be expected to come relatively slowly in the Autonomous Division.

There is another major difficulty with this experiment. Employees were not free to choose the condition they preferred. The results strongly imply that most employees preferred the autonomous condition, but an unknown number of employees would not have chosen the condition in which they were placed. The experimental results might have been more revealing if the employees had been allowed a choice of conditions.

Such results aside, one might object that large organizations admit no alternative to developing elaborate overhead control systems to maintain and increase efficiency. This position seems

---

[44]Nancy C. Morse and Everett Reimer, "The Experimental Change of a Major Organization Variable," *Journal of Abnormal and Social Psychology*, LII (January, 1956), 120-29.

simplistic, however. For example, statistical studies have failed to demonstrate any regularity between the costs of management and productivity in industrial concerns.[45] Such findings suggest that simple, inexpensive, and effective tools of management control can be developed even in large and highly mechanized plants. Moreover, the suggestion is supported by scattered industrial experience. Thus Melman describes a large and mechanically advanced automotive plant in which thousands of workers operated at high levels of efficiency virtually without formal supervision, as commonly understood. At the same time, the plant paid the highest wages in their industry, products were of high quality and of competitive prices, the firm's management overhead was unusually low, and workers had substantial roles in decision-making.[46] A wage-and-salary program was built around the major flows of work in the plant rather than upon individual positions. It provided the general check of performance by which management performed its job with a minimum of fuss, personnel, and overhead cost. Such an approach, of course, is consistent with the Colleague model.

Traditional thought, in sum, stands seriously challenged as the "one-best way," whether in larger units or small.

The Autonomous Group. There exist more extreme examples of the pathway to unity through diversity. Experience with the Autonomous Group approach has been particularly positive, for example, and this experience covers several British industries as well as Indian weaving sheds, some rolling-mill operations in the steel industry, and automated petroleum refining in this country.

The Autonomous Group is typified by an experimental team of seven experienced British coal miners who had responsibility for the complete cycle of operations at the coal face. No team member had a work role which was fixed formally, the men being free to deploy themselves to meet the requirements of the task at any moment. There were certain technological and safety constraints on their behavior, but with these exceptions the members of the Autonomous Group were self-determinative even to the degree that no one of their number held a formal supervisory position. In addition, the formation of the team was based upon self-selection rather than upon management assignment. The team also negotiated a per-ton price for the coal mined and paid its members, equal shares having been given to all members by group agreement.

Most relevantly, the autonomous group of miners was formed at a

---

[45]Seymour Melman, *Dynamic Factors in Industrial Productivity* (New York: Wiley, 1956), Ch. 17.
[46]Melman, *Decision-Making and Productivity, op. cit.,* p. 5.

work site where the principles and the NII model were the prevailing model. Thus the conventional organization of miners set up specialized units separately performing one of the four to eight work roles required on various kinds of coal faces. Not surprisingly, familiar problems bedeviled these operations. As Herbst explains:

> This form of work organization [gave] rise to difficulties in inter-group relations and in the coordination of activities in the various split-up [units], where each [unit] is responsible only for its own small segment of the total work cycle. The problems that arise out of the existence of isolated [units], each concerned with maximizing the earnings obtained by carrying out their task but dependent upon one another to get their work done, are particularly acute in longwall cycle mining, where the various tasks that form part of the coal-getting cycle have to be carried out sequentially. In these circumstances bad conditions left by one [unit] affect the team following them, and disturbances that arise tend to magnify as they spread from one work shift to the next, resulting in breakdowns of the total work cycle and loss of production. The resulting social climate tends to be one of low morale, with tension between the various task [units] and frequent disputes between men and management.[47]

Shades of Figures 13 through 15 (see pp. 182, 184, and 189). All of the symptoms are there, perhaps aggravated by the threat inherent in working underground in the dark and often alone.

The application to coal-mining of the principles and the NII model also generated the growth of a horribly complex system of wage administration. The system's costs included high tension, the development of a considerable staff to administer the system, and substantial pressures toward inefficiency in the bargain. Thus the shift foreman had to negotiate, if not fight about, a large portion of the men's wages. If this were not enough, a special rate was paid for finishing work left over or badly done by a preceding work unit. Consequently, some degree of inefficiency was profitable for the workers, a point that did not escape their attention.[48]

The managers of the mine in question did not foolishly opt for the

---

[47]Herbst, *op. cit.*, p. 9. For similar evidence, see E. L. Trist and K. W. Bamforth, "Some Social and Psychological Consequences of the Longwall Method of Coal-Getting," *Human Relations*, IV (February, 1951), 3-48; A. T. M. Wilson, E. L. Trist, and K. W. Bamforth, *The Bolshover System of Mining* (London: Tavistock Institute, Document 290 [restricted], 1951); and A. K. Rice, "Productivity and Social Organization in an Indian Weaving Shed," *Human Relations*, VI (November, 1953), 297-329.
[48]Herbst, *op. cit.*, p. 33.

proliferation of staff to administer and induce complexity. Given the choice of the "principles," however, there was no real choice of a wage system. (An hourly wage obviously would have reduced complexity, but the mines are dark!) The difficulties observed are predictable, then, and only their absence would be surprising.

The Autonomous Group tended to remedy this imperfect state of affairs. First, the reorganization eliminated the need for the corps of supervisors necessary to monitor the integration of the several monoprocessual units making their partial contributions to the total work cycle. The proliferation of "integrative" supervisors, of course, is implied by the principles and the NII model.

Second, the Autonomous Group negotiated an all-in, per-ton price for the coal extracted from a definite face. The traditional system was not so sensitive, with the probable consequence that a work unit encountering unfavorable working conditions on one face would rush through its work with a haste that would leave either its counterpart unit on the following shift or a unit on the same shift performing a succeeding operation with some "extra" work. Such a work unit then might loll through work at the next face where conditions were more sanguine. This herky-jerky pace led to interunit conflict, difficult supervisory problems, and so on. Relatedly, the wage system in the Autonomous Group did away with the need for the complex payment apparatus, much of the staff that administered it, and the sensitive negotiations with foremen concerning the time spent at various kinds of work which carried different rates.

Third, there were numerous signs that the Autonomous Group developed significant control over its members in ways congruent with the goals of management. The record on absenteeism provides a case in point. The simplified dynamics seem to have been these. Under the traditional theory of organization, the absence of workers does not necessarily affect their fellows. In the Autonomous Group, however, an absentee certainly does affect his fellow team members, who to maintain their income must work harder or longer since no replacements are provided. Or to say much the same thing, the former are not responsible for a discrete sub-assembly and the latter are. Herbst puts the matter less simplistically:

> In a small team where men are highly dependent on one another, the decision to go absent cannot be an entirely private one. The [Autonomous Group], being already one man short from the start, was exceptionally vulnerable to absenteeism and its unusually low absenteeism rate may in part be based on the fact that constraints arising from task requirements were such that it would

not afford the same high level found elsewhere in the pit. In conventional longwall mining [based upon the principles] absentees are generally replaced in order to maintain cycle progress. Also, no one [work unit] is immediately concerned with maintenance of cycle progress, so that there is no firm basis for the control of absenteeism within the [unit] itself.[49]

Consistent with the small-group literature,[50] structural models must be based on a recognition of group properties and their consequences. Organizing via autonomous groups or the Colleague model attempts to meet this requirement; the principles forfeit the contest.

Fourth, in general, the Autonomous Group compared favorably in socioemotional and physical output with the traditionally organized units. On the socioemotional level, the Autonomous Group avoided many of the tensions that plagued the conventionally organized work units. Its members noted favorably the reduction of tension, satisfaction with work seemed high,[51] and the strength of the social relations is amply suggested by such features as the sharp increase in the amount of work done by isolated miners in the Autonomous Group. That is, the unorthodox organization increased the power of the work team over its members, and thus over the work environment, with advantageous consequences for both the team and management.

The favorable comparisons extend beyond such "impractical" features as the socioemotional environment. In physical output, the Autonomous Group produced approximately the same tonnage per man-shift as crews that began work on the same face after the experimental period. The gross production data, however, are misleading. Thus the Autonomous Group "carried out all extra work such as extending and mending their belts and other maintenance and supply work," but additional specialized labor was supplied the conventionally organized unit for such work.

Approaching unity via diversity through the Autonomous Group method had its attractions, then, although not all work can be so handled. Thus a discrete sub-assembly is a prerequisite to management control through the quantity and quality of output. At the very least, large size is not a disqualifying factor. Thus the Standard

---

[49]*Ibid.*, p. 40.
[50]The probability that group power will be turned against the formal goals of an organization when the group is recognized in the breach seems great. For a detailed analysis of the typical dangers of management naivete, see Robert T. Golembiewski, *Behavior and Organization* (Chicago: Rand McNally, 1962), pp. 87-161.
[51]Herbst, *op. cit.*, pp. 5-6.

Organizing for the Colleague Concept:

Motor Company of England bases both its organization and its wage program upon large groupings, or "gangs," each of which includes all of the several contributions necessary for the assembly of motor vehicles. Melman notes that management kept track only of the final output of these gangs, of which there were fifteen. "Indirect workers" also profited from the bonus. As Melman concludes: "The effect of this gang system of production organization and of wage payment had the effect of installing a far-reaching system of production integration...."[52] Standard's approach goes very far toward organizing for the Colleague model, that is, and achieves many of the benefits stressed in the preceding analysis.

The Case for Diversity: One Perspective. Diversity—within rather wide limits—can be an avenue to unity in organizations. The quest for uniformity often has a spottier record. Consider the quest for uniformity as reflected in the matter of "human weakness" which results in an estimated loss of $1 billion per year despite the most elaborate overhead controls which the mind of man has been able to conceive.[53] The common reaction to such losses, of course, is more controls consistent with the NII concept. Thus the American Institute of Accountants suggests an organization based upon "a division of duties and responsibilities [so that] no one person will handle a transaction completely from beginning to end" in its system of "internal control." Given this solution, the Institute then prescribes how these various segments are to be welded into a "smoothly functioning unit." The stress upon unity-through-uniformity leaps through these words:

> Thus, management must always keep its finger on the organization's pulse to detect any tremors arising out of conflicts between departments which might arise, for example, from varying interpretations of authority or reluctance to yield authority as a matter of personal pride. Periodic conferences by management will provide a possible means not only of detecting such differences but also of rectifying them.[54]

Jerome hits the matter on the head when he evaluates these proposals. He notes that safeguarding a firm's property is certainly important, as are minimizing human errors and providing reliable accounting data. But the striking losses from dishonesty suggest the

---

[52]Melman, *Decision-Making and Productivity, op. cit.,* p. 12.
[53]Norman Jaspan and Hillel Black, *The Thief in the White Collar* (Philadelphia: Lippincott, 1960), p. 11.
[54]Committee on Auditing Procedure, American Institute of Accountants, *Internal Control: Special Report* (New York: American Institute of Accountants, 1949), p. 14.

poverty of the reliance on a system of organizational checks and balances. Emphasis upon maximizing productivity rather than minimizing losses attracts him. "Indeed," Jerome observes, "research in this whole area of human relationships indicates the great potential inherent in groups provided they are allowed to work out some of their own problems and to help set some of their own 'controls.' "[55]

Organizing for the Colleague model will help meet Jerome's challenge. Not only will team members tend to develop a conscience about stealing from their team, but organizing for the Colleague concept also sets the general framework within which the controller and the controllee are pulling in the same direction. The development and monitoring of "natural" measures of total performance thus can replace the close supervision of specific actions. As has often been demonstrated, natural measures tend to be accepted as objective and thus avoid the emotional conflict associated with measures that are imposed.[56] In addition, such measures no doubt would make it easier for superiors to intervene when performance lags significantly.[57]

Training and Developing Personnel:
A Side Effect of Organizing for the Colleague Concept

An important set of side effects of organizing for the Colleague concept, fourth, centers on the training and development of personnel. The value of an organization's human resources cannot be overestimated. Training or development programs which are not reinforced by a suitable structure do not realize this value optimally. In fact, frustration may set in as a consequence of the inability to practice on the job what the professors have preached at executive development sessions. Organizing around the Colleague model is aimed at a fuller utilization of an organization's human resources.

These side effects relevant to the training and development of personnel cover a very broad range. Attention here will be restricted to one of the features of organizing work consistent with the Colleague concept, job enlargement. In combination with the wide span of control, job enlargement could be practiced at all levels of organization. Consider a lower-level task with work components a,

---

[55]Jerome, *op. cit.*, p. 121.
[56]Rensis Likert, "Motivational Approach to Management Development," *Harvard Business Review*, XXXVII (July-August, 1959), 65-80.
[57]Villers, *op. cit.*, p. 131.

b, and *c*. Given fifteen workers, the traditional theory prescribes the routinized job pattern depicted in Figure 16A with each individual performing but a single operation under the close direction of a supervisor (*S*). Consistent with the Colleague model, however, each individual performs all (or as many as possible) of the steps *a*, *b*, and *c*, as depicted in Figure 16B. Integration is thereby facilitated, and the responsiblity for defective products can be traced easily. Hence the possible wider span of control. This notion would apply to all jobs whether they are of the program or the sustaining variety. Only the program official, S_{ABC}, is depicted in Figure 16B.

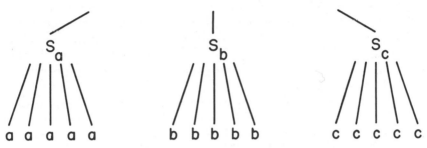

FIGURE 16A.   Two Low Levels of Organization, as Prescribed by the Principles.

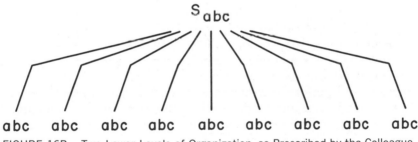

FIGURE 16B.   Two Lower Levels of Organization, as Prescribed by the Colleague Model.

FIGURE 16.   Two Ways of Organizing Jobs.

The structure depicted in Figure 16B may cause some pause for it violates two of the principles: It provides for neither the minute subdivision of tasks nor for a narrow span of control, both of which are central propositions of the traditional theory of organization. Neglect temporarily the question of a limited span of control, which without our attention is violated as often in practice as it is observed.[58] Certainly the specialization of work can be overdone.

<hr>
[58]See Harold Steiglitz, *Corporate Organization Structures*, Studies in Personnel Policy No. 183 (New York: National Industrial Conference Board, Inc., 1961). See

Much research supports the good effects of violations of extreme specialization under a wide variety of conditions. A humble task helps illustrate the point. That task is the answering of letters in a mail-order house. Originally, work had been patterned as in Figure 16A. Each clerk answered only a particular kind of letter, for which prewritten replies were available. The job was reorganized as in Figure 16B. Thus each clerk handled all types of letters, of which there were thirty-two, for all correspondents whose names began with a designated first letter or letters. In addition, the clerks were to make recommendations to their supervisor about that rare letter for which standard replies had not been developed. The two patterns of organizing work had sharply different consequences. In brief, the latter pattern saw output rise by some 30 per cent and turnover fall by two-thirds. Very considerable research further demonstrates that the favorable consequences are not peculiar to the specific case described.[59]

Reinforcing a Convenient Style with Suitable Structure: General Supervision and a Wide Span of Control. These summary results are intriguing, but the broader consequences of organizing work as in Figure 16B are many and (if anything) even more generally favorable. Thus the lesser pressure to integrate an organization's activities under the Colleague model at once encourages general supervision and permits a wider span of control. The present point must be interpreted carefully, however. General supervision may exist independently of the span of control, but a narrow span does not encourage it. Likewise, a wide span of control can mean administrative chaos if it is not coupled with nonarbitrary measures of performance that are at the heart of general supervision. The Colleague model makes the best of these qualified advantages. It facilitates measuring performance, and it implies motivational advantages.

The advantages of a general style of supervision may be adumbrated briefly. Thus it enables the supervisor to cover more territory for he is monitoring things rather than overseeing individuals. This helps avoid "personal criticism" and continuous, detailed instructions. Both set difficult obstacles to the training-and-development role that increasingly has come to characterize contemporary supervision. Moreover, studies reveal a usually pronounced association of general supervision with high output. Considering

also K. K. White, *Understanding the Company Organization Chart*, American Management Association Research Study No. 56 (New York: American Management Association, 1963).

[59]Theo Haimann, *Professional Management: Theory and Practice* (Boston: Houghton Mifflin, 1962), pp. 152-53; Drucker, *op. cit.*, pp. 281-92.

two levels of supervision in one study, only eight supervisors of twenty-seven who utilized close supervision had units with records of high output. "Close supervision" was defined in terms of frequent check-ups, detailed instructions, and very strict limits on the discretion of subordinates. The other side of the coin of supervisory style is no more favorable to close supervision. Thus fourteen of nineteen supervisors identified as using general supervision had work units with high output. "General supervision" implies the development of objectives and standards for performance, with the employee being given considerable leeway so long as his performance is acceptable.[60]

Let one qualification be underscored. For most participants, the possibility of general supervision under the Colleague model has much to recommend it. However, the Colleague model also will accommodate exceptions. That is, close supervision *and* high output *and* high satisfaction may exist simultaneously in a minority of cases. A supervisor under the Colleague model can adapt to a team with members whose personality characteristics are congenial to a close style of supervision. The NII concept and the principles are more jealous masters. These structural guidelines imply close supervision and preempt the question of supervisory style.

A wide span of control provides continuing reinforcement for supervisors to utilize general supervision,[61] and reinforcement is necessary because the role is alien to the training and experience of many supervisors. This observation may be taken as doing-in the present analysis, or very nearly so, but only if one accepts the common argument that the span of control cannot be widened beyond some arbitrary low limit except in those few cases in which the work of subordinates does not interlock.[62] The essence of this point is expanded to an industry-wide basis in such observations:

> Very complex or intricately coordinated operations, such as are found in manufacturing, military, and government organizations, need the discipline that is best maintained by tall structure [based upon the limited span of control.] Flat structure is more appropriate for loosely supervised and technically simple, though individually more challenging, operations, such as those of sales, service, political, and religious organizations.[63]

---

[60]Friedmann, *The Anatomy of Work, op. cit.,* pp. 40-67.
[61]Lawrence, *op. cit.,* pp. 69-129.
[62]Lyndall F. Urwick, "The Manager's Span of Control," *Harvard Business Review,* XXXIV (May-June, 1956), 45.
[63]Herbert E. Krugman, "Organization Structure and Organization Man," *Personnel,* XXXVIII (March-April, 1961), 22.

Does this analysis fall before such reasonably formulated observations? Not in the least. For, in essence, such observations imply this tautological dictum: If you respect the principles and the NII model in one or more respects, you must respect it in others. That is, if function or process is emphasized in organizing, jobs will tend to interlock, and a narrow span of control can be rejected only at the probable cost of considerable administrative chaos. The Colleague model violates the principles and is therefore not heir to these liabilities.

Lest this seem too precious, suggestive evidence permits the conclusion that organizing for the Colleague model can permit extended spans of control even under what seem inhospitable conditions. Consider two comparable plants in the auto industry. One was organized after the model of the principles and the NII concept, and the other was structured in ways consistent with major features of the Colleague model. The former plant had one supervisory foreman per (approximately) every ten production workers. This approaches the usually prescribed limit at low levels of organization. The latter plant, benefitting from such features as the ease of measuring and motivating performance implicit in approaches to the Colleague model, had one supervisory foreman for *every 250 production workers.*[64] At the very least, then, it seems that the full benefits of the Colleague model in the particular of widened span of control can be extended into industrial as well as merchandising contexts.

As with general supervision, a wide span of control can facilitate training and development. For one thing, supervisors must become training-and-development oriented; they have no other reasonable alternative. The virtual necessity has attractive consequences in favorable employee attitudes toward work and in effective performance.[65] A wider span of control also has other endearing features, among them being fewer organizational levels. This feature implies reduced supervisory and executive costs.[66]

Delegation: "Managerial Units" and Their Effects. The lower pressure for integration implicit in organizing for the Colleague model at once permits and rests upon substantial delegation. To recall Worthy's point, each Colleague team is an administrative unit, for it includes "that portion of the organization falling within [a

---

[64]Melman, *Decision-Making and Productivity, op. cit.,* p. 176.
[65]William F. Whyte, *Man and Organization* (Homewood, Ill.: Dorsey Press and Irwin, 1959), pp. 11-16.
[66]Ralph C. Davis, *The Influence of the Unit of Supervision and the Span of Executive Control on the Economy of Line Organization Structure* (Columbus: Ohio State Univ., Bureau of Business Research, 1941).

Organizing for the Colleague Concept:

single] jurisdiction [which] controls enough elements of the total process to make effective decisions regarding the total process." Schematically, the point may be made by contrasting Figures 17A and 17B, where the dotted lines enclose the administrative units in structures patterned after the principles and after the Colleague

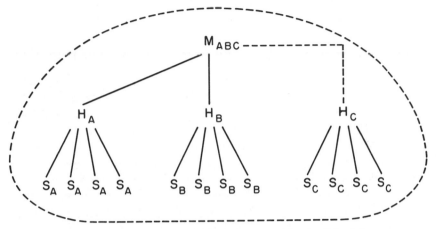

FIGURE 17A.   Managerial Unit Generated by the Principles.

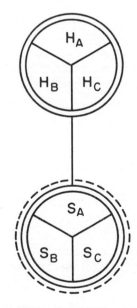

FIGURE 17B.   Managerial Unit Generated by Organizing for the Colleague Concept.

FIGURE 17.   Managerial Units in Different Formal Structures.

model, respectively. Assume that A, B, and C are some mix of program and sustaining activities. M designates the manager; H designates the head of a unit; and S designates a supervisor. Operating employees are not shown.

The possibilities of delegation implied by the different-sized administrative units generated by the two approaches to organizing may be outlined briefly. Roughly, the principles require larger administrative units, a datum that sets rather strict limits on the total size of organizations following this approach. The point is of enormous consequence. Consider Figure 17A. Notice that only M_{ABC}, two levels away from the action level, oversees enough operations to make reasonable decisions concerning some total bundle of activities. In Figure 17B, many such decisions may be made within the lower-level team. This is just the margin by which large organizations often become bureaucratized in the nasty sense of the term: Communication chains are lengthened, time is lost, and decisions are made far away from the action level. The catalog can be extended. Bernard Muller-Thym emphasizes these advantages of reducing the number of levels of supervision, for example:

> The necessary skills are highly concentrated near the point of action instead of being diffused throughout a large organization structure. Working relationships have directness and immediacy. (They are also remarkably free, easy, and effective.) Far more than usual, work controls itself; as a result, fewer people and less paper work are needed to get the work done. There is more flexibility; these units can change, meet daily crises, and adapt to new operating conditions.[67]

The advantages of smaller managerial units have shown up in research. For example, absenteeism seems to vary directly with the size of the administrative unit as Figure 18 shows. Since absenteeism may be regarded as a "leaving of the field" in reaction to a deprivation of needs within the work environment, the findings imply that larger managerial units poorly serve many significant needs of individuals in organizations.

The slim research on managerial units is not all of a piece, be it noted. Consider Worthy's seminal generalization that "mere size is unquestionably one of the most important factors in determining the quality of employee relationships: the smaller the unit the higher the morale and vice versa."[68] Despite the general accep-

---

[67]Bernard J. Muller-Thym, "Reconstructing the Supervisory Job," *Personnel*, XXXI (March, 1954), 404.
[68]James C. Worthy, "Organization Structure and Employee Morale," *American Sociological Review*, XV (1950), 172.

Organizing for the Colleague Concept:

tance of Worthy's proposition, research has provided only qualified support. For example, lower-level executives in small firms reported greater satisfaction than their counterparts in larger organizations. At higher levels, however, executives in large firms oppositely reported greater need fulfillment than executives in smaller firms.[69] If an explanation for this finding seems clear enough, ambiguity seems the order of the day in other findings. Thus Porter and Lawler found that job satisfaction in organizations

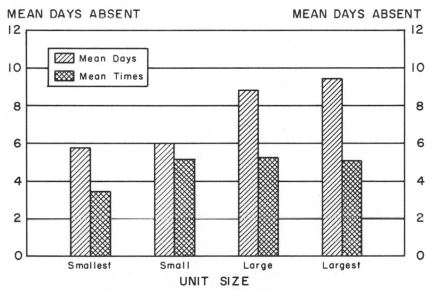

FIGURE 18. Absenteeism and Size of Basic Unit of Organization. From Howard Baumgartel, "Organization Size and Absenteeism," **Kansas Business Review,** X (July, 1958), Sec. 2, 3.

of less than 5000 employees was higher than in "flat" structures like that permitted by Figure 17B. This regularity suggests that the structure in Figure 17A is less in the service of man's needs. However, organizations with more than 5000 employees disturb the pattern. Employees in "flat" structures did not report more job satisfaction than employees in "tall" structures.[70] Sheer company size seemed an important variable in determining the degree to which executives felt their needs were fulfilled at work.

[69]Lyman W. Porter, "Job Attitudes in Management, IV: Perceived Deficiencies in Need Fulfillment as a Function of Size of Company," *Journal of Applied Psychology,* XLVII (1963), 386-97.
[70]Lyman W. Porter and Edward E. Lawler, "The Effects of 'Tall' versus 'Flat' Organization Structures on Managerial Job Satisfaction," *Personnel Psychology,* XVII (1964), 135-48.

What these data at partial sixes-and-sevens mean is uncertain, beyond underscoring the need for further research. Thus Triandis proposes a dual linkage between organization structure and satisfaction outcomes, via the concept of "congruence."[71] Perhaps. Alternatively, the heart of the matter may be that neither "size" nor organizational "flatness" is as important as the size of the "managerial units" in Figure 17.

The need to specify the size of managerial units in predictions about size and flatness may be supported briefly, based upon such unreconciled findings as those above. For example, a relatively small firm might have a "flat" structure with few levels of organization and yet still have large managerial units. Such a firm would not likely induce outcomes in employees like a similar firm with smaller managerial units. Indeed, one might expect a measure of chaos and disaffection.[72] And analytical extrapolations seem fairly convincing on the point that, whenever a choice exists, smaller managerial units are preferable.[73] In addition, the present insistence does not overlook the substantial operational issues involved in testing the suggested relation. The problem was solved by definition in Figure 17, which demonstrates that exactly the same work can be organized so as to yield managerial units of different sizes. Finding such different managerial units producing comparable work, or creating them in the laboratory, seems more than a challenge. But that challenge must be met before true comparative analysis is possible.

The costs of a large managerial unit, then, may more than counterbalance whatever psychic solace is gained from respecting the traditional theory of organization. As Davis notes: "For many organizations the answer is to decentralize into smaller units so that satisfactions may be more readily obtained."[74] This approach is built into the design of a structure for the Colleague concept.

These findings seem reasonable. Thus delegation tends to increase supervisory power. "Power" refers to the supervisors' control over significant aspects of work. Power is no conceptual curiosity, then, although it may seem the product of hairsplitting. Getting recommendations for promotion accepted, for example, is a

---

[71]Harry C. Triandis, "Notes on the Design of Organizations," in *Approaches to Organization Design,* ed. James D. Thompson (Pittsburgh, Pa.: Univ. of Pittsburgh Press, 1966), p. 78.
[72]Howard Baumgartel, "Organization Size and Absenteeism," *Kansas Business Review,* X (July, 1958), sec. 2, p. 3.
[73]Golembiewski, *Men, Management, and Morality, op. cit.,* ch. 7.
[74]Keith Davis, *Human Relations at Work* (New York: McGraw-Hill, 1962), p. 231.

sign of high supervisory power. Power thus conceptually complements "authority." The latter refers to the degree to which the
formal organization legitimates a supervisor's control of the work
environment; the former refers to actual control exercised (which
may or may not be legitimate). Typically, all supervisors at the same
level monitoring similar operations have similar authority. Typically, these supervisors will differ in their power.

Research accords power a prominent role in understanding behavior in organizations. Indeed, it can be said that most people
almost instinctively follow vectors of power.[75] Thus power is associated with the effectiveness of supervision, whether the power is
exercised "upward" (as influence with superiors) or "downward"
(as control of the specific job site). For example, Pelz studied some
fifty measures of supervisory practices and attitudes. He found no
marked relations with employee morale and attitudes until the
influence of a supervisor upward was specified. Then sharp differences appeared. High supervisory power was associated consistently with effective performance.[76] Similarly, power exercised
downwards as control of the work environment also is associated
with effective performance. Likert provides much supporting
data.[77] A comparison between the top third vs. the bottom third of
departments, ranked in terms of their productivity, makes the
present point. Personnel in the top departments attributed greater
influence over "what goes on in your department" than did individuals in the bottom departments to these four sources: higher
management, plant management, department manager, and the
workers themselves. Moreover, the top departments also desired
that greater influence be exercised by all four sources than did the
bottom departments.[78] These results are reasonable. A low-power
supervisor has little leverage for motivating his men via his control
over the job site. That is, the men have little reason to take him all
that seriously.

Power is a significant concept, then, and especially because it is
not governed by scarcity. Indeed, the results suggest that increasing the power of subordinates need not decrease that of the superior. This outlines a topsy-turvy world which much theory and

---

[75]See Dorwin Cartwright (ed.), *Studies in Social Power* (Ann Arbor: Univ. of Michigan, Institute of Social Research, 1959).
[76]Donald C. Pelz, "Interaction and Attitudes Between Scientists and Auxiliary Staff,"
Administrative Science Quarterly, IV (December, 1959), 321-26; and IV (March,
1960), 410-25.
[77]Likert, *op. cit.*, p. 114.
[78]*Ibid.*, pp. 56-57.

Details of Design and Major Side Effects

managerial action do not recognize. Reasonably, however, only a high-power supervisor feels secure enough to allow his subordinates to control their environment.[79] The low-power supervisor, although he may make a great show of "putting on the pressure," most often seems to fight a losing battle. Thus one careful study reported that the *more unreasonable pressure* exerted by a supervisor, the *less power* subordinates attributed to him.[80] Consistently, greater supervisory pressure isolates the supervisor, for he himself increases the danger of communicating.[81] To clinch matters, the degree of pressure seems inversely related to output. For example, ten of eleven departments in one study reporting little outside pressure to control the pace of work were above-average producers. Nine of ten departments reporting great pressure were below-average producers.[82]

Despite these impressive results, organizing by Colleague teams may seem to reduce the power of each of the Colleague group members, for many questions will be collegially decided, especially in the shakedown days. And this may be taken as a lack of power. Such an argument overlooks two points. Thus the subordinate members of any program or sustaining unit are still responsible to their heads, who will see that team decisions are implemented. And the Colleague group will be a prime carrier of recommendations to an upper-level team concerning salary increases and promotions. The lower-level Colleague group's decisions on such matters should carry great weight. Moreover, once a decision is made by a Colleague group, given good faith and the necessary administrative talent, unity of action is likely. That is, the officials can accomplish together what none of them could accomplish alone. This enhances the power of all Colleague group members, individually and collectively.

Moderating Organization By-Play. The argument may seem too tidy to this point or naively unaware of the fierce forces we call "ambition." Therefore, let us admit to argument that toughest of the flesh-and-blood aspects of living and prospering in organizations. The Colleague model may discipline the ways in which ambitious individuals gain high visibility, bluntly, while it also significantly aids the training and development of personnel. The point applies particularly to sustaining officials and may be illustrated by three

[79]James G. March, "Influence Measurement in Experimental and Semi-Experimental Groups," *Sociometry*, X (March, 1956), esp. 266-70.
[80]Likert, *op. cit.*, pp. 56-57.
[81]*Ibid.*, p. 45.
[82]*Ibid.*, p. 20.

techniques with which sustaining officials might seek to cultivate the support of higher-ranking officials.

"Watch Me!" "Show-boating" by sustaining officials to gain the support of high-level officials probably would not be a major problem under the Colleague concept. Compelling pressures upon sustaining personnel would encourage them to work within their team, their fate being closely tied to the performance of their team. Moreover any overenthusiastic attempts to sell programs would be likely to provoke sanctions by other team members, a matter of no little concern when the team evaluation of its members will be of importance to their futures. Indeed, with the premium placed upon cooperation between sustaining and program activities—and with the support of a structure congenial to that end—program officials under the Colleague model might offer less resistance to suggestions for change. Consequently, sustaining officials might strive less for high-level attention. From another point of view, were sustaining officials to avoid the "watch me" technique, program officials might be less predisposed to force them to get top-level approval for a proposal before lower-level program officials move a finger.

Only a choir boy can ignore that high-level officials sometimes tempt sustaining personnel severely to play a "watch me" role. Nor are sustaining officials always above taking credit they deserve, or seeking credit they do not deserve. Perhaps the major saving grace is that sustaining officials will be highly visible in the senses that the contributions to their team in their specialty will be credited to them directly and that they will have the opportunity to display their impact on efficiency over time in competition with sustaining personnel performing the same activities in other teams. The ideal is to assign but a single sustaining official from some single specialty to a team thereby providing a real test of his integrative abilities.

Indeed, it may be the case that, rather than the "watch me" role, Colleague team members may be motivated to hide their bright ideas for as long as possible so that their team might retain a competitive advantage. This possibility must be provided for, as by "tell-all" seminars at semiannual or annual sessions or by arrangements to sell innovations to other teams. Such arrangements would permit a team to profit from its own initiative, a virtual necessity if active innovation is to be encouraged. Suggestion programs may serve the same end. However, such by-pass techniques have their costs, and particularly in that they do not provide for the development of consensus among work-unit members who must implement the suggestion. As a matter of fact, such suggestions often will come from social isolates, since members of informal groups will tend to reserve innovations for their own use as a hedge against decreases in employment or increases in standards.[83]

However things work themselves out in practice, still other features support the Colleague model. Thus the several teams constitute ongoing laboratories in which several methods might be tried and compared. And since one demonstrated success is worth any number of potentials, this feature may be of great significance in encouraging change in organizations. In addition, a uniform approach is not necessarily the best. Two teams might hit upon quite different ways of completing their task that yield similar results. The Colleague model permits each team to try to find its own way. This reduces the need for overhead coordination, discourages pursuit of uniformity, and tends to free powerful creative forces within the teams. Chaos is not advocated, for the teams would be free within an area delimited by applicable general policies. As far as possible, however, the teams should be left to their own devices in determining the "how" of the "what" of policy. The relative rank of a team on performance will supply the crucial check upon the "how."

Finally, the teams are likely to prove very effective training grounds for both program and sustaining officials. This feature should reduce the probability of "watch me" efforts born of tedium and frustration. Decentralization has been the watchword of organizing for the team concept, and the lots of program and sustaining officials should profit. This should reduce the need for middle management to voice such dismal complaints. "We sit here all day pushing papers from top to bottom and back again," one of their number groaned. "All the while we are left out of the actual operations at the bottom, and we don't take part in decisions at the top. *We just push.*"[84] No wonder, then, that some individuals may seek any way to attract the attention necessary to wrench them upwards, whatever the consequences for the future integration of work.

"With a Smile, But Is It Service?" Organizing for the Colleague concept also would moderate attempts by sustaining officials to make a "good impression," thereby staying in the good graces of upper-level program officials. This cynical obsequiousness is often

---

[83]Relevantly, see "Work Group Ownership of an Improved Tool," in Lawrence, *et al., op. cit.,* pp. 260-65.
[84]Davis, *op. cit.,* p. 195.

stressed with distaste by program officials. The pattern of adaptation is understandable, however, given the organizational insecurity fostered by the NII model.

We make no plea that sustaining officials create "bad impressions" under the Colleague concept. Quite the contrary, for the performance of the teams will depend in crucial ways on how well program and sustaining officials find their way together. However, rather less emphasis should be placed on those aspects of the good impression—the dress, the lunch talk, and the like—which may detract from the cooperation of program and sustaining officials at the lower levels while they preserve a paper-thin good impression with upper-level program officials. Some sustaining officials, of course, might dislike losing such differentiae in being assigned to teams on the floor. Such folks are probably not particular catalysts of effective effort, but this does not solve the problem. Hopefully, the increased satisfactions of work will counterbalance the loss of being a marginal appendage of the front office.

In sum, then, the Colleague concept encourages the sustaining official to make his good impression in his work at the job site.

Wink While You Work. There is cooperation and cooperation, and not all of it is desirable. Let us put the matter bluntly. The Colleague concept may encourage the conspiracy of program and sustaining officials, the latter thereby winning the good graces of the former.

The detection of the latter type of cooperation sets a substantial task for upper-level teams and their program and sustaining officials. One of the major responsibilities of the upper-level team collectively and its officials individually, of course, is the development and monitoring of measures of performance. But this does not make the job an easy one. The Colleague concept, however, has its advantages. Thus undesirable cooperation seems endemic under the NII model. This pressure on sustaining and program officials to enter into collusive informal agreements probably will be lessened by organizing for the Colleague concept. To explain, such arrangements often are prompted by a mutual desire to get some breathing room, to gain some control of the environment, and perhaps to compensate for the awkward behaviors required by the principles and the NII model. In any case, the concept does nothing to allay these needs of the sustaining official or to dispel the very strong suspicion that effectiveness often requires behavior not sanctioned by the NII concept.

The Colleague concept provides more elbowroom for lower-level officials, whether program or sustaining. Thus there should be less need to get collusively what is there for the taking. Moreover, collusive arrangements should be inhibited by the facility of measuring the performance of teams. Efforts to hide monstrous errors will soon be found out, an important enough consideration. In addition, sustaining officials will have some measure of their effectiveness reflected in the performance of their teams. Moreover, sustaining officials probably would not face a generalized resistance to their program suggestions in an organization favoring the Colleague concept. Consequently, they would be under less pressure to act collusively as the quid pro quo for a sympathetic reaction to their suggestions.

Perhaps one should not be too pious about this matter, in conclusion. That is, much line-staff collusion is encouraged by the necessity and sanity of avoiding the unenforceable. Perhaps, indeed, "successful chicanery" (i.e., collusion which leads to more effective performance) ought to be tolerated more openly. "Unsuccessful chicanery" — given sensitive measures of team performance — should be more easy to spot in a Colleague-type organization than in an organization following the traditional theory.

Four Summary Emphases

The Colleague concept, then, implies a number of advantages. Four have been emphasized, although not in this order or under these heads. First, the concept patently has as its purpose the horizontal integration of the contributions of program and sustaining units. Ample reasons imply this purpose can be approached more closely in the Colleague concept than under the traditional organization theory and the NII model. Second, the Colleague concept probably would reduce the tendency toward vertically fragmented sub-organizations, a tendency which traditional organization theory and its associated Neutral and Inferior Instrument concept of staff only heighten. Third, the Colleague concept encourages the horizontal integration of the activities required for some discrete sub-assembly. The importance of such an effect should be patent, although it is not encouraged by the traditional staff concept. Fourth, the Colleague concept encourages the reduction of the pressure on sustaining officials to cultivate the support of the upper line in ways which have unsatisfactory effects upon the functioning of organizations. Problems remain, of course, but it seems that on balance the quest for "contacts" need not be so acute in an organization utilizing the Colleague concept.

Chapter 8
The Colleague Concept of Staff:
Its Place in the New Research on Organizations

The preceding chapters have run their longish course toward the redesign of the structural relations of program and sustaining activities. If nothing else, these chapters pay tribute to the tenacity of the simplistic Neutral and Inferior Instrument concept of line-staff relations. Its hold on the minds of organization theorists has been fearsome, and practitioners have given the concept at least passionate lip service. And this despite the fact that the NII model was a rather curious accident. It developed for many convenient reasons, but hardly for any convincing ones.

Of course, the intent of this volume has been to do more than question the methodological ancestry of the NII concept. The detailed development of a structure based upon the Colleague model distinguishes this effort from a considerable literature critical of the traditional staff concept. The case for the usefulness of this new design rests upon two straightforward propositions that are supported by the best available evidence. Given what we know about line-staff relations and what can be inferred reasonably, first, the NII concept suffers from a host of practical difficulties. The Colleague concept, with the same givens, second, fares better when confronted with recurring situations observed in the interaction of program and sustaining activities.

If these propositions were argued too affirmatively, the apparent certainty is held tentatively. The present effort attempts to synthesize considerable managerial practice and a mass of research and is a prelude to much practice and research that is yet to come. For implicit in the present analysis are a host of hypotheses which require more precise verification than the existing descriptive literature provides.

Bows toward tentativeness notwithstanding, the practical question is whether one will support a more, rather than a less, useful theory. This author feels no hesitancy about making a decision in this case.

But the argument thus far may say too much about issues that are relatively clear and too little about other issues which are less obvious. This imbalance will be rectified partially with some considerations in breadth to complement the preceding analysis in depth. The Colleague concept derives from a tradition of research that bids fair to overturn established patterns of thought about organization. Some of the major lines of research that motivated and continue to support this effort are outlined on the following pages, for they supply the philosophical and empirical foundations of the present attempt to redesign a formal structure. This outline, if brief, is necessary to avoid the hidden-ball methodology characteristic of the principles of traditional organization theory and the NII model of staff.

The Empirical Bases of Thinking About Organizations

The traditional theory of organization did not make it on its own. It derived massive support from, as well as reinforced, a body of ideas going back at least as far as the beginning of recorded history. That these ideas often were implicit only added to their power. Suppose that one chooses to argue with proposition 3 in the left-hand column in Theory X which presents the principles of traditional organization theory. These principles are the explicit propositions of what may be called Theory X. Despite the evidence that might be assembled to demonstrate that men do not often behave as proposition 3 requires[1] — and, more convincingly, that efficiency often is low when men do behave that way — one is not likely to disturb overly Theory X. For Theory X continues to draw strong support from a set of propositions, given in the right-hand column, which are often implicit and not usually considered systematically.[2]

Theory X Holds That Efficiency Will Be High When	*Theory X Assumes That*
1. authority flows in a single stream from organization superiors to subordinates;	1. work is inherently distasteful to most people;

---

[1] Chris Argyris, *Personality and Organization* (New York: Harper, 1957), pp. 175-208.
[2] Douglas McGregor developed the parent of this analysis in *The Human Side of Enterprise* (New York: McGraw-Hill, 1960), pp. 33-57.

The Colleague Concept of Staff:

Theory X Holds That Efficiency Will Be High When	*Theory X Assumes That*
2. supervision is detailed and the span of control is narrow;	2. most people prefer to be directed and have little desire for responsibility and little ambition;
3. the individual is considered to be a social isolate and only his physiological properties are respected in organizaing work; and	3. most people have little capacity for creativity in solving organization problems;
4. work is routinized.	4. motivation occurs only at a "bread and butter" level; and
	5. therefore, most people must be closely controlled, and often coerced, to achieve organization objectives.

Even when these usually implicit propositions are listed as has been done here, criticism of Theory X still faces a difficult target. As one student noted:

> The propositions of traditional organization theory, as McGregor demonstrated brilliantly, depend upon an *implicit* world view. This world view, at first glance, seems to describe *how things are*. But, on closer investigation, it dissolves into a melange of wishes about *how the world ought to be*.[3]

Hence the traditional theory of organization cannot lose for winning. If things do not turn out as the theory prescribes, that is, they ought to. Little escapes the nets of such an is/ought dualism.

It has taken students many years to clarify the nature of the implicit support for the explicit principles of traditional organization theory and to untangle the intermingled "is" and "ought" of Theory X. In the interim, any criticism of the principles faced heavy going. Therefore, as one consequence, the NII concept of staff was difficult to attack for it had the support of the principles. Moreover, in turn, the principles were buoyed by the implicit body of ideas outlined in the right-hand column.

The demonstration of the point is not possible here in detail, but Theory X cannot pass muster on an empirical level. Some relevant evidence (e.g., the findings about job enlargement) has been reviewed above; and in any case, a full-dress demonstration of the point has been made elsewhere.[4]

---

[3]Robert T. Golembiewski, *Behavior and Organization* (Chicago: Rand McNally, 1962), p. 75.

[4]Robert T. Golembiewski, "Organizing Work: Theories and Techniques," *Advanced Management — Office Executive*, I (June, 1962), 26-31.

Gradually, support has been growing for what has been called Theory Y. The propositions of this body of thought may be outlined briefly:

Theory Y Holds That Efficiency Will Be High When

1. authority flows from formal and informal sources – up, down, and across the organization – which are oriented in the same direction;
2. supervision is general and the span of control is wide;
3. the individual can behave as a social and psychological being – as well as a physiological being – that is, when work recognizes the fullness of man; and
4. the task is a meaningful whole, providing some variety and requiring some skill and judgment.

Theory Y Assumes That

1. work is as natural as play, if the conditions are favorable;
2. self-control is often indispensable in achieving organization goals;
3. self-control in line with organization objectives is a function of rewards which satisfy ego and social needs, as well as "bread and butter" needs;
4. the capacity for creativity in solving organizational problems is widely distributed in the population; and
5. the capacity for creativity is often underutilized in organizations.

The design of the Colleague structure attempts to reflect the properties and the spirit of Theory Y. Notice its emphasis upon discrete sub-assemblies as the basis for organizing. This emphasis is consistent with propositions 3 and 4 on the left. Similarly, the NII concept reflects the assumption that the capacity for creativity in solving organizational problems is (or should be) narrowly distributed, indeed so much so that the staff is specifically enjoined to "think" while the line must "do." The Colleague concept, of course, goes far in an opposite direction. Illustratively, organizing for the Colleague concept provides substantial room for the officials of a team to shape their own environment. Few would argue that Theory Y is complete and entire.[5] However, the analyst has no alternative but to combat as best he can the comprehensiveness of the body of thought supporting the principles and the NII model.

Acting on Theory Y in organizations very often will require massive attitudinal and behavioral change, and here again attempts to approach the Colleague model may be aided by "laboratory approaches" to organization development. That is to say, the organizational values consistent with laboratory training also are

---

[5]George Strauss, "Some Notes on Power-Equalization," in *The Social Science of Organizations*, ed. Harold J. Leavitt (Englewood Cliffs, N. J.: Prentice-Hall, 1962), pp. 39-84.

congenial to the Colleague model. The major values in question are:

1. full and free communication;
2. reliance on open consensus in managing conflict, as opposed to reliance on coercion or compromise;
3. influence based on competence rather than on whim or on formal authority;
4. expression of emotional as well as task-oriented behavior; and
5. acceptance of conflict between the individual and his organization, conflict that is to be coped with willingly and openly.[6]

As Argyris[7] and others have demonstrated, such values are inconsistent with or actually contradict commonly-held values about organizing work, whether these latter values be expressed as "Theory X" or "the pyramidal values." Implementing the Colleague model commonly will involve demonstrating the awkward consequences of such values in group situations, as well as developing consensus about a replacement set of values. Laboratory training is useful for both purposes.

The Crisis Basis of Organization Structure: Crisis, Neuroticism, and Creativity

There is a sense, subtle in its theory, sometimes gross in its practice, in which Theory X pays a heavy price for the ways in which it seeks to induce effort. The reference here is to the conditions under which men will contribute their efforts to coordinated activity. Needless to say, whatever one's judgment of Theory X, an awkward choice of such conditions implies fantastic costs. At the very least, Theory X and the NII model do not prescribe a set of conditions so useful that it is ridiculous to consider any alternatives.

Crisis as a Credo: Function and Pathology

One of the conditions implied by the traditional theory of organization may be considered in detail to make the present point: the

---

[6]Philip E. Slater and Warren G. Bennis, "Democracy Is Inevitable," *Harvard Business Review*, XLII (March-April, 1964), 51-59.
[7]Chris Argyris, "Interpersonal Barriers to Decision-Making," *Harvard Business Review*, XLIV (March-April, 1966), 84-97.

common practice among managers of creating crises to motivate action. Why are crises necessary? One executive explained the matter this way: "They are," he explained. "Without them the organization would not be alarmed, and without alarm there is not the highest motivation." Other executives noted that in the absence of crisis organizations would become "fat and happy," "sloppy," and "sluggish."[8]

The position invites critical scrutiny. Admittedly, no one has demonstrated that organizations can be run completely without artificial pressure and crisis. But the continual resort to crisis is not supported by compelling evidence, to say the least. Reliance on crisis is consistent with the principles and the NII model, but this does not establish that there is no alternative. Indeed, executives seem to view crisis with mixed emotions. They consider the end to which crisis is directed to be significant, but the means to be a two-edged sword at best. This exchange between a researcher and a group of executives demonstrates both points:

> Researcher: As an outsider I think you would go mad without a crisis.
> No. 5: People enjoy crisis.
> No. 2: Yes.
> No. 3: Yes—that's true.
> No. 11: That's our business....
> Someone: We hate them, but we love them.
> A Lot of People: Yes, yes, this is true. This is us.[9]

Such conflicting evaluations of crisis seem appropriate. For when management by crisis is put to the explicit test, it usually comes off second-best. Recall that close supervision (a kissing kin of management by crisis or pressure) runs a distant second to general supervision when the standard of comparison is the productivity of the work units of foremen employing one style or the other. Similarly, the recent studies by Likert provide no more support for the efficacy of crisis or pressure. Likert determined which departments in one organization felt "unreasonable pressure" from their superiors. These HiP departments compared unfavorably to LoP departments. Thus, paradoxically, HiP departments reported their supervisors had low power. Moreover, HiP departments strongly tended to have low output and also reported that their supervisors had low power. Ten of eleven departments reporting great outside

---

[8]Chris Argyris, *Interpersonal Competence and Organizational Effectiveness* (Homewood, Ill.: Dorsey Press and Irwin, 1962), pp. 115-16.
[9]*Ibid.*, p. 118.

pressure to control the pace of work, in one study, were below-average producers. Nine of ten LoP departments had above-average production records.[10]

The lack of potency of crisis over the longer haul also can be inferred from the reports of executives. Argyris' subtle effort provides a mine of relevant data. He met periodically with a group of executives to explore the relation of their interpersonal competence to organizational effectiveness. As the executives themselves revealed, the steady use of crisis had its substantial costs. First, Argyris' executives stressed the impact upon communications of the mistrust implied by the use of crisis. Communications with a never-never quality, for example, may serve at once to defend and to obscure. There is no calculating the costs of the word that was not spoken to avoid being too open, but the consequences are real enough. [11]

Second, crisis may have the effect of putting greater demands on superiors whose overloading might severely disrupt operations. For example, one junior executive had this reaction to the directiveness and impatience of many superiors: "After awhile, under these conditions, it's easier to go to the boss and say we have a problem and watch him work hard at solving it."[12] There are many convenient reasons why subordinates fall into the habit of dependence, convenience and lack of ability probably being the least among them. For example, the superior may derive great satisfaction from his dominance. The effects on training and development seem great and unfortunate, however, whatever the rationale.

Third, crisis and pressure may reduce the commitment they are designed to foster. Decisions may be forced, and follow-up may suffer thereby. As one executive reported: "If we're sure a decision will wind up in the boss's office, then we lose any sense of responsibility. We don't really feel committed to it."[13] Moreover, some information may be kept secret in order to induce crisis. The Finance Department of the company which supplied Argyris' ex-

---

[10]Rensis Likert, *New Patterns of Management* (New York: McGraw-Hill, 1961), pp. 30, 45. Existing concepts and operations are not adequate for the job, but such findings probably reflect in some part greater tolerance for "pressure" in highly productive groups. Consistently, for example, members of groups with high cohesiveness report lower levels of perceived anxiety than members of low cohesiveness groups. See Stanley Seashore, *Group Cohesiveness in the Industrial Work Group* (Ann Arbor, Mich.: Survey Research Center, Univ. of Michigan, 1954), esp. pp. 60-62.
[11]Argyris, *Interpersonal Competence and Organizational Effectiveness*, p. 121.
[12]*Ibid.*, p. 210.
[13]*Ibid.*, p. 210.

ecutives followed the practice, with many unhappy consequences. Since people did not have the necessary data, extreme bargaining was in order. Humankind being optimistic, the tendency was to think that Finance was being overcautious and that persistence might shake some funds loose. Such a practice can be frustrating, if not positively damaging to commitment to the organization, as an executive spoke of one such unintended consequence: "It's real hard to feel that you are a part of a team if in some plays you cannot get into the huddle."[14]

Fourth, crisis may pollute interpersonal relations. For example, superiors may employ the tactic of encouraging two subordinates to "fight out" some issue while adding the friendly advice that neither should feel obliged to give in. Of course, the decision then must be brought to the superior, which is what he had in mind all along. There is no doubt that the superior gains control in this way, but the costs may be great. Creating administrative situations which are "zero-sum games"—where someone loses and someone else wins —is not likely to encourage cooperative effort. No doubt some extreme efforts may be induced, but it is not clear that such efforts usually are designed to do the job better. Eliminating an opponent may be accomplished by technical superiority, but only one person need begin competing intensely on the social and political margins to set off a round of conflict which will be hard to forget.

Perhaps of great importance, the fostering of interdepartmental rivalries is implicit in the zero-sum strategy. As one executive noted, the strategy forces a great expenditure of "energy spent in building up our own or knocking down some one else's status." If the principles are followed, this often will prove a self-defeating game from an organizational point of view. The traditional theory of organization and the NII model encourage vertical fragmentation, and zero-sum games therefore aggravate an already grave situation.[15]

Organizing for the Colleague model tries to reduce these pressures toward vertical fragmentation. And if zero-sum games do exist between the teams under the Colleague concept, the stresses are bearable because the teams are performing parallel and comparable operations rather than sequential operations. In short, the stresses will not complicate the problems of integration, for the teams perform the necessary integration internally in the ideal case.

---

[14] *Ibid.*, p. 211.
[15] *Ibid.*, p. 209.

The Colleague Concept of Staff:

Crisis → Neuroticism → Creativity:
The Basic Organizational Sequence?

If perhaps more controversial, the impact of crisis upon the creative process deserves consideration. The organization structure certainly has an impact on behavior, and that includes creative thought. The traditional theory of organization implies that creative thought is encouraged by pressure upon the individual, by the induction of selective frustration that will trigger and sustain effort. The use of crisis as a management technique is consistent with this philosophy of motivation. The same notion also has far wider manifestations, as in the assumptions that genius is associated with neuroticism if not insanity, or that creativity is associated with illness or at least unusual behavior.

Such elements of folk mental science seem expendable. The old saw applies, if at all, only within narrow limits. The distinguished psychiatrist Kubie, for example, concludes that the "culturally noxious assumption" of the relation of creativity and mental instability has very strict limits indeed. The "ancient cliche," he reports, is devoid "as far as I can see of the least fragment of truth."[16] This conclusion shakes the spirit of the traditional theory of organization to its roots. For coercion and frustration figure prominently in the principles. Consider these conditions that have been found to be frustrating in experimental situations:

1. arbitrary change of a condition desired by a subject;
2. preventing the completion of a task;
3. inducing a feeling of failure and a sense of low ability;
4. interfering with the expression of a subject; and
5. leadership that is unsatisfactory to the subject.[17]

The principles do a noteworthy job of inducing these conditions, and the consequence often will be frustration:

> Traditional organization theory, then, cannot claim a low potential for frustration: for specialization has the effect of inducing Situation 2 [see p. 165 of this volume], and the limited span of control seems based upon the necessity of inducing Situations 3 and 4. Moreover, the directive style of supervision ... often will encourage em-

---

[16]Lawrence S. Kubie, *Neurotic Distortion of the Creative Process* (Lawrence: Univ. of Kansas Press, 1958), p. 4.
[17]Hilde Himmelweit, "A Review of Recent Experimental Work," in *Psychological Factors of Peace and War*, ed. T. H. Pear (New York: Philosophical Library, 1950), pp. 164-70.

ployees to conclude that Situation 5 exists. Finally, traditional organization theory assumes that Situation 1 has favorable consequences, as [in lack of participation in decision making].[18]

The NII model is an application of this underlying psychology of motivation. Staff is by intention an extension of the faculties of the line and as such often plays a punitive role as opposed to a role which positively facilitates work. The "up, over, and down" reporting required by the model sharply demonstrates the point.

The trick of unleashing man's creative potential seems not so much one of forcing out as of permitting expression, however. Kubie sees our neuroses, which all humankind must combat, as the prime repressive factor. As Kubie expressed the point:

> ... Man's actual creative productivity, as compared to his potential productivity, is pitifully reduced by the ubiquitous, masked, neurotic ingredients of what is euphemistically called "normal" human nature. Furthermore, the fragment of potential creativity which survives these neurotic inhibiting influences is first distorted in content and then is made rigid and stereotyped by these same veiled processes. What men succeed in creating is in spite of their struggles to overcome their neuroses, and not in any sense the fruit of these struggles.[19]

An organization theory generates stressful conditions at some cost, then, for two major reasons. First, the neurotic processes are shaped by experiences universal in infancy and early childhood, e.g., by the very fact that parents are big and formidable. Second, these processes might be triggered by events that (as Kubie notes) are not "exceptional or even especially stressful," and this with fearsome consequences. Thus there exists striking evidence that, even under "normal" conditions, the efficiency of the human organism has tremendous potential for improvement if man's total powers can be unchained. Consider the phenomenon of hypermnesia. Thus an individual, several minutes after being brought into a strange room, is asked to list every item he observed. Typically, a subject may reproduce twenty or thirty items. Given a similar command under hypnosis, which tends to free the individual from his restricted conscious self, the typical subject can go on to list perhaps another two hundred items.[20]

---

[18]Golembiewski, *Behavior and Organization, op. cit.*, p. 137.
[19]Kubie, *op. cit.*, p. 6.
[20]*Ibid.*, pp. 34, 35-36.

It is not being overly hasty to extend such data toward a provisional conclusion. The substantial contributions of the traditional theory at less complex stages of organized life under certain cultural conditions may be gainsaid. But matters have almost reached the stage at which this reworking of Kubie seems justified: What men succeed in creating is in spite of their struggles to work within the traditional theory of organization, and not in any significant sense the fruit of these struggles.

Stress as an End-Product: Some Wages of Stressful Structure

The preceding heading is not merely flamboyant. For many of the "unfavorable" factors in organized life — low satisfaction, low output, high interdepartmental conflict, and the like — reasonably are reactions to stressful situations. The principles and the NII model cannot win for losing in this case. They are cornucopias of stress-inducing forces, and as such they bet against long odds. For most individuals will avoid stress if possible,[21] or will develop defenses against stress if avoidance is not possible.

This point may be illustrated briefly. Assume that organization members feel great stress due to vertical fragmentation. Various tactics to avoid the stress — changing work relations, resigning, or the like — might be tried. If such tactics do not prove effective or are not convenient, defenses against the stress will be developed. Thus output might be low, or absenteeism high, or satisfaction low. Concurrently, sub-organization members might make a virtue of necessity. That is, they could develop highly cohesive social groups which would contribute to their members' mental health by reducing threat via the groups' control of the environment.[22] In turn, these groups heighten any tendencies toward vertical fragmentation.

The concept "stress," however, poses challenges as well as provides explanations. That is, stress has proved a valuable concept in the physical and biological[23] sciences where its meaning has been quite clear. The concept's meaning in the social sciences has

---

[21]Harry Stack Sullivan, "Tensions, Interpersonal and International," in *Tensions That Cause Wars*, ed. Hadley Cantril (Urbana: Univ. of Illinois Press, 1950), p. 95.
[22]Stanley E. Seashore, *op. cit.*, pp. 49, 67, 71.
[23]Hans Selye, *The Stress of Life* (New York: McGraw-Hill, 1956).

been less precise, a symptomatic reflection of which is the long-standing dispute over whether[24] or not[25] there is a "bridge of meaning" that connects social and physico-biological stress. Two items of conceptual unclarity deserve particular note. First, "stress" in the social sciences has been applied to a wide variety of cases exhibiting various intensities and durations. Thus battle conditions may be characterized as of severe intensity and extended duration,[26] bereavement in cultures emphasizing replaceable patterns of mutual obligations often seems of moderate intensity and intermediate duration,[27] and annoying insects imply mild intensity and brief duration.[28] Yet all have been used as examples of stress. Patently, the 6 x 6 table implicit in the three examples demonstrates that stress has been forced to cover vast conceptual ground in the social sciences. Second, "stress" has been used both as subject and object, as it were. Thus it has been defined as "the discomforting responses of persons in particular situations,"[29] that is, as an object. And stress has been defined as the stimulus or stimuli which at least by inference underlay such responses.[30] The difference can be significant for many purposes.

This minianalysis must plead guilty on both counts, although present purposes do not suffer greatly because of the fact. Given these imprecisions, it is still possible to suggest the impact of stress upon organized life. Thus some consequences favorable to an organization and its personnel may accrue from extreme stress, as in the intense attachments developed under combat conditions.[31] Most often, it is problematic whether the mixed consequences of stress benefit the individual or the organization. A case-in-point is provided by Mechanic's longitudinal study of graduate students taking their written general examinations.[32] In many cases, stress has consequences that seem deleterious to both individuals and (if

[24]Irving L. Janis, *Psychological Stress* (New York: Wiley, 1958), esp. pp. 11-13.
[25]Howard B. Kaplan and Samuel W. Bloom, "The Use of Sociological and Social Psychological Concepts in Physiological Research," *The Journal of Nervous and Mental Disease*, CXXXI (August, 1960), 128-134.
[26]Roy R. Grinker and J. P. Spiegel, *Men Under Stress* (New York: McGraw-Hill, 1945).
[27]Edmund H. Volkart, in collaboration with Stanley T. Michael, "Bereavement and Mental Health," in *Explorations in Social Psychiatry*, ed. Alexander H. Leighton, John A. Clausen, and Robert N. Wilson (New York: Basic Books, 1957), pp. 281-304.
[28]David Mechanic, *Students Under Stress* (Glencoe, Ill.: Free Press, 1962), p. 7n.
[29]*Ibid.*, p. 7.
[30]Harold Basowitz, Harold Persky, and Roy R. Grinker, *Anxiety and Stress* (New York: McGraw-Hill, 1955), p. 7.
[31]Grinker and Spiegel, *op. cit.*, pp. 21-22.
[32]Mechanic, *op. cit.*, esp. pp. 180-91.

by implication) to their organizations. This seems the import of findings such as those of Hinkle and Wolff,[33] who demonstrated the relation of illness with social and occupational conditions that the individuals perceived as stressful, that is, as frustrating their needs and aspirations.

There are methodological reservations concerning some of this work on the effects of social stress, and a direct and rigorous demonstration that the stresses induced by organization structure have significant psychoemotional consequences has seldom been attempted. All available evidence presses toward support of the point,[34] however, and organizational folklore is replete with cases-in-point. With it all, the leads are suggestive only (if frightening). Thus there is substantial evidence that even minor changes in the flow of work can induce extraordinary behavioral changes for good or ill. To a similar point, changes in organization structure may prove acutely stressful. Strauss presents some supporting data covering a twelve-month period after substantial changes were made in the structural relations of a group of twelve set-up men. The data imply a high incidence of emotional disturbances associated with prolonged stress:

Set-up Man A: Died of heart attack that was attributed to overwork.

Set-up Man B: Developed nervous twitches that became substantially more serious; is hospitalized with a painful back injury.

Set-up Man C: Had constant complaints of stomach pains; was taken to hospital reportedly for an emergency appendicitis operation, but after three days of observation, no organic faults were detected.

Set-up Man D: Had nervous breakdown; on advice of doctor left plant to work as bartender.

Set-up Man E: Developed stomach condition.

Set-up Man F: Was out sick for various reasons for twenty-three days in rush season quarter.

Set-up Man G: Developed hernia, was out for thirty-four days.[35]

---

[33]Lawrence E. Hinkle, Jr., and Harold G. Wolff, "Health and the Social Environment: Experimental Investigations," in *Explorations in Social Psychiatry, op. cit.*, pp. 105-32.

[34]Robert Kahn, *et al., Organizational Stress* (New York: Wiley, 1964). Descriptively, see Paul R. Lawrence, *The Changing of Organizational Behavior Patterns* (Boston: Graduate School of Business Administration, Harvard Univ., 1958), pp. 69-129.

[35]George Strauss, "The Set-Up Man: A Case Study of Organizational Change," *Human Organization*, XIII, No. 2 (1954), 23.

Similarly, various other significant complaints seem to have their origin in stress derived from structure.[36] More generally, adaptive reactions to stress may persist long after the stressful conditions have disappeared. Everyone familiar with organizations has encountered his share of the "overly careful" who, having been burned for administrative adventuresomeness, are forevermore reticent about making even trivial adaptations to their environment. Rats illustrate the point as well.[37]

Stress cannot and should not be eliminated. In organizing around teams in the Colleague model, in fact, a degree of constructive stress is patently retained. However, there seems far less potential for destructive stress under the Colleague model. Thus the retained potential for stress resides in the work and does not derive from the emotional and interpersonal sources aggravated by the NII model and the principles. Stress occurs naturally in the performance of work under the Colleague model. In contrast, stress must be created and sustained under the traditional model to force the integration of activities necessary for the performance of work. The difference is not niggling. For in the latter case, at least, someone (e.g., staff budget officials) must induce and sustain the stressful conditions. Stress then takes on a variety of unfortunate properties: It gets involved with questions of power and sub-organization development, it becomes more or less personal and more or less artificial, and, most important, the stressful conditions become very difficult to sustain and therefore will tend to appear capricious and arbitrary. These characteristics define "arbitrary stress."

Firm conclusions should not become our masters yet, although there seem convenient guides to understanding significant phenomena in organizations. For the research technology is not yet so developed that one may predict which type of structure will prove particularly stressful for which particular individual. But the principles and the NII model are culprits in the case of most individuals in organizations.[38] Moreover, a particular type of structure has proved less stressful to most individuals studied thus far. Argyris'

[36]Reginald Bennett, "Why Executives Die Young," *Scope*, (London, April, 1952), 115-16; William F. Whyte, *Human Relations in the Restaurant Industry* (New York: McGraw-Hill, 1948), pp. 64-81, support this proposition. More broadly, Kubie observes that "There is a widespread conviction that close interdependence exists between individual psychopathology and the pathology of social structure and of cultural forces." "Social Forces and the Neurotic Process," in *Explorations in Social Psychiatry, op. cit.*, p. 78.
[37]N. E. Miller, "Learnable Drives and Rewards," in *Handbook of Experimental Psychology*, ed. S. S. Stevens (New York: Wiley, 1951), pp. 435-72.
[38]Robert H. Guest, *Organizational Change: The Effect of Successful Leadership* (Homewood, Ill.: Dorsey Press and Irwin, 1962).

work is seminal on the point. He argues that stress will be reduced only as the organization structure permits the individual "to actualize his potential as much as possible." Argyris has translated this reasonable and general proposition into relatively specific characteristics of an effective organization structure. Thus a structure will approach the ideal for mental health as it increases the probabilities that employees can:

1. experience the wholeness of the organization;
2. be required to be self-responsible, self-directed, and self-motivated;
3. aspire toward excellence in problem-solving;
4. strive to decrease compulsive behavior and organization defenses and to increase control of the work environment;
5. utilize their abilities, especially their cognitive and interpersonal abilities; and
6. increase their time perspective.[30]

Organizing for the Colleague concept attempts to increase just such probabilities in restructuring line-staff relations. If it is not yet certain that the Colleague model is adequate for the job, this much seems clear: The Colleague model is a step toward a structure which will provide for personal self-actualization while it induces behavior well-suited to organizational success as measured by such criteria as high output, low cost, and high employee satisfaction.

The Perspective of Thinking About Organization: The Logics of Centralization and Decentralization

Thinking about the act of organizing also is undergoing a radical transition in terms of the angle from which it is to be viewed. Two such angles-of-view vie for attention, a "top, downward" view consistent with centralization and a "bottom, upward" view which is consistent with decentralization. The struggle is not inconsequential. For in organization theory, as elsewhere, the angle of view determines what one sees. The "top, downward" approach attempts to fit work to the organizer's preconceptions which usually derive from the principles. The "bottom, upward" approach attempts to tailor organization to the flow of work. The contrast could not be more marked.

---

[39]Chris Argyris, "The Integration of the Individual and the Organization," in *Social Science Approaches to Business Behavior,* ed. George B. Strother (Homewood, Ill.: Dorsey Press and Irwin, 1962), p. 76.

The Centrality of the "Flow of Work"

More sharply, the principles describe a "trickle down" type of organizing. That is, below the level of the chief executive, the organizer isolates the major functions (personnel, engineering, legal, and the like). And each of these functions is divided in terms of sub-functions (e.g., wage and salary administration), and then at lower levels in terms of processes (e.g., filing). This vertical emphasis is wonderful in the classic sense of the term. For emphasis tends to monopolize attention, despite the fact that the flow of work and the horizontal relations associated with it seem of great significance in understanding organized life.[40] Landsberger put the matter directly in terms of these three propositions:

1. that horizontal relations and flows of work across the organization may rival the vertical flow of authoritative orders both in incidence and significance;
2. that these horizontal relations and flows of work may be found at all levels; and
3. that these horizontal relations and flows of work at the several organizational levels may be considered as "relatively independent and qualitatively different from each other."[41]

Organizational behavior, as viewed in its horizontal dimensions, may be motivated by a wide variety of factors. Thus horizontal relations may result from the complex amalgams of personal ambitions and personal and group rivalries that characterize much of organized life. The glue of such relations may have little or nothing to do with work-relevant factors, i.e., the importance of membership in the Masonic Order in understanding horizontal relations in an organization. Or horizontal relations may be induced as a particular consequence of *some specific flow of work* as it relates units, for good or ill, in some flow of effort. Landsberger also stressed what he calls "genuine objective dilemmas" that encourage horizontal relations, such dilemmas being illustrated by the always-present choice between the short-run and the long.[42] Such dilemmas may be thought of as more or less universal consequences of *any general flow of work*. And several sources may foster such relations simultaneously. That is, horizontal relations encouraged

---

[40]Leonard R. Sayles, *Managerial Behavior* (New York: McGraw-Hill, 1964), esp. Chs. 4-6.
[41]Henry A. Landsberger, "The Horizontal Dimension in Bureaucracy," *Administrative Science Quarterly*, VI (December, 1961), 299-332.
[42]*Ibid.*, pp. 299-300.

by a specific flow of work may be reinforced by race, or religion, or what have you.

Horizontal relations are a terra incognita in their largest part, but our ignorance is far from total. First, many advocates of the principles were aware of the horizontal dimension of work. The overwhelming tendency, however, was to attempt to design work so as to preclude such relations or to treat them as permissible only in exceptional cases and/or as empirically unusual.[43] In any case, horizontal relations have been of marginal concern.[44]

Second, horizontal relations are "there," and prominently so. Various attempts have been made of late to measure the incidence of "across" transactions. Table 8 presents some typical data. It indicates a substantial volume of horizontal interactions, while there seem significant differences between functions. This dual pattern obviously sets a difficult chore for organization design and no less obviously demonstrates the mischievous myopia of the principles in neglecting horizontal relations.

Third, the prevalence of horizontal relations implies that much of the work of organizations must be carried out informally and, as it were, illegally. For the principles do not legitimate horizontal relations, although such relations exist and apparently often must exist for the organization to function effectively. No doubt the conflict between the stress on the legitimacy of the formal organization and the necessity of (largely) extralegal horizontal relations constitutes a severe conflict situation for many individuals. As Dubin concludes:

> A remarkable amount of total time is spent by all ranks of management with organizational peers, which, by inference, leads to the conclusion that much of the active coordination of actual work of the organization is carried out through nonformal relations [as defined by the principles of organization].[45]

This feature may make organized life generally upsetting for many, a fact of enormous significance.

Organizing for the Colleague concept does not treat the flow of work as a bastard child at a family outing. The flow of work is of central concern. This is the significance of the emphasis throughout on discrete sub-assemblies or products. The emphasis requires that

---

[43]*Ibid.*, pp. 301-5.
[44]Eliot D. Chapple and Leonard R. Sayles, *The Measure of Management* (New York: Macmillan, 1961), p. 20.
[45]Robert Dubin, "Business Behavior *Behaviorally* Viewed," in *Social Science Approaches to Business Behavior, op. cit.,* p. 25.

one begin organizing in terms of the flow of work, the primary level of organization being composed of Colleague teams performing chunks of work whose operations constitute meaningful and manageable wholes. The common consequence of the traditional approach is unmanageable organizational units at all levels. In contrast to the common approach, also, overhead levels in the Colleague model are added *as needed* to monitor the management of teams producing a discrete sub-assembly. In the principles, the organization of work is the residual of organizing top management rather than its guide.

Organizing for the Colleague concept, then, presumes that structure will be built upward from the flow of work, rather than downward from some a priori principles. Fitting structure to work, rather than vice versa, seems reasonable, even if it does not permit the codification of a brief and simplistic set of rules of how one organizes always and ever. And this says it all. For the reasonable is no general match for the convenient.

The intention of the Colleague design, then, is dual. First, the attempt is to legitimate those relations required by any flow of work. The principles go against the grain of work. Relatedly, the hope is that each Colleague team will be the locus for horizontal relations tying together all of the operations necessary to perform some discrete sub-assembly. Personal ambitions, in short, may be served only as a team succeeds. One need be under no allusions that some utopia will shortly follow the inauguration of the Colleague approach. But there seems ample hope of a significant moderation of behaviors that perhaps once served organization purposes but presently tend to be dysfunctional in the sociologist's sense of the term.

Second, organizing for the Colleague concept attempts to follow through the logic of decentralization in respecting the flow of work.

TABLE 8. HORIZONTAL INTERACTIONS OF THREE DEPARTMENT HEADS
IN SEVERAL PLANTS

| | Horizontal Interactions As Percentages of Total Interactions Originated and Received | | | |
| | Originated | | Received | |
Organizational Unit	Plant A %	Plant B %	Plant A %	Plant B %
Production Planning and Control	31.5	40.1	30.7	48.9
Production	16.8	41.2	22.4	40.2
Sales Liaison	61.7	61.5	56.9	63.7
Total	39.1	48.2	38.4	51.9

From Henry A. Landsberger, "The Horizontal Dimension in Bureaucracy," **Administrative Science Quarterly**, VI (December, 1961), 315.

The Colleague Concept of Staff:

Decentralization has been a major remedy for what ails large organizations, but it seldom has been carried below the plant level in any comprehensive way. Where decentralization has been applied widely in organizations—as in Sears or IBM—experience seems quite favorable. Organizing for the Colleague concept attempts to capitalize on the full potential implicit in the placing of responsibility and authority for the management of work where that work is to be done.

The Flow of Work and Decentralization:
Organizing for the Colleague Concept Illustrated

The interacting salubrious effects of focusing on the flow of work, of decentralization, and of organizing for the Colleague concept may be illustrated by an extended example. The example does not deal with a full-fledged approach to organization by Colleague teams. It approaches the new model developed here, however. In addition, the example demonstrates again the vertically fragmenting tendencies of the traditional theory of organization and the attractive pay-offs of organizing in ways consistent with the Colleague concept.

A Case Study of Integrative Problems: Plant S. Integrative problems at work are common. By design, moving toward the Colleague model intends to reduce integrative problems that can create difficulties impeding the flow of work. Therefore, approaching the Colleague model would seem to have much to recommend it.

Life has a perverse habit of avoiding such logical nets, however. Therefore, at the expense of belaboring the already-established, the focus here is upon a typical integrative difficulty that developed in a set of assembly operations and upon the ways in which integration was enhanced by approaching the Colleague model. To set the stage, Figure 19 outlines the original structure of the several activities, the tidy formal organization of several line and staff units. The NII concept governs their relations. Only the inspection activity presents any novelty, and it will be discussed later in some detail. For the rest, the organizational separation of the four functions follows the traditional theory of organization. These assembly operations, then, may serve to illustrate the general integrative problems posed by the principles.

Figure 19, if it has a certain pleasing symmetry, did not in all significant senses facilitate the flow of work. Indeed, it hindered

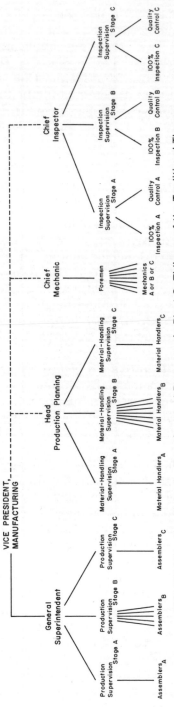

FIGURE 19. Organizing by Functions and Processes in Plant S: Tidiness of the Traditional Theory.

the flow of work in almost all ways. This is a grievous indictment, of course. Figure 20 takes a first step in supporting this indictment. It reveals that, rather than being organizationally divisible into functional and processual units, the flow of work demanded a complex linkage of the several functions and processes at several points. Discrete centers of activity in the flow of work could be distinguished in the sets of activities required for the three stages of production. But these centers of activity did not coincide with the organization units prescribed by the formal structure.

Experience in Plant S, as elsewhere, supports the reasonable proposition that the integration of activities cannot be expected in the absence of suitable structural arrangements. The specific difficulties in Plant S of integrating the component activities may be detailed conveniently by considering each of the three staff units in turn. Generally, as Chapple and Sayles note: "... foremen, general foremen, and superintendents were constantly calling each other ... to straighten things out. The constant arguments could only be settled by the vice-president in charge of manufacturing."[46] Such vertical fragmentation of organization units — both line and staff — is an expected consequence of the traditional pattern of organization.

Inspection and Integrative Problems. Inspection was one of the three activities separated organizationally from the line chain of command connecting the assembly operations. Two types of inspection were involved: A 100 per cent, if cursory and visual, check of output as a part of the finishing process was performed by one set of inspectors, and a quality-control inspection, utilizing sampling methods, was performed by other inspectorial units.

The traditional theory requires the organizational separation of production and inspection on the grounds that production people might not give due attention to quality, but the theory often pays a stiff price for its way of assuring that such due attention is given. The application of the point to Plant S may be made tersely: The 100 per cent inspection was "the source of frequent holdups that seriously aggravated the relationship of production and inspection personnel." This inspection was in the midst of the work flow and had to be performed in close time-sequence with at least two assembly steps. The intramanagement feud, then, resulted from the necessity of balancing operations of two organizationally separate units whose common superior was three or four levels removed from the action level. The superior's intervention often was nec-

---

[46]Chapple and Sayles, *op. cit.*, p. 29.

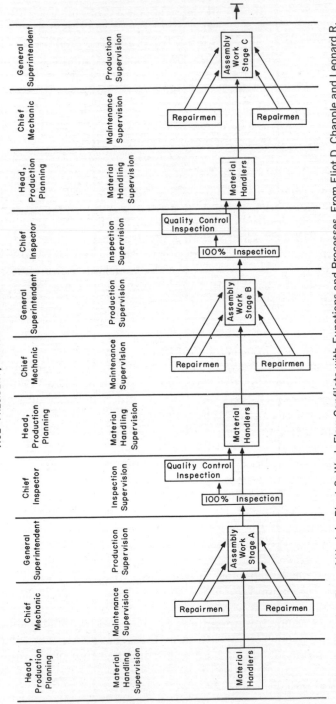

VICE PRESIDENT, MANUFACTURING

FIGURE 20. The Flow of Work in Plant S: Work Flow Conflicts with Functions and Processes. From Eliot D. Chapple and Leonard R. Sayles, **The Measure of Management** (New York: Macmillan, 1961), p. 28.

The Colleague Concept of Staff:

essary to settle (at least temporarily) squabbles between the lower-level supervisors of the three production stages and of the two types of inspections.

Significantly, the quality-control inspection in Plant S was not a source of great difficulty. It was on a different production sequence, thereby reducing the need for the close coordination of their efforts and those of the assemblers. In the terminology of this analysis, the 100 per cent inspection was part of the "discrete sub-assembly" which included the three assembly operations. The quality-control inspection was not part of this flow of work and, indeed, provides management with one of the measures of performance required by the Colleague model.

The situation was volatile in Plant S. Line supervisors could legitimately demand service from the inspection units, given their organizational superiority. But sustaining units did have their sources of power. Thus they could affect the record of any line unit, as by a slowdown of the 100 per cent inspection. Moreover, staff was directly responsible to a staff official rather than to someone in the lower line. This exemplifies how "power without responsibility" reinforces a high potential for vertical fragmentation.

Maintenance and Integrative Problems. The integrative difficulties in Plant S were compounded by tensions between production and maintenance personnel. As the traditional theory prescribes, repairmen were organized under a Chief Mechanic who reported directly to the Vice-President of Manufacturing. The assembly workers reported to the General Superintendent, who in turn reported to the manufacturing vice-president. The underlying expectation of the principles is that efficiency is thereby increased and money saved. The expectation heavily leans on the position that, *all other things being equal,* such serial organization implies less loss due to overstaffing than does a parallel organization in which mechanics are assigned directly to each assembly unit and report directly to the unit's foreman and thence to the General Foreman. The latter approach, it is commonly argued, is prone to suffer from overstaffing in all units, or too much in some units and too little in others. A serial organization saves on this possible "fractional loss" by assigning workers to a central pool and sending them where they are needed rather than by assigning them to a work station permanently. Maintenance activities are more episodic than production activities and therefore are commonly organized separately from production units. The two activities have a common superior only one or more levels above that of their immediate supervisors.

In Plant S, "all other things" were not equal. The expectations of the principles were not realized, therefore. The costs of integration, tersely, outweighed whatever advantages were realized from reduction of fractional loss. Thus Plant S operated its mechanics' services on a first-come, first-served basis. If a breakdown occurred in some program unit, the foreman signaled by a call light. Problems arose if the light flashed when mechanics were otherwise occupied, however, which was often. The resulting conflict set line against staff and program unit *vs.* program unit. Consider two conditions. First, when all mechanics were busy in another department, the "first-come, first-served" basis was not likely to be satisfactory to the foreman with a rush order facing him. Second, a mechanic often would be performing some regular activities in Department A when he was needed for an emergency in Department B. The supervisor of Department B then would request the mechanic's foreman for a reassignment. These requests were not always honored without resistance. For the regular program of the mechanics was being disrupted and the mechanics could argue that most breakdowns could be avoided if the line gave a little more attention to preventive maintenance. Line supervisors could counter with the charge that the mechanics were stubborn, did not appreciate production problems, and were there to help rather than to get in the way. The force of such charges, however, was much diluted. For line supervisors argued with one another about informal priorities as much as with the mechanics.[47]

Such difficulties created by a firm devotion to the principles and to the NII concept resisted easy solution. The manufacturing vice-president attempted to encourage the development of priorities for repair of machines and schedules of preventive maintenance, all to little avail. The assembly foremen and the mechanics' foreman often ended up in the vice-president's office with grievances, and the latter made the decision.

The reasons for such unabated tension are far from trivial. Thus the mechanics' supervisor had to preserve his influence over his subordinates. No doubt, in addition, "who got service when" was a major source of control over the environment by sustaining officials. The mechanics' supervisor also had to beware of offending powerful program supervisors. This respect for reality is necessary for the former's well-being and for that of his mechanics, as in promotions and perhaps in pay increases. Such respect also may be a source of discontent for less-endowed supervisors. If this seems too unvar-

---

[47] Strauss, "The Set-Up Man," *op. cit.*, pp. 17-25.

The Colleague Concept of Staff:

nished, legitimate conflicts of interest make matters worse. That is, program officials can complain that "repairing the wrong machines" hurts their productivity, which is certainly the case. The mechanics, in turn, can complain that a little more time spent on preventive maintenance by program officials would allow the mechanics to respond to emergencies with fewer disruptions to the maintenance program. This was a point of some significance for maintenance, although not of great interest to program officials.

Materials Handling and Integrative Problems. The story was similar for materials handling. The department reported to the Head of Production Planning who developed and monitored the master schedule for production. Variations from this master schedule were at the heart of the integrative problems induced, and the common variations were compounded by the lack of coordination between the four organizationally-separate hierarchies involved in the flow of work. The vice-president had to handle the disturbances occasioned, for example, by the lack of materials resulting from output levels higher than the master schedule assumed. In terms of earlier analysis, the managerial unit in Plant S was a very large one and only the vice-president could make reasonable decisions about integrating the several activities required for the flow of work. No wonder, then, that he was a man in much demand. The structure of work made it highly probable that most non-trivial issues would end up on his desk.

Organizing for the Colleague Concept in Plant S. Such problems in Plant S are precisely those for which the Colleague model of program and sustaining relations has been developed. It is a simple matter to fit the Colleague model to the work flow in Plant S, as in Figure 21. The nature of the work load, the technology, or other factors might require adaptations of this general model. For example, there might not be enough mechanics' work to warrant a Maintenance Supervisor for each team. Such a supervisor then might be given an assignment on two or more teams. This is consistent with the Colleague concept, although it might dilute the intensity of a supervisor's identification with *a* team. This dilution has costs and benefits, whose weight will vary from case to case. Similarly, it might not be possible technically to have each operator perform all steps *a, b,* and *c.* This would be a substantial loss, for such job enlargement—extending decentralization to its logical conclusion—can be a powerful motivator of work. Job rotation might be a feasible alternative, however, with many favorable consequences.

These may be overly fussy reservations. For the Colleague pattern seems generally applicable. Notice only that Quality-Control Inspection, an activity outside the flow of work in question, provides one of the sources of overhead general supervision consistent with the Colleague model. This design feature illustrates

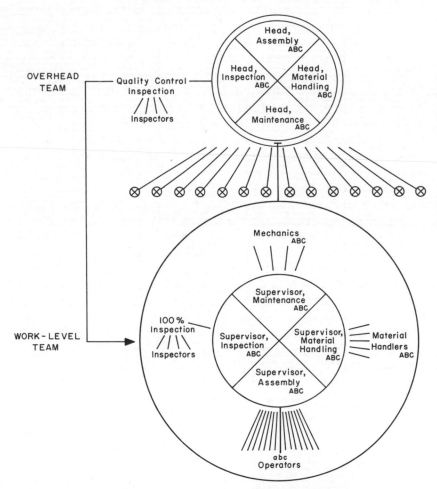

FIGURE 21. Ideal Colleague Relations for Plant S.

how an overhead team can monitor performance without clogging the flow of work.

Actual Reorganization in Plant S: The Colleague Concept Approach and Avoided. The stresses in Plant S precipitated an actual reorganization whose general character is reflected in Figure 22. The reorganization approached the Colleague concept in a number of respects and avoided it in others. Detailing the senses in which this is the case should demonstrate how the pressure of

The Colleague Concept of Staff:

events encouraged rejection of the logic of the traditional theory and precipitated a reorganization that did not fully exploit the logic of the Colleague model. Figure 22 helps establish both rejection and redesign.

In some particulars, the reorganization of Plant S was complex. The task here may be simplified by concentrating on the mechanics. Notice that mechanics have been assigned to program superiors, more precisely to general foremen in some cases and to supervisors in others. This moved toward the Colleague concept. Although no provisions were made for the equal representation of a mechanic's foreman on the assembly units to which the mechanics had been assigned, greater consultation probably was encouraged. In addition, although the Chief Mechanic was not formally made a partner of an overhead team, his responsibilities were focused upon the training of mechanics and the development and monitoring of standards for the work of the individual mechanics. The long-run danger is that the Chief Mechanic will lose power and, consequently, that maintenance will be slighted. The Colleague model guards against such an outcome.

These few details permit useful characterization of the two structural patterns. Decentralization was encouraged in the reorganization in two ways. First, mechanics were assigned to each of the assembly operations. Second, performance was monitored in terms of general objectives. The old structural arrangement, in contrast, encouraged centralization as program and sustaining officials struggled to control their operatives closely and to marshal their forces for appearances before the vice-president in charge of manufacturing. Paradoxically, the vice-president's intervention had the perverse effects of encouraging further centralization and of reducing the power of lower-level program and sustaining officials alike. The results suggest the usefulness of even more ambitious approaches toward the Colleague model. As Chapple and Sayles conclude:

> As a result, the conflicts ended, and the vice-president was able to devote time to more constructive activities than settling intramanagement rows. In terms of cost, the company was better off than before. Although the original centralization of facilities appeared efficient, no additional mechanics were needed for the reorganization, and it reduced delays in the work flow because of mechanical failure, actually saving money for the company.[48]

This is powerful encouragement for even more decisive breaks with the traditional theory of organization and with the Neutral and Inferior Instrument concept of line-staff relations.

---

[48]Chapple and Sayles, *op. cit.*, p. 32.

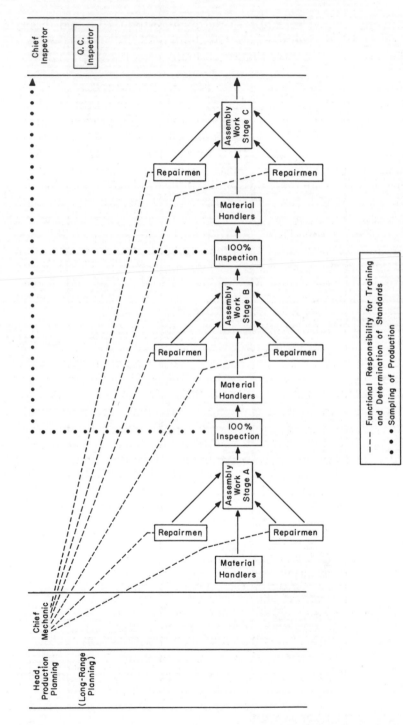

FIGURE 22. Actual Reorganization of Plant S. From Eliot D. Chapple and Leonard R. Sayles, **The Measure of Management** (New York: Macmillan, 1961), p. 30.

The Colleague Concept of Staff:

The Integrative Basis of Organization Theory:
Organizing for the Colleague Concept

Organizing for the Colleague model attempts, within limits presently realizable, to move away from unnecessary stress and repression, and this by maximizing the chances of horizontal integration. This dictates the choice of parallel teams. It also permits the exploitation of such research findings as the common efficacy of general supervision and the wide span of control.

Surprisingly, the emphasis upon integration has received little notice. The principle of specialization has had the lion's share of attention. Although defenders of the unity of command are not lacking, it has been accommodated to specialization only via such devices as the NII concept of staff. The result is an organization structure fragmented around "partial" specialized contributions to a total work cycle, an effort legitimated in terms of the unity of command it subverts.

In extreme opposition, this analysis has attempted to accommodate both the unity of command and specialization. That is, the guiding question has been: How can the various program and sustaining specialties be formally organized so as to encourage that most personnel will be oriented in the same direction as often as possible? The Colleague structure was the answer.

Notice that in this effort to accommodate the principle of unity of command to specialization, the meaning of the former concept has been changed. The traditional notion is that unity of command means direction by a single head. Proponents of this point of view did not seem to have envisioned that a Dr. Jekyll/Mr. Hyde might be in command. Less facetiously, no complex organization can approach this notion of monolithic direction, although the meaning is still the most current one. The definition of unity of command here has been changed to that of some organized group working so as to encourage the achievement of a similar goal. As is common in our paradoxical social and psychological worlds, interteam competition was the most convenient approach to unity of command defined as pulling in a similar direction rather than as dictation by a single head.

There has been much trite talk and writing about "working together." This pious effort is impoverished by the failure to reinforce preachment with suitable structure. The structural design for the Colleague model attempts to achieve the same end, albeit in two apparently conflicting ways. That is, team members work together in the accepted sense. However, the relations between several teams at the same level of organization may be described as working together toward the same goal, although autonomously if not competitively. In this respect, as in others, the secret of successful organized life lies not in logically overcoming such apparent paradoxes but in making use of them. That is, the task of organizational design imposes contradictory demands, and they must be met on their own ground. As Maier and Hayes observe, the "unique and optimal condition" in organizations requires avoiding "the pitfalls of irresponsible individualism ... and blind conformity." They conclude: "The objective is to find a synthesis: a new creative climate within the framework of organization."[49] This analysis accepted that challenge.

Revolution by Computer:
Effects on Organization Structure

Literally within the last few years, the computer has risen to occupy a significant place in the arsenal of management tools. The power of the computer is very considerable, and the boundaries of its potential applications are dimly recognized at best. Two propositions seem relatively safe, however. Thus the computer will have a major impact upon the organization structure appropriate for guiding behavior. In addition, in broad outline at least, the computer does not seem congenial to the principles or to the NII concept of staff. If the point must be made somewhat hesitantly, organizing for the Colleague concept seems consistent with the demands of the computer and, more generally, of automated operations.[50] The computer can be used to support the new centralization as well as the new decentralization.[51] Thus the point here is not that the

---

[49]Norman R. F. Maier and John J. Hayes, *Creative Management* (New York: Wiley, 1962), p. 37.

[50]Confirmation of many of the emphases of this section may be found in such sources as: John Diebold, *Automation* (New York: Van Nostrand, 1952), esp. conclusions at p. 53; Charles R. Walker, *Toward the Automated Factory* (New Haven: Yale Univ. Press, 1957); and many others.

[51]Many commentators have predicted a re-centralization spurred by computers, as did Herbert Simon, *The New Science of Decision-Making* (New York: Harper & Bros., 1960). However, experience has generally violated the prediction. Thus, less than one in ten executives in some 200 major corporations felt that electronic data processing would reverse the trend toward decentralized management. See "Will New Methods of Data Processing Affect Organization Planning?" *American Business*, XXV (November, 1955), 9ff. Relatedly, even firms having extensive experience with computers reported no great structural changes. "The Impact of A.D.P. on Organization Structure," *O & M Bulletin*, XVII (August, 1962), 124-32.

The Colleague Concept of Staff:

computer requires the Colleague model. Rather, the computer does not imply organizational demands that are inconsistent with that model while, in a number of important particulars to be detailed soon, these demands are at odds with the traditional theory of organization and the NII model.

Stress on Flow of Information

Although the consequences of the computer have not worked themselves out completely, first, the use of the tool permits an information flow consistent with the requirements of the Colleague concept. This is meant in two senses. Thus the computer permits a speed of measurement thoroughly in keeping with the monitoring of the performance of teams required by the Colleague concept. In no small part, in contrast, the principles are grounded in resignation to the tardy measurement of performance. Hence the prescription of continuous and detailed supervision and of a limited span of control. These are prescribed, that is, to supplement traditional techniques of measuring performance that provide data often in the category of ancient history. Similarly, the speedy measurement of performance via computers is consistent with the spirit of openness and cooperation between functions implied by the Colleague concept.

Both of these characteristics of the flow of information induced by computers may be illustrated by Argyris' report of the consequences of putting a computer in one firm on "real time."[52] One major effect was a drastic shortening of the gestation period of certain reports. The computer provided the required information in two or three days, while previously the information was a month or so in reaching the president's desk. A week or so of this preparation period, however, was spent by vice-presidents "politicking" in order to find ways and means of softening the president's reaction to the report. The president of the firm expressed satisfaction with the computer's speed: "I'll now be able to nail things down and find out who are the real culprits." And this could be done without close supervision or the intervention of staff agents. The vice-presidents, however, were more undecided about the computer. One reported: "I simply won't have time to politic anymore." Another vice-president went to the heart of the matter. "Having this damn computer on real time," he observed, "means that there has

---

[52] Argyris, "The Integration of the Individual and the Organization," *op. cit.*, p. 77.

to be a hell of a lot of trust, confidence, and leveling among people."

Such features of the computer technology support organizing for the Colleague concept. For the approach assumes techniques of effective overhead control which do not require that officials of lower-level teams be continually hamstrung by close and detailed direction from above. The computer also permits more reasonable overhead control of, for example, system-wide inventory levels. Lower-level officials, that is, may be relieved of the burden of controlling such factors, as well as of the guesswork and busywork often associated with efforts to make such judgments. The technology, of course, will determine which areas are chosen for such overhead control. Even if most supervisors would resent being relieved of such difficult burdens, retraining in the subtle arts of motivating and communicating could more than take up the slack. This reorientation also is consistent with the Colleague concept.

Stress on Flow of Work

Second, evidence strongly suggests that the application of computers requires a "flow of work" approach. That is, the systems analysis which must precede successful computer installations often gives the lie to the vertical bias of the principles of organization since systems analysis follows the horizontal flow of work. The mischief of the principles is commonly observed, for example, in that data tend to be gathered vertically for the individual functions. What happens horizontally in the integration of interrelated functions tends to be neglected, and data in this horizontal "no-man's land" often is required to provide accurate measures of the flow of work. Warren Alberts, Vice-President, United Air Lines, puts the matter this way in summarizing the path-finding experience of his firm with computers: "It appears to us — and I think it is generally true in industry — that much of today's information is designed to satisfy governmental, legal, and accounting requirements, with little recognition of what the various levels of management need as a base for the types of decisions which they are called upon to make."[53]

In any case, the use of computers can tolerate little of the vertical fragmentation of the principles when the flow of work is across

[53]Warren E. Alberts, "United Air Lines," in *Management Organization and the Computer*, ed. George P. Shultz and Thomas L. Whisler (Glencoe, Ill.: Free Press, 1960), p. 163.

departmental barriers. Melvin Grosz, of Standard Oil of New Jersey, speaks directly from his firm's experience: "The effects on the organization of drawing together formerly separate units become irresistible. The walls of departments really do crumble. Once you have changed the system, people simply can't resist doing what then appears to be logical in an organizational sense."[54]

Organizing for the Colleague concept is patently congenial to this integrative bias of computer applications. That is, the Colleague concept is organized around the flow of work, which should lay the firm groundwork of systems analysis upon which computer applications depend. The Colleague concept and the computer, then, seem highly compatible. Or to put the matter another way, one can organize for the Colleague concept without using a computer. However, it does not seem that computers can be used as general-purpose tools without the systems analysis of horizontal flows of work that is required by the Colleague model.[55]

The principles of organization seem less congenial to the computer technology. John E. Hines makes the point when he summarizes the history of the use of computers in the General Electric Company. The computer certainly affects organization structure, he notes, but the relation is not one-way. Hines thus concludes that "being preoccupied with organization charts [based upon the principles makes] it difficult to cut across departmental lines in developing the kind of system which ties together different departments and divisions."[56]

Both the computer technology and the Colleague model have a structural bias-in-common, then. The principles and the NII model induce patterns of power that fragment organizations structured around functions or processes. Organizing for the Colleague concept, in contrast, intends to integrate patterns of power around discrete flows of work. In the former case, power can disrupt effective performance; in the latter case, power contributes to effective performance.

Stress on New Organizational Forms

Third, the introduction of the computer raises significant questions of the validity of the line-staff dichotomy and the placement of

---

[54]*Ibid.*, p. 219.
[55]Alberts, *op. cit.*, pp. 177-78.
[56]John E. Hines, "A Department of the General Electric Company," in *Management Organization and the Computer, op. cit.*, p. 153.

the computer specialists in one or the other. The question is hardly academic. For given the cost and the power of the computer, one can question relegating its supporting personnel to a staff role patterned after the NII concept. On the other hand, however, the work of computer specialists does not seem very much like the work implied in the NII caricature of line.

Only the foolhardy will predict how this dilemma will be resolved. The Atwood Vacuum Machine Company, however, took an interesting approach. Following the introduction of IBM RAMAC equipment, the firm reorganized into six divisions: Manufacturing, Finance, Sales, Personnel, Purchasing, and Planning (which handles the RAMAC installation). As Atwood's president, Seth G. Atwood, Jr., notes: "With this divisional arrangement, we have eliminated the concept of staff people. We have been able to avoid the kinds of problems that the existence of staff creates by simply not having staff around."[57] The mechanics of the approach of Atwood may be outlined. Thus Planning determines the purchase requirements and the delivery dates of various items. Purchasing, then, determines the vendor and the price to be paid. Atwood's plan seems to have the atmosphere necessary to sustain this approach, and the company is relatively small. One can expect that relations are not always smooth as the several divisions integrate their efforts, but Atwood's approach does not bind any division with organizational inferiority. As President Atwood explains: "Planning, then, in our company, is a line function. It was not always such. We once had all kinds of staff people, but we could see no reason for continuing to have the kinds of problems that staff people create. So we eliminated staff [as traditionally defined]."[58]

Certainly, there seems no unmistakable trend toward the resolution of line-staff problems as at Atwood. One point, however, seems of general validity. The NII concept does not seem well-suited to provide the organizational framework for the computer-equipped firm. On this point, at least, agreement seems to exist among those who have midwifed computer installations in their organization.

Toward the Colleague Model: A Conclusion

There seem, in sum, ample reasons to approach the Colleague concept in organizing. The argument may be outlined in terms of a

---

[57]Seth G. Atwood, "The Atwood Vacuum Machine Company," in *Management Organization and the Computer, op. cit.*, p. 237.
[58]*Ibid.*, p. 237.

few emphases. First, methodologically, the NII concept of staff rests on a curious foundation, if that foundation usually has escaped critical analysis. Second, the NII concept often poses difficult operating problems. Third, the Colleague concept provides a reasonable alternative for organizing program and sustaining activities. The problems of design do not seem insurmountable, and there is ample reason to expect that the Colleague model will avoid the severity of the problems occasioned or worsened by the NII model. Fourth, and finally, the Colleague approach seems consistent with a wide range of the recent research on organizations, ranging from sharper insights into behavior in cooperative systems to revolutionary applications of the computer.

This anaysis can rest on the evidence relevant to these four emphases while it awaits empirical testing and replication. Some of this research is presently underway among "natural" populations,[59] but it seems clear that it will also be necessary to bring some of this work into the social laboratory, as has been done successfully in other areas.[60]

---

[59]Robert T. Golembiewski, "Personality and Organization Structure: Staff Models and Behavioral Patterns," *Journal of the Academy of Management*, IX (September, 1966), 217-32.
[60]James D. Barber, *Power In Committees: An Experiment in the Governmental Process* (Chicago: Rand McNally, 1966).

Author Index

Adams, John, 24
Adams, Stuart, 137, 140
Alberts, Warren E., 264, 265
Almond, Gabriel, 102
Anderson, Lynn R., 192
Argyle, Michael, 191
Argyris, Chris, 45, 69-70, 103, 145, 187, 209, 210, 234, 237, 238, 239-40, 247, 263
Atwood, Seth G., Jr., 266

Baker, Alton W., 25
Bales, Robert F., 137
Bamforth, K. W., 214
Barber, James D., 267
Barnes, Louis B., 4
Basowitz, Harold, 244
Bass, Bernard M., 165
Baumgartel, Howard, 106, 135, 225, 226
Beaumont, Richard A., 44
Bennett, Reginald, 246
Bennis, Warren G., 145, 152, 237
Bibby, D. L., 123, 125, 167
Black, Hillel, 217
Blackwell, R., 157
Blair, Clay, Jr., 45
Blake, Robert R., 29
Blau, Peter M., 37, 71, 82, 92
Bloom, Samuel W., 244
Bowers, Raymond V., 192
Boyd, Thomas A., 26, 70
Brech, E. F. L., 3
Brown, Alvin, 11
Brown, Wilfred, 149, 150
Buckingham, Walter, 43
Burack, Elmer H., 44
Burke, Ronald J., 145

Calhoon, Richard P., 69
Calvin, Allen D., 209
Cantril, Hadley, 243
Cartwright, Dorwin, 35, 98, 138, 174, 191, 201, 227
Chandler, Alfred D., Jr., 26, 55, 56, 70, 139, 186, 187
Chapple, Eliot D., 104, 105, 249, 253, 254, 259, 260
Chekhov, Anton P., 41
Cioffi, Frank, 191
Clausen, John A., 244
Clausewitz, Baron von, 17
Cleland, David I., 124
Coch, Lester, 201
Cole, Taylor, 71
Cooper, William W., 187
Corbin, Arnold, 42
Cordiner, Ralph J., 39
Cronin, T. C., 123

Dahl, Robert A., 29
Dale, Ernest, 8, 12, 56, 62, 161, 186
Dalton, Melville, 63, 66, 68, 71, 72, 74, 78, 90, 94, 113-14, 200, 208
Daniel, D. Ronald, 147
Davis, Keith, 19-20, 21, 83, 226, 230
Davis, Louis E., 210
Davis, Ralph C., 25, 222
Dearborn, DeWitt C., 99
DeSpelder, Bruce E., 25
Deutsch, Morton, 174
Diamant, Alfred, 82
Diebold, John, 262
Dill, William R., 195, 207
Drucker, Peter F., 4, 47, 84, 147, 192, 204
Dubin, Robert, 97, 131, 192, 249
Dutton, J. M., 142

Maier, Norman R. F., 262
March, James G., 92, 140, 193, 228
Mareson, Simon, 122
Marrow, Alfred J., 153
McCormick, Cyrus, 26
McFarland, Dalton E., 26, 85
McGregor, Douglas, 6, 7, 37, 47, 84, 104, 234
Mechanic, David, 244
Melman, Seymour, 140, 161, 199, 213, 217, 222
Meyer, Herbert A., 100
Michael, Stanley T., 244
Miller, N. E., 246
Mitchell, Don G., 41
Montgomery, Bernard Law, 10-11
Mooney, James D., 13
Morse, Nancy C., 212
Mosel, James N., 65
Mouton, Jane S., 29
Mueller, R. A. H., 165
Mulder, Mark, 166
Muller-Thym, Bernard, 75, 224
Myers, Charles A., 47
Mylander, William H., 125, 134

Newcomb, Robert, 162

O'Donnell, Cyril, 27

Parkinson, C. Northcote, 3, 67
Parsons, Talcott, 82
Patchen, Martin, 138, 191
Pelz, Donald C., 227
Persky, Harold, 244
Ponder, Q. D., 97
Pondy, L., 152
Porter, Lyman W., 64, 225
Provost, Normand, 15

Randall, Frederick D., 81
Reiley, Alan C., 13
Reimer, Everett, 212
Reitman, Walter R., 195, 207
Rice, A. K., 214
Richardson, F. L. W., Jr., 158
Ronken, Harriet O., 88-89, 127
Ross, M. G., 192
Russell, Bertrand, 24

Sammons, Marg, 162
Sampson, Robert C., 3, 5, 6, 14, 75, 121, 169, 171
Sayles, Leonard R., 64, 79, 104, 105, 140, 151, 202, 248, 249, 253, 254, 259, 260
Schein, Edgar H., 145, 152
Schellendorf, Bronsart von, 16
Schleh, Edward C., 47, 99-100, 101
Schutz, William C., 136
Schwartz, Milton M., 145
Scott, William G., 107-9
Scott, W. Richard, 37, 71
Scoutten, E. F., 38
Seashore, Stanley, 137, 165, 211, 239, 243
Seeckt, Hans von, 9
Selye, Hans, 243
Selznick, Philip, 129
Shelly, Maynard W., II, 187
Shepard, Herbert A., 29, 152
Sherman, Harvey, 124, 151
Shils, Edward A., 82
Shultz, George P., 37
Simon, Herbert A., 3, 33, 47, 58, 92, 99, 193, 262
Slater, Philip E., 237
Smithburg, Donald V., 33, 47
Sommer, R., 86
Spiegel, J. P., 244
Sproat, Audrey T., 85
Stahl, O. Glenn, 47, 48-54, 60
Stark, Harry, 145
Steiglitz, Harold, 219
Stein, Harold, 76
Stevens, S. S., 246
Stewart, Frank M., 47
Stewart, John M., 124
Strauss, George, 64, 79, 177-79, 236, 245, 256
Strother, George B., 97, 247
Sullivan, Harry Stack, 243
Suojanen, Waino W., 28, 137

Talacchi, Sergio, 106
Tead, Ordway, 12-13
Thayer, Clarence H., 130
Thompson, James D., 226
Thompson, Victor A., 33, 37, 47, 82, 126, 206-7
Traxler, Ralph N., Jr., 16, 17, 18

Triandis, Harry C., 226
Tripp, L. Reed, 102
Trist, E. L., 214
Turk, Herman, 94
Turk, Theresa, 94
Turnbull, John G., 47
Turner, Arthur N., 209
Turner, Ralph H., 64

Uris, Auren, 123
Urwick, Lyndall F., 8, 58, 221

Van Riper, Paul P., 171
Van Zelst, Raymond M., 211
Villers, Raymond, 46, 218
Vlcek, Adolph, Jr., 43, 100
Volkart, Edmund H., 244
Vroom, Victor H., 192, 210

Waldo, Dwight, 65
Walker, Charles R., 158, 262

Walker, Nigel, 21
Walton, Eugene, 145
Walton, Richard E., 142
Weber, Max, 82
Whinston, Andrew, 192
Whisler, Thomas L., 37, 186
White, K. K., 220
White, Leonard D., 11
Whyte, William F., 61, 72, 98, 186,
    187, 209, 222, 246
Wickesberg, A. K., 123
Wilson, A. T. M., 214
Wilson, Robert N., 244
Wolff, Harold G., 245
Woodward, Joan, 44
Worthy, James C., 97, 98, 102, 105,
    106, 138, 147, 160, 222, 224

Zander, Alvin, 35, 98, 138, 174, 191,
    201
Zeigarnik, Bluma, 165

Subject Index

Absolute standards, 193
Alter Ego Model, 10-18
  general properties, 10-11
  in German General Staff, 16-18
Atwood Vacuum Machine Co., 266
Authority, 35-51, 122
  and line vs. staff, 34-35
  and responsibility, 50-51
  colleague concept of, 122
  environmental changes relevant
    to, 35-39
  impact of technology on, 41-45
  in the NII model, 34-35
  ownership concept of, 34
  See also Centralization; Decen-
    tralization; and Delegation
Automation, 43, 147, 262-67
  and the Colleague model, 262-64
  and emphasis on flow of work,
    264-67
  and impact on structure, 43, 147
  See also Computers; Centraliza-
    tion; Decentralization; and
    Flow of work
Autonomous Group, 214-17
  advantages over NII model,
    214-17
  as analog of Colleague model,
    215-16

Budget department, 69-70
  bias toward change, 69-70
Bureaucratic organizations, 82-83

Centralization, 248-57
  and the NII model, 251-57
  neglect of flow of work, 248-50
  See also Decentralization; and
    Flow of work

Civil Service Commission, U. S., 48
Cliques, types of, 94-95
  horizontal, 95
  random, 95
  vertical, 94
Cohesiveness, 201-2
  See also Groups
Collaboration, patterns for, 28-30
  in various types of organizations,
    28-29
Colleague Model, 16-18, 118-232
  and horizontal integration, 155-56,
    162-63, 166-68, 173-76
  approached via behavioral
    change, 142-46
  approached via structural change,
    146-51
  basic structure for, 118-19
  detailed design of, 183-87
  general properties, 8-10
  guidelines for, 119-41
  in German General Staff, 16-18
  laboratory approach to, 151-53
  major side effects of, 188-232
  testing of, 154-76
  See also Integration, horizontal;
    and NII Model
Command, staff participation in,
    62-65
  sources of staff influence, 62-64
  via control over scarce resources,
    62-65
Command, unity of, 32, 131-33,
    206-9
  in the Colleague model, 131-33
  traditional prescription, 32
  vs. uniformity, 206-9
  See also Organization theory,
    traditional

as neglecting environmental change, 35-39
as neglecting power, 21-24, 46-54
impact on supervisory job, 107-10, 177-79
in German General Staff, 16-18
testing of, 76-89
See also Colleague Model; and Fragmentation, vertical
New York Port Authority, 124
Norms, 139-40

Objectives, major managerial, 128-29
Organization theory, traditional, 34-45, 58-59
as underlying the NII model, 33-34
internal contradictions in, 58-59
methodological problems with, 34-45
properties of, 32-33
See also Centralization; and Flow of work
Organizations, types of, 28
crisis-oriented, 28
knowledge-oriented, 28
routine-oriented, 28
See also Collaboration

Performance, measurement of, 99-110, 193-200
difficulties under NII model, 99-110, 193-96
ease of under Colleague model, 194, 196-200
Personality predispositions, 136-37
Personnel Department, 169-73
alternative organizations of, 169-71
and personnel generalists, 171-73
Personnel Management, charges against, 84-86
Power, 21-25
general concept of, 23-24
neglect of in NII staff, 21-24, 46-54
provisions for in *The Federalist Papers*, 24-25

Power, supervisory, 227-28
and pressure, 228
relation to output, 227-28
Pressure, 98-107, 135, 190-91
and the Colleague model, 190-91
and the NII model, 98-107, 135
Professionalism and staff behavior, 71-72, 82-83
Program management, 123-24
Project ACORD, 152-53
Project management, 43, 123-24

RAMAC, 266
Raytheon, 171-72
Resonance, 104-5
  See also Groups
River Rouge, 55

Sears, Roebuck, 26, 147-49
Self-choice, 211
Sensitivity training, 151-53
Service/Control dualism, 61-62
Span of cognition, 144
Specialist staff, 19-21
as advisory, 19
as control, 20-21
as service, 19-20
Staff, analysis of, 2-12, 25-27
models for, 7-12
reasons for, 2-4
significance of, 25-27
Staff Officers' Field Manual, U. S. Army, 10-11
Staff services, 5-21
in German General Staff, 15-18
new role of, 5
three models of, 7-14
varieties of, 18-21
Standard Oil of New Jersey, 26, 265
Strategic Air Command, 29
Stress, 243-47
and the Colleague model, 247
and the NII model, 245-46
concepts of, 243-44
consequences of, 245-47
See also Crisis
Structural integration, 137-38
Sub-organizations, 93-97, 137-38, 200-2
development of under NII model, 93-97

management of by Colleague model, 137-38, 200-2
Substantive vs. technical issues, 119-20, 131-33, 159
Sun Oil Co., 130
Supervision, close, 32, 98-105, 190-91, 208-9
  traditional prescription, 32
  under the NII model, 98-105, 190-91, 208-9
Sylvania Corporation, 11

Tall structures, 125-26, 224-25
  See also Centralization; Delegation; and Flow of work
Technical vs. substantive issues, 119-20, 131-33, 159

Technology, levels of, 44
Tension systems, 165-67
  and unfinished tasks, 165-66
  as increased by NII model, 166-67
Texas Instruments, 123
Theory, central role of, 7-8
Theory X, as support for NII model, 234-35
Theory Y, as support for Colleague model, 236-37
Training and development, 104-5, 218-27
  and the Colleague model, 218-27
  and the NII model, 104-5, 221-22

United Air Lines, 264

Working supervisor, 177-79